GREEK FICTIONAL LETTERS

Greek Fictional Letters

A Selection with Introduction, Translation and Commentary by

C. D. N. COSTA

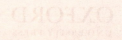

OXFORD
UNIVERSITY PRESS

Greek Fictional Letters

A Selection with Introduction, Translation
and Commentary by

C. D. N. COSTA

OXFORD
UNIVERSITY PRESS

OXFORD

UNIVERSITY PRESS

Great Clarendon Street, Oxford OX2 6DP

Oxford University Press is a department of the University of Oxford.
It furthers the University's objective of excellence in research, scholarship,
and education by publishing worldwide in

Oxford   New York

Athens Auckland Bangkok Bogotá Buenos Aires Cape Town
Chennai Dar es Salaam Delhi Florence Hong Kong Istanbul Karachi
Kolkata Kuala Lumpur Madrid Melbourne Mexico City Mumbai Nairobi
Paris São Paulo Shanghai Singapore Taipei Tokyo Toronto Warsaw

with associated companies in Berlin Ibadan

Oxford is a registered trade mark of Oxford University Press
in the UK and in certain other countries

Published in the United States
by Oxford University Press Inc., New York

British Library Cataloguing in Publication Data

Data available

Library of Congress Cataloging in Publication Data

Greek fictional letters / a selection with introduction, translation,
and commentary by C.D.N. Costa.
p. cm.
Texts in Ancient Greek and English; commentary in English.
Includes bibliographical references and index.
1. Greek letters—Translations into English. 2. Imaginary letters—Translations
into English. 3. Imaginary letters—History and criticism. 4. Greek letters—
History and criticism. 5. Letter writing, Greek—History. 6. Letters in literature.
7. Imaginary letters. 8. Greek letters. I. Costa, Charles Desmond Nuttall.

PA3637.L4 G74 2002   883'.0108—dc21   2001021841

ISBN 0-19-924001-9

ISBN 0-19-924546-0 (pbk)

1 3 5 7 9 10 8 6 4 2

Typeset by Newgen Imaging Systems (P) Ltd., Chennai, India
Printed in Great Britain
on acid-free paper by
T.J. International Ltd., Padstow, Cornwall

PREFACE

This book aims to explore an interesting and attractive but not very familiar field of late Greek literature, the fictional letter. Examples are offered from two of the main types of these letters, the 'comic' and the 'philosophical', with translations for those who may need them, and commentaries to assist both with grammatical interpretation and with the literary and cultural background. I have done no major work in establishing the texts, but have based them on existing older editions (listed in the Bibliography), making such alterations of readings as seemed necessary. Whenever an apparatus is appended it is extremely selective, and it is preceded by a reference to the edition on which it is based and from which the sigla are derived.

I am grateful to many friends and colleagues who helped me by answering my questions; but my biggest debt is to Emeritus Professor Donald Russell. He read the whole book, made many wise and constructive suggestions, and generally saved me from myself. I am also glad to thank the staff of the Oxford University Press for their encouragement, their vigilance and their friendly courtesy. The flaws that remain in the book are mine.

May 2001   C.D.N.C.

CONTENTS

Philostratus

Aristaenetus

Anacharsis

Diogenes

Crates

Socrates

Socratics

Euripides

Themistocles

Hippocrates

Chion

INTRODUCTION

The letter was an extremely popular literary form in the Graeco-Roman world. That is true both of real letters (genuine communications between writer and recipient) and of fictional or imaginary letters, the type which this book is concerned with. From the Hellenistic period onward the Greeks themselves were interested in the theory of letter-writing, the most important surviving critic being Demetrius, whose work *On Style* includes a section on letter-writing (223–35).[1] This is a most perceptive analysis, in which Demetrius stresses the immediacy and intimacy of the letter, and suggests that the letter is the εἰκών, the image, of the writer's mind. He also quotes one Artemon, who edited the letters of Aristotle, as comparing a letter to one half of a conversation. We shall see that this informal, chatty element is carefully preserved in what are undoubtedly fictitious letters as well. Moreover, the lasting popularity of the letter is attested by nearly 150 major collections of letters surviving from the Byzantine period. The attitude to the letter as something very precious is expressed memorably by Leo of Synnada in the tenth century, when he likened a friendship without letters to a lamp without oil.[2]

Some reasons for the popularity of the fictitious letter as a literary form can be seen if we look at the educational and scholastic background of the period in which most of them seem to have been written. They are generally very hard to date with any approach to accuracy, but most of those we are concerned with were perhaps written between *c*.100 BC and *c*. AD 250 (Aristaenetus seems to be somewhat later). This period, especially the Imperial age, was the time of the dominance of the sophists and rhetors, the professional teachers and practitioners of rhetoric, who were profoundly influential in the political and educational life especially of the cities of the Greek East. They not only attracted pupils as famous and respected teachers, but they often acted as trusted emissaries and secretaries to rulers and other powerful men. There are vital links between these rhetors and their work and the two main types of fictional letters we are looking at. The 'imaginary' (sometimes called 'comic') letters of the type written by Aelian, Alciphron, and Philostratus are themselves the work of rhetors and explore the same range of themes as do the rhetors' own professional declamations or *meletai*, at least the lighter variety which were based on character (ἦθος). They relate even more closely to earlier study at school of comedy and other poetry, where instruction began under the *grammatikos*. Our other category of letters, those attributed to famous historical characters (Phalaris, Themistocles), especially philosophers (Anacharsis, Hippocrates, Socrates), whether or not they were written by professional rhetors, have obvious rhetorical purposes which show a clear affinity with the historical declamation, in which a famous figure is made to speak 'in character' in some defined situation. This presentation of character (*ethopoiia*) was one of the most widely practised of the rhetorical exercises. As a variation on this, to reproduce convincingly what Socrates, Themistocles, or Diogenes would have felt and thought and put into a letter was obviously an enjoyable challenge, and, to judge by the number of collections of such letters we have, they must have had an appreciative readership. From an earlier age we might also compare Ovid's studies in characterization in his fictitious verse letters, the *Heroides*.

Apart from these clear links with the rhetors and their work we can detect some more general reasons for the popularity of letters in the late Hellenistic and Imperial periods. One is the attractiveness of epistolography as a literary form. The real letter is by its nature generally short, informal, intimate, allusive, an unpredictable mixture of the urbane and the chatty, as the mood of the writer takes him. There is also the obvious point that the letter was a vital means of communication in ancient society. Moreover, given the exceptionally easy communications of the Imperial age, letter-writing to distant addressees was common.[3] All these factors made the letter a satisfyingly challenging form to reproduce fictitiously. Rhetorical teachers had the opportunity to demonstrate the range of skills which they both used in their public lives and tried to impart to their pupils. But there must also have been other writers, who were not professional sophists, who enjoyed the challenge of fictitious letter-writing.

So far as we can establish a likely span of dates for our fictional letters, we may note too that though this was not a period of creative giants in Greek literature, we find two other genres now establishing themselves: biography (Plutarch—though apparently a lone figure in his particular field of moral biography) and the novel (five complete surviving examples by Chariton, Xenophon of Ephesus, Achilles Tatius, Longus, and Heliodorus). The novels too are notoriously hard to date,[4] but there is general agreement that the genre peaked around the second century AD, and we can make important comparisons between the fictional letters and the novels. One strong link is the use both make of New Comedy (characters, the recurrent theme of the love-intrigue): this influence can be seen everywhere in the novels, while among the epistolographers Aelian and Alciphron, for example, show a particular debt to New Comedy, especially Menander. It is also relevant to remember the many letters we find as part of the fictional structure of the novels, e.g. Chariton 4. 4 and 6, 8. 4; Heliodorus 5. 9, 8. 3, 10. 2 and 34; and the extensive correspondence that lies behind the compilation of the *Alexander Romance*.

The second century was also the period which has been called the Second Sophistic, when the dominant aim of writers was to emulate what they regarded as the golden age of Greek style—the Attic which had been written four or five hundred years before. This classical style was widely taught and practised as the canonical form of Greek prose, and we duly find evidence of this in our letter-writers, though more noticeably in the 'imaginary' letters of Aelian, Alciphron, and Philostratus. Here we might say that the *mimesis* of earlier Greek language which these authors are practising matches the *mimesis* of earlier Greek society which is an obvious aim of their letters. The extent and the success of the Atticizing we find in the letters varies quite a lot, but the fact that this was an important and pervasive goal of writers in the Imperial period must never be forgotten when we read their works. A familiar example of an expert Atticizer is Lucian (second century AD), a sophist and a brilliantly witty and entertaining satirist. His comic dialogues and other writings almost certainly had a strong influence, for example, on Alciphron, though the details of that literary relationship are not entirely clear (see below).

So there can be no doubt that the fictitious letter was popular both as a rhetorical exercise and as a literary form, and the large corpus of surviving examples illustrates the wide range of motives and seriousness to be found in them, from the intense philosophical spirit professed by Chion to the frivolities of Alciphron. If we try now to classify these letters we can distinguish three groups:

1. There are letters which form part of fictional and historical narratives. We have already seen that the surviving Greek novels are full of letters, and to those already quoted can be added the letter from Cyrus to Cyaxares in Xenophon, *Cyropaedia* 4. 5. 27, formally a historical work, but one which could more accurately be described as a vast novel. There is also the letter Nicias wrote from Sicily in Thucydides (7. 10–15), which has been the subject of much scholarly argument: did Nicias write it as it stands, or is it a Thucydidean construct to add documentary realism and interest to the narrative? At any rate the letter became famous and was often quoted up to Byzantine times. Another well-known example is the letter of Lysias to Felix in Acts 23: 26–30, where there is the same uncertainty whether the author Luke reproduced an existing letter of Lysias or invented one to fit his character and the situation. In these two examples, if Thucydides and Luke did compose the letters themselves, it is important not to see this as a piece of deception but rather as a technique of verisimilitude and characterization—a shot at *ethopoiia* to illuminate their narratives.

2. The second group of letters, in contrast with the first, consists of independent compositions which do not form part of a narrative, and are somewhat loosely called 'comic' or 'imaginary'. These terms are used to indicate that they are not primarily moralizing or didactic in intent (like our third group), but aim to portray character and various levels of society, or to evoke a past age. This is the group to which our authors Aelian, Alciphron, Philostratus, and the later Aristaenetus belong. The writers are rhetors or sophists, and many of the topics of these letters are much like those we find in the exercises in declamation (*meletai*) which the rhetors practised and taught: New

Comedy in particular, and Greek myth and history are fully exploited in both letters and *meletai*.

3. Thirdly there is a large group of letters which are attributed to famous philosophers and other historical characters. Nobody nowadays seriously maintains that any of these collections are genuine, since Richard Bentley in 1697–9 proved that the so-called letters of Pharlaris and others are spurious.[5] There are of course genuine surviving letters of this class. Best known are the three letters of Epicurus to his disciples, though we should no doubt include in this group the letters of St Paul in the New Testament.[6] The extant letters of Plato are the subject of much dispute, but most of them are probably spurious; while Aristotle, in spite of his fame in antiquity as a letter-writer, certainly did not write those that survive under his name. Generally speaking the authors of the letters allegedly by Diogenes, Socrates, Anacharsis, Hippocrates, and so on, have a didactic aim and offer more or less obliquely a moralizing or philosophical lesson, while at the same time trying to convey what was traditionally known of the character and personality of the supposed author. 'Anacharsis' caustically offers some home truths to the Athenians; 'Crates' shows Diogenes reacting nonchalantly to captivity; 'Socrates' counsels Xenophon about his plan to help Cyrus, and so on.

Our selection is of letters from the second and third of these classes, and we turn now to a brief consideration of each of the authors represented, using the rather loose labels 'comic' and 'philosophical'.

THE 'COMIC' LETTERS

AELIAN (flourished c. AD 200): a professional Roman sophist, among whose surviving works are twenty Ἐπιστολαὶ ἀγροικικαί, 'Letters of farmers'. These purport to give vignettes of the life of the Attic farmer in around the fourth century BC. It must be said that Aelian is not a distinguished writer, but the letters are worth reading as an exercise in Atticizing diction (for which Aelian was praised by Philostratus, *VS* 2. 31), and in evoking an earlier society (as do Alciphron and Philostratus). He has many echoes of earlier Greek authors from Homer to Menander, with New Comedy seemingly a particularly popular source.

ALCIPHRON (*c.* late second/early third century AD): another sophist and competent Atticizer, but nothing is known of him otherwise. He has left us a collection of four groups of letters supposedly by Athenian fishermen, farmers, parasites, and courtesans, which again evoke social life in the fourth century. There are many striking resemblances of theme and language between Alciphron and Lucian, and though it is hard to decide which one influenced the other, or whether both followed common sources, the likelihood is that Alciphron drew extensively on Lucian (see a good discussion of this point in the Benner–Fobes Loeb edition, 7–17). Like Aelian he was also indebted to New Comedy, particularly Menander. A particular interest in Menander is strongly suggested by the two most famous letters, those between Menander and Glycera (4. 18 and 19), included in this selection.

PHILOSTRATUS (*c.* AD 170–240s): it is difficult to disentangle the four Philostrati known to us, but our letter-writer is generally agreed to be Flavius Philostratus, who was born at Athens and taught by the celebrated orators Damianus of Ephesus and Antipater of Hierapolis. He went to Rome during the principate of Septimius Severus and was associated with the philosophical circle patronized by the emperor's wife Julia Domna (see his Letter 73 below). He also wrote the *Life of Apollonius of Tyana* and *Lives of the Sophists*, a mine of information for us about the sophists and their activities up to and including his own contemporaries.

ARISTAENETUS (writing probably *c.* AD 500): nothing whatever is known of Aristaenetus, and the estimate of his date depends on one or two internal references and his habit of writing rhythmical clausulae based on word-accent rather than quantity.[7] But though he is thus the latest author in our collection, he is another keen Atticizer, and he alludes to and even quotes liberally from a range of classical and later authors, notably Plato, Lucian, Alciphron, Philostratus, and the novel writers. We have two books of his letters, fifty in all.

THE 'PHILOSOPHIC' LETTERS

ANACHARSIS: the historical Anacharsis was a Scythian prince of the sixth century BC, who visited Greece in his travels and acquired such a reputation for wisdom that he was counted among the Seven Sages. There is disagreement in our sources about his attitude to the Greeks, but the prevailing view was that he had a low opinion of all except the Spartans. In the spurious letters ascribed to him he is portrayed as a spokesman for Cynic ideals against corrupt Greek culture, and they thus have strong links with the letters attributed to Crates and Diogenes. Of the ten 'Anacharsis' letters 1–9 are written predominantly in Koine rather than Attic, and are probably to be dated to the third century BC; 10 seems to be by a different author and may be a bit earlier.[8] These letters also have some interesting later associations. Cicero translated no. 5 (*Tusc.* 5. 90); on them Montesquieu based his *Lettres persanes* (1721), in which two Persian travellers give a satirical picture of Parisian culture under Louis XIV; and Montesquieu in turn influenced Goldsmith's *Citizen of the World* (1762), an imagined Chinese view of English society.

DIOGENES of Sinope (*c.*400–*c.*325 BC): influenced by Antisthenes to found the Cynic sect. His great notoriety as a sturdy individualist and the most famous of the Cynics must have been an important stimulus to the large corpus of fifty-one letters attributed to him. They are probably the work of several authors, they predominantly indulge in Cynic propaganda, and they date perhaps from around the first century BC to the first century AD.[9]

CRATES of Thebes (*c.*365–285 BC): another Cynic and the most famous pupil of Diogenes. We know from Diogenes Laertius (6.98) that he wrote a collection of letters which were highly regarded, but those are not the surviving corpus of thirty-six attributed to him. These, like the 'Diogenes' letters, may be the work of more than one author, there are many similarities between the two groups, and they probably date from the first or second century AD.[10]

SOCRATICS: a collection of thirty-five letters, the first seven attributed to Socrates himself and the rest to various of his disciples. Because of differences in style and content the two groups are probably by different authors. The author of 1–7 is an Atticizer and shows an interest in Cynicism; the other, larger group is more varied in theme and interest and not consistently Atticist in style. Possible dates are *c.* AD 200 or earlier for 1–7 and a bit later for the rest.[11]

EURIPIDES: a group of five letters attributed to Euripides, all but one addressed to or concerned with his visit to Archelaus of Macedonia. They are very hard to date, but the language, which is Koine rather than Atticist, seems to put them perhaps around AD 100.[12]

THEMISTOCLES: a collection of twenty-one letters, which purport to give an account of Themistocles' ostracism from Athens in around 472 and his flight by a circuitous route to Persia. The language is not consistently Atticist, with an apparently capricious use of both Attic and non-Attic forms, and the best guess at a date is probably *c.* AD 100.[13]

HIPPOCRATES: a set of twenty-four letters ascribed to the great fifth-century doctor. The two offered here (14 and 17 only in part) come from the series 10–17 within the collection, which are concerned with Democritus and Hippocrates' visit to Abdera to cure him of his alleged madness. The language is the Ionic dialect (but without complete consistency), as would be appropriate for the Coan Hippocrates,[14] and a very tentative date is some time before or in the first century AD.[15]

CHION: a very interesting collection of seventeen letters ascribed to Chion of Heraclea in Pontus, who was famous for having killed Clearchus, the tyrant of his native city, in about 353/2 BC, when he himself was killed by the bodyguard. Most of the letters are written to his father Matris while Chion is away in Athens and elsewhere, and they discuss his thoughts and strategy regarding the planned assassination. Chion is also a pupil and associate of Plato, and so the correspondence has a philosophical theme, that students of philosophy—and particularly of Plato—can be men of action and champions of their country's liberties. The final letter, indeed, is a valedictory address to Plato himself in which Chion presages his own death. Language and style show only fumbling and sporadic attempts at classical Attic, mixed with Hellenistic and poetical forms, and a reasonable guess at a date for the letters is late first century AD.[16]

For some time interest in the letters of Chion has centred on the idea that the collection forms a deliberate novel-in-letters or *Briefroman*, that the author intentionally ordered the letters in a sequence so as to tell the story of Chion's plans and movements prior to assassinating Clearchus. This theory has also been applied to other collections of letters—Themistocles, Hippocrates, the Socratics—but on the face of it the arguments look stronger in the case of the Chion correspondence.[17]

Some plausibility is given to this theory by the sequence itself of the letters, which do unfold a narrative. Letter 1 from Byzantium on Chion's way to Athens reassures his father about the journey. Letter 3 (below) recounts a meeting with Xenophon, who is on his way back from Persia. Letter 4 tells of an exciting adventure at Perinthos during his voyage. Letters 5 and 6 indicate arrival at Athens and gratitude for food and money sent by his father. Letters 7 and 8 (also to his father) are an interesting pair, though less relevant to the story: 8 is a letter of recommendation for someone, but it is effectively sabotaged by 7, which warns his father privately that the man concerned is a thoroughgoing rascal. By Letter 14 (below) he has reached Byzantium on his way home, and in this and 15 he enlists his father's help in his plans against Clearchus and in diverting the tyrant's suspicions of him. Letter 16 (below) is addressed to Clearchus himself, and 17, as we have seen, is a farewell to Plato.

Where the theory of a *Briefroman* falls down is in the chronological details of the letters. The dramatic time span of the whole collection is nearly fifty years: Chion would have met Xenophon (3) in 400/399, and he killed Clearchus around 353/2. Letters 11 and 12 offer further difficulties. In 11 he has been in Athens for five years (so the date is now 394), and he plans to stay for five more (i.e. until 389). But in 12 he decides to come home sooner than planned since learning about Clearchus' tyranny—yet that did not start until 364/3, thirty years after Letter 11.

So it seems safer to say that what we have here is not so much a novel-in-letters as a roughly maintained narrative line, interspersed with some less relevant but familiar letter-types: the thank-you letter (6), which also reveals the character of the writer (a philosopher does not need presents of money); and the letter of recommendation (8). The writer cannot have thought he was keeping to a credible chronology. Rather we must think of him as more interested in using the letter-form to explore the ἦθος, the character and moral make-up, of a young philosopher with a burning ambition to rid his city of a tyrant. We are still in the world of the declaimers and their favourite themes.

Similar arguments can be used even more strongly against viewing the letters of Themistocles and others as novels-in-letters. Yet the fact that it is possible to regard some of these collections as such may have had a distant influence on the early development of the novel in England and France. Richardson's *Pamela* (1740) and *Clarissa* (1747/8), Rousseau's *La Nouvelle Héloïse* (1761), and Laclos's *Les Liaisons dangereuses* (1782) are all written in the form of letters, and could thus be regarded as late echoes of some of our epistolographers.[18] An even later echo is Walter Savage Landor's *Pericles and Aspasia* (1836), an imaginary series of letters between those two; and we have already seen that the Anacharsis letters inspired Montesquieu and through him Goldsmith. The Greek fictional letter has a lot to answer for, and much of that is fascinating and distinguished.

NOTES TO THE INTRODUCTION

1. Demetrius' dates are uncertain, but he may belong to the 1st cent. BC, and he is clearly using earlier material.

2. *Ep.* 34: J. Darrouzès, *Epist. byz. du Xe siécle* (Paris, 1960), 137.

3. On genuine public letters see C. B. Welles, *Royal Correspondence in the Hellenistic Period* (London, 1934), pp. XXXV–1.

4. Reardon, 5.

5. The letters of 'Phalaris' are a particularly interesting group in this class of letter, and the most complex and ambitious of the surviving collections. Bentley's *Dissertation* is still well worth reading as a classic exposé of their status. On some of the issues see D. A. Russell in *JHS* 108 (1988), 94–106, with further references given there.

6. One should note here the importance of letters in the early spread of Christianity and the establishment of its communities in distant cities.

7. Mazal, pp. iii–iv.

8. Reuters, 3–5.

9. Capelle, 17–19.

10. Capelle, 51–4.

11. Köhler, 5; Malherbe, 27–9.

12. Gösswein, 29.

13. See the detailed discussion in Doenges, 49–63.

14. C. D. Buck, *Greek Dialects* (Chicago, 1955), 15.

15. W. D. Smith, 29, 43–4.

16. Düring, 22–4: see also below, Chion 13 and n.

17. See Düring's edn., and for detailed discussions and arguments in favour of the theory, N. Holzberg and others in N. Holzberg (ed.), *Der griechische Briefroman* (Tübingen, 1994).

18. For further discussions of the origins of the novel-in-letters see: F. G. Black, *The Epistolary Novel in the Late Eighteenth Century* (Eugene, Ore., 1940); R. A. Day, *Told in Letters: Epistolary Fiction before Richardson* (Ann Arbor, 1966); L. Versini, *Le Roman épistolaire* (Paris, 1979).

SELECT BIBLIOGRAPHY

(References to these works will generally be to the author's name only. A more extensive bibliography on both epistolography in general and the individual authors can be found in Holzberg.)

ARNOTT, W. G., 'Imitation, Variation, Exploitation: a study in Aristaenetus', *GRBS* 14 (1973), 197–211.

——'Pastiche, pleasantry, prudish eroticism: the letters of "Aristaenetus"', *YCS* (1982), 291–320.

BENNER, A. R., and FOBES, F. H., *The Letters of Alciphron, Aelian and Philostratus* (Loeb: Cambridge, Mass., and London, 1949).

BOWERSOCK, G. W., *Greek Sophists in the Roman Empire* (Oxford, 1969).

BUNGARTEN, J. J., *Menanders und Glykeras Brief bei Alkiphron* (Diss. Bonn, 1967).

CAPELLE, W., *De Cynicorum epistulis* (Diss. Göttingen, 1896).

DOENGES, N. A., *The Letters of Themistocles* (New York, 1981).

DÜRING, I., *Chion of Heraclea: A Novel in Letters* (Göteborg, 1951).

GIANNANTONI, G., *Socratis et Socraticorum Reliquiae* (Naples, 1990).

GÖSSWEIN, H.-U., *Die Briefe des Euripides* (Beiträge zur klassischen Philologie 55; Meisenheim am Glan, 1975).

HERCHER, R., *Epistolographi Graeci* (Paris, 1873).

HOLZBERG, N. (ed.), *Der griechische Briefroman: Gattungstypologie und Textanalyse* (Tübingen, 1994).

HOUT, M. VAN DEN, 'Studies in early Greek letter-writing' *Mnemosyne* 2 (1949) 19–41, 138–53.

KÖHLER, L., *Die Briefe des Sokrates und der Sokratiker* (Philologus Suppl. 20.2; Leipzig, 1928).

KOSKENNIEMI, H., *Studien zur Idee und Phraseologie des griechischen Briefes bis 400 n. Chr.* (Helsinki, 1956).

LESKY, A., *Aristainetos: Erotische Briefe* (Zürich, 1951).

MALHERBE, A.J., *The Cynic Epistles* (Missoula, Mont., 1977).

MAZAL, O., *Aristaeneti Epistularum Libri II* (Stuttgart, 1971).

REARDON, B.P. (ed.), *Collected Ancient Greek Novels* (Berkeley, Los Angeles, and London, 1989).

REUTERS, F. H., *Die Briefe des Anacharsis* (Berlin, 1963).

RUSSELL D. A., *Greek Declamation* (Cambridge, 1983).

SCHEPERS, M. A., *Alciphronis Rhetoris Epistularum Libri IV* (Leipzig, 1905).

SCHMID, W., *Der Atticismus* (Stuttgart, 1887–96).

SMITH, W. D., *Hippocrates: Pseudepigraphic Writings* (Leiden, etc., 1990).

SYKUTRIS, J., 'Epistolographie', *RE* Suppl. 5 (1931), 185–220.

USSHER, R. G., 'Love letter, novel, Alciphron and Chion', *Hermathena* 143 (1987), 99–106.

REFERENCE WORKS

ARNDT W. F.–GINGRICH, F. W., *A Greek-English Lexicon of the New Testament* (Chicago, 1957).

DENNISTON, J. D., *The Greek Particles* (2nd edn., Oxford, 1954).

LAMPE G. W. H., *A Patristic Greek Lexicon* (Oxford, 1961).

LEUTSCH, E. L. VON–SCHNEIDEWIN, F. G. *Corpus Paroemiographorum Graecorum* (Repr. Hildesheim, 1965).

LIDDELL H. G.–SCOTT, R.–JONES, H. STUART, *Greek–English Lexicon* (Oxford, 1925–40). (LSJ)

Oxford Classical Dictionary (3rd edn., Oxford, 1996). (OCD)

OTTO, A., *Die Sprichwörter und sprichwörtlichen Redensarten der Römer* (Repr. Hildesheim, 1964).

PAULY, A. F. VON–WISSOWA, G.–KROLL, W., *Real-Encyclopädie der classischen Altertumswissenschaft* (Stuttgart, 1893–). (*RE*)

WEIR SMYTH, H., *Greek Grammar* (rev. G. M. Messing: Cambridge, Mass., 1956).

TEXTS AND TRANSLATIONS

GREEK FICTIONAL LETTERS

AELIAN

5

Βαίτων Ἀνθεμίωνι

Τὰ σμήνη μοι τῶν μελιττῶν κενά, καὶ ἀπεφοίτησαν τῆς ἑστίας οὐκ
οὖσαι τέως δραπέτιδες, ἀλλὰ γὰρ καὶ πισταὶ διέμενον καὶ ᾤκουν ὡς
οἴκους τοὺς αὐτῶν σίμβλους, καὶ εἶχον λειμῶνα εὔδροσον καὶ δὴ καὶ
ἀνθῶν εὔφορον, καὶ εἱστιῶμεν αὐτὰς πανδαισίᾳ· αἱ δὲ ὑπὸ τῆς φιλ-
5 εργίας τῆς ἄγαν ἀνθεῖστίων ἡμᾶς πολλῷ καὶ καλῷ τῷ μέλιτι,
κοὐδέποτε τῆσδε τῆς ὠδῖνος τῆς γλυκείας ἦσαν ἄγονοι. νῦν δὲ
ᾤχοντο ἀπιοῦσαι λυπηθεῖσαι πρὸς ἡμῶν οὐδέν, οὐ μὰ τὸν Ἀρισταῖον
καὶ τὸν Ἀπόλλω αὐτόν. καὶ αἱ μέν εἰσι φυγάδες, ὁ δὲ οἶκος αὐτῶν
χῆρός ἐστι, καὶ τὰ ἄνθη τὰ ἐν τῷ λειμῶνι περὶ αὐτὰ γηρᾷ.
10 Ἐγὼ δὲ αὐτῶν ὅταν ὑπομνησθῶ τῆς πτήσεως καὶ τῆς
εὐχαρίστου χορείας, οὐδὲν ἄλλο ἢ νομίζω θυγατέρας ἀφῃρῆσθαι.
ὀργίζομαι μὲν οὖν αὐταῖς· τί γὰρ ἀπέλιπον τροφέα αὐτῶν καὶ ἀτε-
χνῶς πατέρα καὶ φρουρὸν καὶ μελεδωνὸν οὐκ ἀχάριστον; δεῖ δέ με
ἀνιχνεῦσαι τὴν πλάνην αὐτῶν καὶ ὅποι ποτὲ ἀποδρᾶσαι κάθηνται
15 καὶ τίς αὐτὰς ὑπεδέξατο καὶ τοῦτο· ἔχει γάρ τοι τὰς μηδὲν
προσηκούσας. εἶτα εὑρὼν ὀνειδιῶ πολλὰ τὰς ἀγνώμονας καὶ
ἀπίστους.

13

Καλλιπίδης Κνήμωνι

Ἀγροίκου βίου τά τε ἄλλα ἐστὶ καλὰ καὶ δὴ καὶ τὸ ἥμερον τοῦ
τρόπου· ἡ γὰρ ἡσυχία καὶ τὸ ἄγειν σχολὴν τοῖς[a] τῆς γῆς καλὴν
πραότητα ἐνεργάζεται. σὺ δὲ οὐκ οἶδ' ὅπως ἄγριος εἶ καὶ γείτοσιν
οὐκ ἀγαθὸς πάροικος. βάλλεις οὖν ἡμᾶς ταῖς βώλοις καὶ ταῖς
5 ἀχράσι καὶ μέγα κέκραγας ἰδὼν ἄνθρωπον ὡς διώκων λύκον καὶ
ἀργαλέος εἶ καὶ τοῦτο δὴ τὸ λεγόμενον ἁλμυρὸν γειτόνημα. ἐγὼ δὲ εἰ

Benner and Fobes   [a] τοῖς: τὴν M

AELIAN

5

BAITON TO ANTHEMION

My hives are deserted by the bees: they have left hearth and home, though they weren't runaways before. In fact they used to remain loyal and lived in their hives as their very own homes. They had a dewy meadow too, one that was rich in flowers, and we used to feast them on the richest of banquets. They, in turn, with excessive industry would feed us on lots of lovely honey, and never failed to produce this sweet fruit of their labours. But now they have gone off and away, though we did nothing to annoy them: I swear it by Aristaeus and by Apollo himself. So they have fled, and their home is bereft, and the meadow flowers are deserted and wasting away.

As for me, whenever I think of their flights and their graceful dancing I can only consider that I have lost my daughters. I am indeed angry with them (why did they desert their foster-father—quite simply their father, their guardian, and their keeper, who was not unwelcome to them?), but I must track down their wanderings, and find out where the fugitives have settled, and who has taken them over—that too must be found out. For he is keeping bees that don't belong to him. Then, when I've found them, I shall scold them mightily for being ungrateful and disloyal.

13

CALLIPIDES TO CNEMON

Among the many pleasant aspects of living in the country is the civilized behaviour: for peace and quiet and devoting one's leisure to the land create a fine sort of gentleness. But for some reason you are fierce and not a good neighbour to those living near you. You throw lumps of earth and wild pears at us, and you let out a tremendous yell at sight of anyone, as if you were chasing a wolf; you just cause trouble and embody the proverbial 'salty neighbourhood'. If it wasn't my father's

μὴ πατρῷον τὸν[b] ἀγρὸν ἐγεώργουν, ἄσμενος ἂν αὐτὸν ἀπεδόμην
φυγῇ φοβεροῦ γείτονος. ἀλλ᾽, ὦ βέλτιστε Κνήμων, τὸ σκαιὸν τοῦ
τρόπου κατάλυσον, μηδέ σε ὁ θυμὸς εἰς λύτταν[c] προαγέτω, μὴ καὶ
10 μανεὶς σεαυτὸν λάθῃς. ταῦτά σοι φίλα παρά φίλου παραγγέλματα
ἔστω καὶ ἴαμα τοῦ τρόπου.

[b] τὸν add. Wilamowitz　　[c] λύτταν L. A. Post: λύπην A: λήθην M Ald.

14

Κνήμων Καλλιπίδῃ

Ἔδει μὲν μηδὲν ἀποκρίνασθαι· ἐπεὶ δὲ εἶ περίεργος καὶ βιάζῃ με
ἄκοντά σοι προσδιαλέγεσθαι, τοῦτο γοῦν κεκέρδαγκα τὸ δι᾽
ἀγγέλων σοι λαλεῖν ἀλλὰ μὴ πρὸς αὐτὸν σέ. ἔστω σοι τοίνυν ἡ ἀπὸ
Σκυθῶν λεγομένη ἀπόκρισις αὕτη. ἐγὼ μαίνομαι καὶ φονῶ καὶ
5 μισῶ τὸ τῶν ἀνθρώπων γένος. ἔνθεν τοι βάλλω τοὺς εἰσφοιτῶντας
εἰς τὸ χωρίον καὶ βώλοις καὶ λίθοις. μακάριον δὲ ἥγημαι τὸν
Περσέα κατὰ δύο τρόπους ἐκεῖνον, ὅτι τε πτηνὸς ἦν καὶ οὐδενὶ
συνήντα, ὑπεράνω τε ἦν τοῦ προσαγορεύειν τινὰ καὶ ἀσπάζεσθαι.
ζηλῶ δὲ αὐτὸν καὶ τοῦ κτήματος ἐκείνου εὖ μάλα ᾧ τοὺς συναντῶν-
10 τας ἐποίει λίθους· οὗπερ οὖν εἴ μοί τις εὐμοιρία κατατυχεῖν ἐγένετο,
οὐδὲν ἂν ἦν ἀφθονώτερον λιθίνων ἀνδριάντων, καὶ σέ γ᾽ ἂν
εἰργασάμην τοῦτο πρῶτον. τί γὰρ μαθὼν ῥυθμίζεις με καὶ πρᾶον
ἀποφῆναι γλίχῃ οὕτως ἐχθρὰ πᾶσι νοοῦντα; ἔνθεν τοι καὶ τοῦ
χωρίου τὸ παρὰ τὴν ὁδὸν ἀργὸν εἴασα καὶ τοῦτό μοι τῆς γῆς χῆρόν
15 ἐστι καρπῶν. σὺ δὲ ἕνα σεαυτὸν τῶν ἀναγκαίων ἀποφανεῖς, καὶ
σπεύδεις με φίλον ἔχειν μηδὲ ἐμαυτῷ φίλον ὄντα. τί γὰρ καὶ μαθών
εἰμι ἄνθρωπος;

19

Μορμίας Χρέμητι

Ἐγὼ μὲν ἔθυον γάμους ὁ χρυσοῦς μάτην καὶ περιῄειν
ἐστεφανωμένος οὐδὲν δέον καὶ τούς τε ἔνδον καὶ τοὺς ἔξω θεοὺς
ἐκολάκευον, ὁ δὲ παῖς κατήγαγε μὲν καὶ αὐτὸς τὸ ζεῦγος ἐκ τῶν

property that I was farming, I would gladly have got rid of it to escape such a frightful neighbour. Come, my dear Cnemon, stop this stupid behaviour and don't let your anger lead you into a frenzy, in case you actually go mad without knowing it. Treat this as friendly advice from a friend and a remedy for your behaviour.

14

CNEMON TO CALLIPIDES

I didn't have to reply, but since you are being a busybody and forcing me to start a discussion with you against my will, at least I have the advantage that I can talk to you through messengers and not face to face. So here is my Scythian reply, as they say. I am feeling mad and murderous and I loathe the human race. That is why I throw clods and stones at intruders on my land. And I consider that famed Perseus lucky in two ways: he had wings and met nobody, being too high up to greet and talk politely to anyone; and I envy him also for that truly famous gift he had of turning those he met into stone. If I had the good fortune to possess that gift there would be nothing more plentiful than stone statues of men—and you would have been the first I made. What do you mean by trying to run my life, and why so keen to tame me, when my mind is so hostile to everyone? Of course that is the reason I've let my roadside bit of land go wild, and that part of my property doesn't bear crops. But you'll be proclaiming yourself a relation of mine, and you're eager to make a friend of me even though I'm not even a friend to myself. Why on earth am I a human being?

19

MORMIAS TO CHREMES

Like a fine fool, there I was offering wedding sacrifices pointlessly, and going around wearing a garland without any need for it, and trying to appease both the household gods and those outside it. Meanwhile, my son had himself brought in a

ἀγρῶν ὡς τὴν νύμφην ἐξ ἄστεος εἰς τὸ πατρῷον χωρίον ἐπανάξων,
5 αὐλητρίδα δὲ λυσάμενος, ἧς ἔτυχεν ἐρῶν, νύμφης στολὴν αὐτῇ
περιβαλὼν ἐπανήγαγέ μοι φάτταν ἀντὶ περιστερᾶς, φασίν, ἑταίραν
ἀντὶ νύμφης. καὶ τὰ μὲν πρῶτα αἰδουμένη κορικῶς εὖ μάλα καὶ
κατὰ^α τὸν [τῶν παίδων]^α τῶν γαμουμένων νόμον ἀπέκρυπτε τὴν
τέχνην, μόλις δὲ ἀπερράγη ἡ σοφία τε αὐτῶν καὶ αἱ κατ' ἐμοῦ
10 μηχαναί. οὐ μὴν εἰς τὸ παντελές μου καταφρονήσουσιν ὥσπερ οὖν
πλινθίνου, ἐπεί τοι τὸν μὲν καλὸν νυμφίον ἐς κόρακας ἀποκηρύξω
ἐὰν μὴ τῆς ὑπερβαλλούσης τρυφῆς παυσάμενος σὺν ἐμοὶ ταφρεύῃ καὶ
βωλοκοπῇ· τὴν δὲ νύμφην ἀποδώσομαι κἀκείνην ἐπ' ἐξαγωγῇ ἐὰν
μή τι καὶ αὐτὴ τῶν ἔργων τῇ Φρυγίᾳ τε καὶ τῇ Θράττῃ
15 συναπολαμβάνῃ.

Benner and Fobes   ^{a-a} τὸν τῶν παίδων om. M, τῶν παίδων om. Ald.

20

Φαιδρίας Σθένωνι

Φύεται μὲν ἐν τοῖς ἀγροῖς καλὰ πάντα, κεκόσμηταί τε ἡ γῆ τούτοις
καὶ τρέφει πάντας· καὶ τὰ μέν ἐστι τῶν καρπῶν διετήσια, τὰ δὲ
καὶ πρὸς ὀλίγον ἀντέχοντά ἐστιν τρωκτὰ ὡραῖα· πάντων δὲ τούτων
θεοὶ μὲν ποιηταί, ἡ γῆ δὲ μήτηρ ἅμα καὶ τροφὸς αὕτη· φύεται δὲ
5 καὶ δικαιοσύνη καὶ σωφροσύνη καὶ ταῦτα ἐν τοῖς ἀγροῖς, δένδρων τὰ
κάλλιστα, καρπῶν τὰ χρησιμώτατα. μὴ τοίνυν γεωργῶν καταφρόνει·
ἔστι γάρ τις καὶ ἐνταῦθα σοφία, γλώττῃ μὲν οὐ πεποικιλμένη οὐδὲ
καλλωπιζομένη λόγων δυνάμει, σιγῶσα δὲ εὖ μάλα καὶ δι' αὐτοῦ
τοῦ βίου τὴν ἀρετὴν ὁμολογοῦσα. εἰ δὲ σοφώτερα ταῦτα ἐπέσταλταί
10 σοι ἢ κατὰ τὴν τῶν ἀγρῶν χορηγίαν, μὴ θαυμάσῃς· οὐ γάρ ἐσμεν
οὔτε Λίβυες οὔτε Λυδοὶ ἀλλ' Ἀθηναῖοι γεωργοί.

yoke of oxen from the farm to bring his bride from the town to his family property. He'd happened to fall in love with a pipe-playing music girl, bought her freedom, put a bride's robe on her and brought her home to me—a wild pigeon for a tame one, as they say, a courtesan instead of a bride. At first she was very modest and maidenly and, behaving as newly wed brides do, she kept the trick a secret; but eventually their cunning device and their schemes against me were suddenly revealed. However, they are not going to treat me with utter contempt, as if I were clay in their hands; for I'll renounce with curses that fine bridegroom, unless he gives up his outrageous wantonness and helps me with digging ditches and breaking up the earth. As for that bride of his, I'll sell her for export, unless she too does her share of the work along with the Phrygian and the Thracian maidservants.

20

PHAEDRIAS TO STHENON

All that is lovely grows in the country: thereby the earth is adorned and gives nourishment to everyone. Some of its products last through the year; others keep for a short time and are eaten in season. The gods create all these things, but the earth is their mother and also their nurse. As for justice and temperance, these too grow in the country—the most beautiful of trees and the most useful of fruits. So don't despise farmers; for they too have a kind of wisdom, not embellished in speech or displaying itself in powerful oratory, but remarkably silent and proclaiming its virtue through its own life. If this letter to you looks too clever for the country to offer, don't marvel at it: we aren't Libyan or Lydian but Athenian farmers.

ALCIPHRON

I.I

Εὔδιος Φιλοσκάφῳ

Χρηστὴν ἡμῖν ἡ θάλαττα τὸ τήμερον εἶναι τὴν γαλήνην ἐστόρεσεν.
ὡς γὰρ τρίτην ταύτην εἶχεν ὁ χειμὼν ἡμέραν, καὶ λάβρως κατὰ τοῦ
πελάγους ἐπέπνεον ἐκ τῶν ἀκρωτηρίων οἱ βορεῖς, καὶ ἐπεφρίκει μὲν
ὁ πόντος μελαινόμενος, τοῦ ὕδατος δὲ ἀφρὸς ἐξηνθήκει, πανταχοῦ
5 τῆς θαλάσσης ἐπ᾽ ἀλλήλων ἐπικλωμένων τῶν κυμάτων (τὰ μὲν γὰρ
ταῖς πέτραις προσηράσσετο, τὰ δὲ εἴσω ἀνοιδοῦντα ἐρρήγνυτο),
ἀεργία παντελὴς ἦν· καὶ τὰ ἐπὶ ταῖς ἠόσι καταλαβόντες καλύβια,
ὀλίγα ξυλισάμενοι κομμάτια ὅσα οἱ ναυπηγοὶ πρώην ἐκ τῶν δρυῶν
ἃς ἐξέτεμον ἀπέλιπον, ἐκ τούτων πῦρ ἀνάψαντες τὸ πικρὸν τοῦ κρυ-
10 μοῦ παρεμυθούμεθα. τετάρτη δὲ αὕτη ἐπιλαβοῦσα ἡμᾶς ἀλκυονίς,
ὡς οἶμαι, ἡμέρα (ἔστι γὰρ τοῦτο τῷ καθαρῷ τῆς αἰθρίας
τεκμήρασθαι) πλοῦτον ἀθρόον ἀγαθῶν ἔδειξεν. ὡς γὰρ ὤφθη μὲν ὁ
ἥλιος, πρώτη δὲ ἀκτὶς εἰς τὸ πέλαγος ἀπέστιλβε, τὸ πρώην
νεωλκηθὲν σκαφίδιον σπουδῇ κατεσύραμεν, εἶτ᾽ ἐνθέμενοι τὰ δίκτυα
15 ἔργων εἰχόμεθα. μικρὸν δὲ ἄπωθεν τῆς ἀκτῆς χαλάσαντες, φεῦ τῆς
εὐοψίας, ὅσον ἰχθύων ἐξειλκύσαμεν· μικροῦ καὶ τοὺς φελλοὺς ἐδέησε
κατασῦραι ὑφάλους τὸ δίκτυον ἐξωγκωμένον.
    Εὐθὺς οὖν ὀψῶναι πλησίον, καὶ τὰς ἀσίλλας[a] ἐπωμίους ἀνελόμενοι
καὶ τὰς ἑκατέρωθεν σπυρίδας ἐξαρτήσαντες καὶ ὑπὲρ αὐτῶν κατα-
20 βαλόντες τἀργύριον, ἄστυδ᾽ ἐκ Φαλήρων ἠπείγοντο. πᾶσι δὲ τούτοις
ἠρκέσαμεν ἡμεῖς καὶ πρὸς τούτοις ἀπηνεγκάμεθα γαμεταῖς καὶ
παιδίοις ὄγκον οὐκ ὀλίγον ἔχειν τῶν λεπτοτέρων ἰχθύων, οὐκ εἰς μίαν,
ἀλλ᾽ εἰ χειμὼν ἐπιλάβοιτο καὶ εἰς πλείους ἡμέρας ἐμφορῆσαι.

Benner and Fobes   Schepers
[a] ἀσίλλας *Hemsterhuys*: ὕλας χ: εἴλας *Neap.* [b] *Vat*1: εἶλας *cet.*

ALCIPHRON

1.1

EUDIUS TO PHILOSCAPHUS
('FAIRWEATHER' TO 'BOATLOVER')

It was useful for us that the sea became smooth and calm today. For when the storm continued into the third day, the north winds blowing furiously from the headlands over the sea, the deep rippling and turning black, and the foam flowering on the water's surface, as the waves of the sea broke against each other—here they dashed against the rocks, there they swelled up within themselves before breaking in spray— there was no possibility of work at all. We took over the little huts along the shore, and collecting a few chips of wood which the shipwrights had recently left after cutting down the oaks, we lit a fire with them and relieved ourselves of the bitter cold. This fourth day that has come is a 'halcyon', I think (you can judge by the clear sky), and it has given us a wealth of good things all at once. For when the sun appeared and the first beam shone on the sea, we eagerly launched our boat, which had recently been beached; then stowing our nets on board we set to work. A short distance offshore we let out the nets, and, my goodness, what a catch of good food! What masses of fish we hauled in!—the bulging net almost dragged the cork-floats under the water.

Well, the fishmongers were right on the spot: they lifted up their yokes on their shoulders, hung their baskets from each end and, paying us cash in return, hurried away from Phalerum to the city. We had enough to satisfy them all, and in addition we took away for our wives and children a fair load of the smaller fry, enough for them to have their fill not just for one day, but for several if bad weather comes.

1.4

Κυμόθοος Τριτωνίδι

Ὅσον ἡ θάλαττα τῆς γῆς διαλλάττει, τοσοῦτον καὶ ἡμεῖς οἱ ταύτης
ἐργάται τῶν κατὰ πόλεις ἢ κώμας οἰκούντων διαφέρομεν. οἱ μὲν γὰρ
ἢ μένοντες εἴσω πυλῶν τὰ δημοτικὰ διαπράττονται, ἢ γεωμορία
προσανέχοντες τὴν ἐκ τῆς βώλου πρὸς διατροφὴν ἀναμένουσιν
5 ἐπικαρπίαν· ἡμῖν δέ, οἷς βίος ἐν ὕδασι, θάνατος ἡ γῆ καθάπερ τοῖς
ἰχθύσιν ἥκιστα δυναμένοις ἀναπνεῖν τὸν ἀέρα. τί δὴ οὖν παθοῦσα, ὦ
γύναι, τὴν ἀκτὴν ἀπολιποῦσα καὶ τὰ νήματα τοῦ λίνου ἄστυδε
θαμίζεις Ὠσχοφόρια καὶ Λήναια ταῖς πλουσίαις Ἀθηναίων
συνεορτάζουσα; οὐκ ἔστι τοῦτο σωφρονεῖν οὐδ᾽ ἀγαθὰ διανοεῖσθαι.
10 οὐχ οὕτω δή σε ὁ πατὴρ ἐκ τῆς Αἰγίνης, οὗ τεχθῆναί σε καὶ τραφῆναι
συνέβη, μυεῖσθαι ὑπ᾽ ἐμοὶ γάμῳ παρέδωκεν. εἰ τὴν πόλιν ἀσπάζῃ,
χαῖρε καὶ ἄπιθι· εἰ τὸν ἄνδρα, εἰ τὰ ἐκ θαλάττης ἀγαπᾷς, ἐπάνιθι τὸ
λῷον ἑλομένη, λήθη δέ σοι ἔστω μακρὰ τῶν κατ᾽ ἄστυ τούτων
ἀπατηλῶν θεαμάτων.

1.11

Γλαυκίππη Χαρόπῃ

Οὐκέτ᾽ εἰμὶ ἐν ἐμαυτῇ, ὦ μῆτερ, οὐδὲ ἀνέχομαι γήμασθαι ᾧ με
κατεγγυήσειν ἐπηγγείλατο ἔναγχος ὁ πατήρ, τῷ Μηθυμναίῳ μειρακίῳ
τῷ παιδὶ τοῦ κυβερνήτου, ἐξ ὅτου τὸν ἀστικὸν ἔφηβον ἐθεασάμην τὸν
ὠσχοφόρον, ὅτε με ἄστυδε προὔτρεψας ἀφικέσθαι Ὠσχοφορίων ὄντων.
5 καλὸς γάρ ἐστι, καλός, ὦ μῆτερ, καὶ ἥδιστος, καὶ βοστρύχους ἔχει
βρύων οὐλοτέρους, καὶ μειδιᾷ τῆς θαλάττης γαληνιώσης χαριέστερον,
καὶ τὰς βολὰς τῶν ὀφθαλμῶν ἐστι κυαναυγής, οἷος τὸ πρῶτον ὑπὸ τῶν
ἀκτίνων τῶν ἡλιακῶν ὁ πόντος καταλαμπόμενος φαίνεται. τὸ δὲ ὅλον
πρόσωπον—αὐτὰς ἐνορχεῖσθαι ταῖς παρειαῖς εἴποις ἂν τὰς Χάριτας τὸν
10 Ὀρχομενὸν ἀπολιπούσας καὶ τῆς Ἀργαφίας κρήνης ἀπονιψαμένας·
τὼ χείλη δὲ τὰ ῥόδα τῆς Ἀφροδίτης ἀποσυλήσας τῶν κόλπων

1.4

CYMOTHOUS TO TRITONIS
('WAVESWIFT' TO 'TRITON'S DAUGHTER')

As the sea is different from the land, so are we who toil on the sea unlike those who live in cities and villages. They either remain within the gates busy in public affairs, or devote themselves to farming and for their sustenance await the produce of the soil. But to us who live among the waters the land means death, just as it does to the fish who cannot breathe in air at all. So what's got into you, wife, deserting the shore and your threads of flax, and constantly rushing off to the city to join the rich Athenian ladies in celebrating the Oschophoria and Lenaea? This isn't modest behaviour or keeping a decent frame of mind. It surely wasn't for this that your father in Aegina, where you happened to be born and bred, entrusted you to be initiated by me into the mysteries of marriage. If you are so fond of the city, good-bye and be off with you; but if you are content with your husband and with what the sea has to offer, choose the better course and come back, and may you long forget those beguiling city shows.

1.11

GLAUCIPPE TO CHAROPE
('GREY-EYED' TO 'BRIGHT-EYED')

I can no longer control myself, mother: I cannot bear the thought of marrying the boy from Methymna, the boat-pilot's son to whom my father lately promised to betroth me. This is since I noticed that young man from the city, who carried the vine-branch when you sent me to Athens to be present at the Oschophoria. He is lovely, mother, lovely; he is really sweet, with hair that is more curly than seaweed; his smile is more charming than the sea when it's calm; and his flashing eyes gleam like the sea when first it appears dazzling under the rays of the sun. As for his whole face—you could say that the Graces themselves have deserted Orchomenus and their baths in the Argaphian spring to dance in his cheeks. And his lips!—he has stolen the roses from Aphrodite's bosom and touched his own

διήνθισται ἐπὶ τῶν ἄκρων ἐπιθέμενος. ἢ τούτῳ μιγήσομαι ἢ τὴν
Λεσβίαν μιμησαμένη Σαπφὼ οὐκ ἀπὸ τῆς Λευκάδος πέτρας, ἀλλ᾽ ἀπὸ
τῶν Πειραϊκῶν προβόλων ἐμαυτὴν εἰς τὸ κλυδώνιον ὤσω.

1.15

Ναυσίβιος Πρυμναίῳ

Ἠγνόουν ὅσον εἰσὶ τρυφερὰ καὶ ἁβρόβια τῶν Ἀθήνησι πλουσίων
τὰ μειράκια· ἔναγχος δὲ Παμφίλου μετὰ τῶν συνηλικιωτῶν
μισθουμένου τὸ σκαφίδιον, ὡς ἂν ἔχοι γαληνιῶντος τοῦ πελάγους
περιπλεῖν ἅμα καὶ συμμετέχειν ἡμῖν τῆς ἄγρας τῶν ἰχθύων,
5 ἔγνων ἡλίκα αὐτοῖς ἐκ γῆς καὶ θαλάττης πορίζεται τρυφήματα. οὐ
γὰρ ἀνεχόμενος τῶν ξύλων τῆς ἁλιάδος ἐπί τε ταπήτων τινῶν
ξενικῶν καὶ ἐφεστρίδων κατακλιθείς (οὐ γὰρ οἷος ἔφασκεν εἶναι
κεῖσθαι ὡς οἱ λοιποὶ ἐπὶ τῶν καταστρωμάτων, τὴν σανίδα, οἶμαι,
νομίζων λίθου τραχυτέραν) ᾔτει παρ᾽ ἡμῶν σκιὰν αὐτῷ
10 μηχανήσασθαι τὴν τοῦ ἱστίου σινδόνα ὑπερπετάσαντας, ὡς οὐδαμῶς
οἷός τε ὢν φέρειν τὰς ἡλιακὰς ἀκτῖνας. ἡμῖν δὲ οὐ μόνον τοῖς
ταύτην ποιουμένοις τὴν ἐργασίαν, ἀλλὰ καὶ πᾶσιν ἁπαξαπλῶς ὅσοις
μὴ περιουσία πλούτου πρόσεστιν ἢ σπουδάζεται, ἔστιν οὗ δυναμένοις
τῇ εἴλῃ θέρεσθαι· ἐν ἴσῳ γὰρ[a] κρυμὸς καὶ θάλασσα.
15 Φερομένων δὲ ἅμα[a] (οὐ μόνος οὐδὲ μετὰ μόνων τῶν ἑταίρων ὁ
Πάμφιλος, ἀλλὰ καὶ γυναίων αὐτῷ περιττῶν τὴν ὥραν πλῆθος
συνείπετο, πᾶσαι μουσουργοί. ἡ μὲν γὰρ ἐκαλεῖτο Κρουμάτιον καὶ
ἦν αὐλητρίς· ἡ δὲ Ἐρατὼ καὶ ψαλτήριον μετεχειρίζετο· ἄλλη δὲ
Εὐεπίς,[b] αὕτη δὲ κύμβαλα ἐπεκρότει) ἐγένετο οὖν μοι μουσικῆς ἡ
20 ἄκατος πλέα, καὶ ἦν ᾠδικὸν τὸ πέλαγος καὶ πᾶν θυμηδίας
ἀνάμεστον. πλὴν ἐμέ γε ταῦτα οὐκ ἔτερπεν· οὐδὲ γὰρ οὐκ ὀλίγοι
τῶν ὁμοβίων καὶ μάλιστα ὁ πικρὸς Γλαυκίας Τελχῖνος ἦν μοι
βασκαίνων βαρύτερος. ἐπεὶ δὲ τὸν μισθὸν πολὺν κατεβάλετο,
τἀργύριόν με διέχει καὶ νῦν ἐκείνου τοὺς ἐπιθαλαττίους ἀγαπῶ
25 κώμους καὶ τοιοῦτον ἕτερον ἐπιστῆναί μοι ποθῶ δαπανηρὸν καὶ
πολυτελῆ νεανίσκον.

Benner and Fobes   Schepers
[a-a] κρυμὸς–ἅμα *Ald.*: θάλπος φέρομεν φερομένων δὲ x¹: θάλατταν φερομένων δὲ
ἅμα x²: θάλασσαν φέρομεν ἅμα. φερομένων δὲ ἅμα *cet.*
[b] Εὐεπὶς *Nauck*: Εὐεπὴς *codd.*: Εὐτέρπη *Hercher*

lips with their bloom. Either I will have this man, or I'll follow Lesbian Sappho's lead and throw myself, not from the Leucadian cliff, but from the rocks of the Peiraeus into the surging sea.

1.15

NAUSIBIUS TO PRYMNAEUS ('BOATLIFE' TO 'STERN')

I had no idea how delicate and effeminate are the rich men's boys at Athens. But recently Pamphilus and his pals hired my little boat, so that they could sail about while the sea was calm, and at the same time take part in our fishing. Then I learnt what extraordinary luxuries they are provided with from land and sea. For he couldn't bear the planks of my fishing-boat, and lay down on some imported rugs and cloaks, saying he couldn't lie on the decks like the others—I suppose he imagined that the timbers were rougher than rock. Then he asked us to organize some shade for him by stretching a sail over him like an awning, since he absolutely couldn't bear the rays of the sun. For the likes of us, however—not just those working at this trade, but all those in general who do not have or aim at abundance—it is possible sometimes to get warm by sunning ourselves: for cold and sea go together.

So we sailed around together, and Pamphilus wasn't alone, nor accompanied by his friends only, for a bunch of extremely attractive girls had joined him, all musicians. There was one called Kroumation, who played the pipes; another one, Erato, plucked the harp; and another was Euepis, and she clashed the cymbals. So my little boat was full of music, the sea echoed with melody, and everywhere delight filled the heart. But I wasn't too pleased myself at all this; for several of my colleagues were looking at me enviously—especially that spiteful Glaucias, who is more overbearing than a Telchis. But since Pamphilus paid me well, the silver cheered me up and now I rather like his nautical revels, and even long to come across another such lavish and extravagant young man.

2.2

Ἰοφῶν Ἐράστωνι

Ἐπιτριβείη καὶ κακὸς κακῶς ἀπόλοιτο ὁ κάκιστος ἀλεκτρυὼν καὶ
μιαρώτατος, ὅς με ἡδὺν ὄνειρον θεώμενον ἀναβοήσας ἐξήγειρεν.
ἐδόκουν γάρ, ὦ φίλτατε γειτόνων, λαμπρός τις εἶναι καὶ βαθύπλουτος,
εἶτα οἰκετῶν ἐφέπεσθαί μοι στῖφος, οὓς οἰκονόμους καὶ διοικητὰς
5 ἐνόμιζον ἔχειν. ἐῴκειν δὲ καὶ τὼ χεῖρε δακτυλίων πεπληρῶσθαι καὶ
πολυταλάντους λίθους περιφέρειν· καὶ ἦσαν οἱ δάκτυλοί μου
μαλακοὶ καὶ ἥκιστα τῆς δικέλλης ἐμέμνηντο. ἐφαίνοντο δὲ καὶ οἱ
κόλακες ἐγγύθεν· Γρυλλίωνα εἴπαις ἂν καὶ Παταικίωνα παρεστάναι.
ἐν τούτῳ καὶ ὁ δῆμος Ἀθηναίων εἰς τὸ θέατρον παρελθόντες ἐβόων
10 προχειρίσασθαί με στρατηγόν. μεσούσης δὲ τῆς χειροτονίας ὁ
παμπόνηρος ἀλεκτρυὼν ἀνεβόησε καὶ τὸ φάσμα ἠφανίσθη. ὅμως
ἀνεγρόμενος περιχαρὴς ἦν ἐγώ· ἐνθύμιον δὲ ποιησάμενος τοὺς φυλλοχόους ἑστάναι μῆνας ἔγνων εἶναι τὰ ἐνύπνια ψευδέστατα.

2.8

Δρυαντίδας Χρονίῳ

Οὐκέτι σοι μέλει οὔτε τῆς εὐνῆς ἡμῶν οὔτε τῶν κοινῶν παιδίων
οὔτε μὴν τῆς κατ᾽ ἀγρὸν διατριβῆς, ὅλη δὲ εἶ τοῦ ἄστεος, Πανὶ μὲν
καὶ Νύμφαις ἀπεχθομένη, ἃς Ἐπιμηλίδας ἐκάλεις καὶ Δρυάδας καὶ
Ναΐδας, καινοὺς δὲ ἡμῖν ἐπεισάγουσα θεοὺς πρὸς πολλοῖς τοῖς
5 προϋπάρχουσι. ποῦ γὰρ ἐγὼ κατ᾽ ἀγρὸν ἱδρύσω Κωλιάδας ἢ
Γενετυλλίδας; οἶδ᾽ ἀκούσας ἄλλα τινὰ δαιμόνων ὀνόματα, ὧν διὰ τὸ
πλῆθος ἀπώλισθέ[a] μου τῆς μνήμης τὰ πλείονα. οὐ σωφρονεῖς ὡς
ἔοικεν, ὦ γύναι, οὐδὲ ὑγιές τι διανοῇ, ἀλλὰ ἀμιλλᾶσθαι[b] ἐν ταῖς
ἀστικαῖς[c] ταυταισὶ ταῖς ὑπὸ τρυφῆς διαρρεούσαις, ὧν καὶ τὸ
10 πρόσωπον ἐπίπλαστον καὶ ὁ τρόπος μοχθηρίας ὑπεργέμων· φύκει

Benner and Fobes   Schepers
  [a] ἀπώλισθέ *Hemsterhuys*: ἀπολεῖσθαί *codd.*
  [b] ἀμιλλᾶσθαι *Beaudoin*: ἀμιλλᾶσαι *Bx*[1]: ἄμιλλαι *Ven.*: ἀμιλλᾶς *Harl.*
  [c] ἀστικαῖς *Ruhnken*: ἀττικαῖς *codd.*

2.2

IOPHON TO ERASTON
(? 'VENOMOUS' TO 'LOVERMAN')

Damn that vile and abominable cock, and may he come to a horrible end! His crowing woke me from a sweet dream, where I thought, dear neighbour, that I lived in grand style and was enormously rich, with a retinue of servants attending me, whom I imagined to be my overseers and stewards. I thought my hands were covered with rings and that I was wearing stones worth a fortune. And my fingers were delicate and had quite forgotten the mattock. Flatterers, too, seemed to be around me: you could say that Gryllion and Pataecion were at my side. Meanwhile, the people of Athens had come into the theatre and were shouting out that I should be appointed general. But in the middle of the voting the villainous cock crew and the vision vanished. However, when I woke up I was very happy—until I remembered that it was the time of year when the trees shed their leaves, and I realized that my dreams were completely false.

2.8

DRYANTIDAS TO CHRONIUM
('OAKMAN' TO 'LINGERER')

You care no longer for our marriage bed, nor for the children we share, nor indeed for our rural way of life. You are utterly intent on the city; you loathe Pan and the Nymphs you used to call Epimelides and Dryads and Naiads; and you are bringing strange new gods to us to add to the many we have already. Where on earth can I find room on the farm to put up shrines to the Coliades and the Genetyllides? I'm sure I've heard the names of some other divinities, but there are so many most of them have slipped my memory. This doesn't seem a reasonable attitude or sound thinking in you, wife: you're just competing with those fashionable women who are demoralized through luxury. Their faces are all plastered over and their characters stuffed with vice; they outdo even clever

γὰρ καὶ ψιμυθίῳ καὶ παιδέρωτι δευσοποιοῦσι τὰς παρειὰς ὑπὲρ τοὺς
δεινοὺς τῶν ζωγράφων. σὺ δὲ ἢν ὑγιαίνῃς, ὁποίαν σε τὸ ὕδωρ ἢ τὸ
ῥύμμα τὸ πρὶν ἐκάθηρε, τοιαύτη διαμενεῖς.

2.9

Πρατίνας Ἐπιγόνῳ

Μεσημβρίας οὔσης σταθερᾶς φιλήνεμόν τινα ἐπιλεξάμενος πίτυν
καὶ πρὸς τὰς αὔρας ἐκκειμένην, ὑπὸ ταύτῃ τὸ καῦμα ἐσκέπαζον.[a]
καί μοι ψυχάζοντι μάλ᾽ ἡδέως ἐπῆλθέ τι καὶ μουσικῆς
ἐπαφήσασθαι, καὶ λαβὼν τὴν σύριγγα ἐπέτρεχον τῇ γλώττῃ, στενὸν
5 τὸ πνεῦμα μετὰ τῶν χειλέων ἐπισύρων, καί μοι ἡδύ τι καὶ νόμιον
ἐξηκούετο μέλος. ἐν τούτῳ δὲ οὐκ οἶδ᾽ ὅπως ὑπὸ τῆς ἡδυφωνίας
θελγόμεναι πᾶσαί μοι πανταχόθεν αἱ αἶγες περιεχύθησαν, καὶ
ἀφεῖσαι νέμεσθαι τοὺς κομάρους καὶ τὸν ἀνθέρικον ὅλαι τοῦ μέλους
ἐγίνοντο. ἐγὼ δὲ ἐν μέσαις τὸν Ἡδωνὸν ἐμιμούμην τὸν παῖδα τῆς
10 Καλλιόπης. ταῦτά σε οὖν εὐαγγελίζομαι, φίλον ἄνδρα συνειδέναι
βουλόμενος ὅτι μοι μουσικόν ἐστι τὸ αἰπόλιον.

Benner and Fobes Schepers   [a] ἐσκέπαζον *Meineke*: ἐσκίαζον *codd.*

2.15

Εὔσταχυς Πιθακνίωνι

Τοὐμοῦ παιδίου γενέσια ἑορτάζων ἥκειν σε ἐπὶ τὴν πανδαισίαν, ὦ
Πιθακνίων, παρακαλῶ, ἥκειν δὲ οὐ μόνον ἀλλ᾽ ἐπαγόμενον τὴν
γυναῖκα καὶ τὰ παιδία καὶ τὸν συνέργαστρον·[a] εἰ βούλοιο δέ, καὶ τὴν
κύνα, ἀγαθὴν οὖσαν φύλακα καὶ τῷ βάρει τῆς ὑλακῆς ἀποσοβοῦσαν
5 τοὺς ἐπιβουλεύοντας τοῖς ποιμνίοις. ἡ δὲ τοιαύτη οὐκ ἂν ἀτιμάζοιτο
δαιτυμὼν εἶναι σὺν ἡμῖν. ἑορτάσομεν δὲ μάλ᾽ ἡδέως, καὶ πιόμεθα
εἰς μέθην καὶ μετὰ τὸν κόρον ᾀσόμεθα, καὶ ὅστις ἐπιτήδειος κορδακίζειν εἰς μέσους παρελθὼν τὸ κοινὸν ψυχαγωγήσει. μὴ μέλλε
οὖν, ὦ φίλτατε· καλὸν γὰρ ἐν ταῖς κατ᾽ εὐχὰς ἑορταῖς ἐξ ἑωθινοῦ
10 συντάττειν τὰ συμπόσια.

Benner and Fobes Schepers
    [a] συνέργαστρον *codd.*: σύργαστρον *Reiske*: συνεργάτην *Seiler*

artists in smearing their cheeks with rouge and white lead and paint. If you're sensible, you'll stay as you were, when soap and water kept you clean.

2.9

PRATINAS TO EPIGONUS

It was high noon when I found myself a wind-loving pine tree, exposed to the breezes, and under it I took shelter from the heat. While I was very much enjoying the cool I thought I'd play myself a tune. So I took my pipe and ran my tongue over it, letting out a gentle breath as my lips moved along it, and I caught the sound of a sweet pastoral air. Meanwhile, all my goats were somehow charmed by the sweet sounds and came crowding round me from all sides. They stopped grazing on the arbutus and the asphodel and were completely absorbed in the music; while in the midst of them, there was I, playing the part of the Edonian son of Calliope. So I pass on to you this bit of cheerful news, as I want my good friend too to know that my herd of goats likes music.

2.15

EUSTACHYS TO PITHACNION
('GOODCORN' TO 'LITTLEJAR')

I am giving a party for my son's birthday and invite you to come to our fine banquet, Pithacnion—not just you, but bring your wife, your children, and your hired man too. And if you like, bring your dog as well: she is a good watchdog, and with her deep barking scares away those who have designs on your flocks. She is not the sort to be thought unworthy of being our guest. We shall have a very pleasant party: we shall drink till we are drunk, and when we have had our fill we shall sing; and anyone who is skilled in dancing the cordax can take the stage and entertain the assembled company. So, don't be late, dear friend: for an ideal party it's a good thing to organize the drinking early in the day.

2.17

Ναπαῖος Κρηνιάδῃ

Οἶσθά με ἐπισάξαντα τὴν ὄνον σῦκα καὶ ᵃπαλάθας. καταγαγόντα οὖν ἕως οὗ ταῦταᵃ ἀπεδόμην τῶν τινι γνωρίμων, ἄγει μέ τις λαβὼν εἰς τὸ θέατρον καὶ καθίσας ἐν καλῷ διαφόροις ἐψυχαγώγει θεωρίαις. τὰς μὲν οὖν ἄλλας οὐ συνέχω τῇ μνήμῃ, εἰμὶ γὰρ τὰ τοιαῦτα καὶ εἰδέναι
5 καὶ ἀπαγγέλλειν κακός· ἓν δὲ ἰδὼν ἀχανὴς ἐγώ σοι καὶ μικροῦ δεῖν ἄναυδος. εἷς γάρ τις εἰς μέσους παρελθὼν καὶ στήσας τρίποδα τρεῖς μικρὰς ἐπετίθει παροψίδας· εἶτα ὑπὸ ταύταις ἔσκεπε λευκά τινα καὶ μικρὰ καὶ στρογγύλα λιθίδια, οἷα ἡμεῖς ἐπὶ ταῖς ὄχθαις τῶν χειμάρρων ἀνευρίσκομεν· ταῦτα ποτὲ μὲν ἓνᵇ κατὰ μίαν ἔσκεπε
10 παροψίδα, ποτὲ δὲ οὐκ οἶδ' ὅπως ὑπὸ τῇ μιᾷ ἐδείκνυ, ποτὲ δὲ παντελῶς ἀπὸ τῶν παροψίδων ἠφάνιζε καὶ ἐπὶ τοῦ στόματος ἔφαινεν. εἶτα καταβροχθίσας τοὺς πλησίον ἑστῶτας ἄγων εἰς μέσονᶜ τὴν μὲν ἐκ ῥινός τινος τὴν δὲ ἐξ ὠτίου τὴνᶜ δὲ ἐκ κεφαλῆς ἀνῃρεῖτο, καὶ πάλιν ἀνελόμενος ἐξ ὀφθαλμῶν ἐποίει. κλεπτίστατος ἄνθρωπος ὑπὲρ
15 ὃν ἀκούομεν Εὐρυβάτην τὸν Οἰχαλιέα. μὴ γένοιτο κατ' ἀγρὸν τοιοῦτον θηρίον· οὐ γὰρ ἁλώσεται ὑπ' οὐδενός, καὶ πάντα ὑφαιρούμενος τἄνδον φροῦδά μοι τὰ κατ' ἀγρὸν ἀπεργάσεται.

Benner and Fobes   Schepers
ᵃ⁻ᵃ παλάθας <ἄστυδε> καταγαγόντα; ὡς οὖν ταῦτα... *Schepers*
ᵇ ἓν add. *Beaudoin*   ᶜ⁻ᶜ τὴν... τὴν... τὴν *codd.*: τὸ... τὸ... τὸ *Hirschig*

2.36

Εὔδικος Πασίωνι

Φρύγα οἰκέτην ἔχω πονηρόν, ὃς ἀπέβη τοιοῦτος ἐπὶ τῶν ἀγρῶν· ὡς γὰρ τῇ ἕνῃ καὶ νέᾳ κατ' ἐκλογὴν τοῦτον ἐπριάμην, Νουμήνιον μὲν εὐθὺς ἐθέμην καλεῖσθαι, δόξαντα δὲ εἶναι ῥωμαλέον καὶ ἐγρηγορὸς βλέποντα μετὰ περιχαρείας ἦγον ὡς ἐπὶ τῆς ἐσχατιᾶς μοι ἐσόμενον.
5 ἦν δὲ οὗτος μάλαᵃ λαμπρὰ ζημία. ἐσθίει μὲν γὰρ τεσσάρων

Benner and Fobes   Schepers
ᵃ μάλα *Ruhnken*: ἅμα B: ἄρα *Bergler*

2.17

NAPAEUS TO CRENIADES
('WOODY' TO 'FOUNTAINSON')

You know that I loaded my donkey with figs and fruit cakes.
Well, I stabled him until I was due to deliver the stuff to one of
my friends, and then somebody got hold of me and took me off
to the theatre. He found me a good seat and entertained me
with all kinds of shows. I can't remember the others, as I'm no
good at keeping in mind and reporting such things; but let me
tell you I saw one thing that made my jaw drop and I was
almost speechless. A man came among us, set down a three-
legged table, and put three little bowls on it. Then under these
bowls he hid some little round white pebbles—the sort we find
on the banks of fast-flowing streams. Sometimes he would hide
one of these under each bowl; sometimes, goodness knows how,
he would reveal them all under one bowl; then again he would
make them completely vanish from the bowls and produce them
in his mouth. Next, he would swallow them, and then, drawing
forward the bystanders near to him, he would take a pebble
from one man's nose, another from another man's ear, another
from another man's head; and then, gathering them up, he
would make them disappear again. A most dexterous thief!—
superior even to the notorious Eurybates of Oechalia. I hope
such a creature doesn't appear on my farm: nobody could catch
him, and he would filch all my household goods and do his
vanishing trick with everything I have on the farm.

2.36

EUDICUS TO PASION
('JUST' TO 'RICH')

I have a Phrygian slave who is worthless—that's what he
turned out to be on the farm. Since I chose and bought him
on the last day of the month, I straightway named him
Numenius; and as he seemed to be sturdy, with a wide-awake
look to him, I was very pleased when I took him off to live on
my up-country estate. But the man has proved to be a spec-
tacular loss. For he eats as much as four ditchers; and he

σκαπανέων σιτία, ὑπνοῖ δὲ ὅσον ἤκουσα τετυφωμένου σοφιστοῦ
λέγοντος Ἐπιμενίδην τινὰ Κρῆτα κεκοιμῆσθαι, ἢ ὡς ἀκούομεν τὴν
Ἡρακλέους τριέσπερον. τί ἂν οὖν ποιοίην, ὦ φίλτατε ἑταίρων καὶ
συγγεωργῶν, ἴθι φράσον, ἐπὶ τοιούτῳ θηρίῳ καταβαλὼν ἀργυρίδιον;

2.38

Εὐθύδικος Φιλίσκῳ

Ἐγὼ μὲν τὸν παῖδα ἀποδόσθαι εἰς ἄστυ ξύλα καὶ κριθὰς ἀπέπεμψα,
ἐπανήκειν τὴν αὐτὴν τὰ κέρματα κομίζοντα παρεγγυῶν. χόλος δέ,
ἐμπεσὼν ἐξ ὅτου δαιμόνων εἰς αὐτὸν οὐκ ἔχω λέγειν, ὅλον παρήμειψε
καὶ φρενῶν ἔξω κατέστησε. θεασάμενος γὰρ ἕνα τουτωνὶ τῶν
5   μεμηνότων, οὓς διὰ τὸ μανιῶδες πάθος, λύτταν,[a] κύνας ἀποκαλεῖν
εἰώθασιν, ὑπερέβαλε τῇ μιμήσει τῶν κακῶν τὸν ἀρχηγέτην. καὶ ἔστιν
ἰδεῖν θέαμα ἀποτρόπαιον καὶ φοβερόν, κόμην αὐχμηρὰν ἀνασείων, τὸ
βλέμμα ἰταμός, ἡμίγυμνος ἐν τριβωνίῳ, πηρίδιον ἐξηρτημένος, καὶ
ῥόπαλον ἐξ ἀχράδος πεποιημένον μετὰ χεῖρας ἔχων, ἀνυπόδητος,
10 ῥυπῶν, ἄπρακτος, τὸν ἀγρὸν καὶ ἡμᾶς οὐκ εἰδὼς τοὺς γονεῖς, ἀλλ᾽
ἀρνούμενος, φύσει λέγων γεγονέναι τὰ πάντα καὶ τὴν τῶν στοιχείων
σύγκρασιν αἰτίαν εἶναι γενέσεως, οὐχὶ τοὺς πατέρας. εὔδηλον δέ ἐστι
καὶ χρημάτων περιορᾶν καὶ γεωργίαν στυγεῖν. ἀλλὰ καὶ αἰσχύνης
αὐτῷ μέλει οὐδὲν καὶ τὴν αἰδῶ τῶν προσώπων ἀπέξυσται. οἴμοι οἷόν
15 σε, ὦ γεωργία,[b] τὸ τῶν ἀπατεώνων τουτωνὶ φροντιστήριον
ἐξετραχήλισε. μέμφομαι τῷ Σόλωνι καὶ τῷ Δράκοντι, οἳ τοὺς μὲν
κλέπτοντας σταφυλὰς θανάτῳ ζημιοῦν ἐδικαίωσαν, τοὺς δὲ
ἀνδραποδίζοντας ἀπὸ τοῦ φρονεῖν τοὺς νέους ἀθώους εἶναι τιμωρίας
ἀπέλιπον.

Benner and Fobes   Schepers
  [a] λύτταν *Vahlen:* λυττάναν B   [b] γεωργέ *Hercher*

3.2

Ἐκτοδιώκτης Μανδαλοκολάπτῃ

Χθὲς δείλης ὀψίας Γοργίας ὁ Ἐτεοβουτάδης συμβαλών μοι κατὰ
τύχην χρηστῶς ἠσπάσατο καὶ κατεμέμφετο ὅτι μὴ θαμίζοιμι παρ᾽
αὐτόν. καὶ μικρὰ προσπαίξας, "ἴθι πρὸς Διός," εἶπεν, "ὦ βέλτιστε,

sleeps as long as I heard a crazy sophist say that Epimenides the Cretan slept, or as long as the triple night of Hercules we hear about. So, do tell me what I am to do, my dear friend and fellow-farmer, since I've paid good money for such a creature?

2.38

EUTHYDICUS TO PHILISCUS
('RIGHTEOUS' TO 'FRIEND')

I sent my son to the city to sell wood and barley, charging him to come back the same day with the cash. But some emotional fit seized him, sent by who knows what evil spirit, which altered his whole being and drove him out of his wits. What happened was that he was watching one of those lunatics who, as they suffer from a frenzy like rabies, are usually called Cynics, and through imitation he has surpassed even the founder of that wicked sect. And now he presents a revolting and horrible sight—tossing back his filthy hair, staring around him insolently, half naked in a tattered cloak, a pouch hanging by his side, a pear-wood stick in his hands, barefoot, dirty, idle, not knowing the farm or us his parents, but denying us and saying that all things come about through nature, and that the cause of birth is not parents but a combination of the elements. And it's pretty obvious that he despises money and hates farming. What is more, he has no sense of shame and he has wiped modesty from his countenance. Alas, O Farming, how has the thinking-shop of these rogues perverted you! I blame Solon and Draco, who thought fit to give the death penalty to men who steal grapes, but let off scot-free men who deprive the young of their wits and enslave them.

3.2

HECTODIOCTES TO MANDALOCOLAPTES
('SIX-O'CLOCK-CHASER' TO 'DOORBOLT-PECKER')

Late yesterday afternoon Gorgias the Eteoboutade happened to meet me, greeted me kindly, and took me to task for not visiting him more often. After a little teasing he said, 'By

καὶ μετὰ βραχὺ λουσάμενος ἧκε Ἀηδόνιον ἡμῖν τὴν ἑταίραν ἄγων.
5 ἔστι δέ μοι συνήθης ἐπιεικῶς καὶ μένει, πάντως οὐκ ἀγνοεῖς, μικρὸν
ἄπωθεν τοῦ Λεωκορίου. δεῖπνόν τε ἡμῖν ηὐτρέπισται γεννικόν, ἰχθὺς
τεμαχίτης καὶ σταμνία τοῦ Μενδησίου νέκταρος, εἴποι τις ἄν,
πεπληρωσμένα." καὶ ὁ μὲν ταῦτα εἰπὼν ᾤχετο. ἐγὼ δὲ παρὰ τὴν
Ἀηδόνιον δραμὼν καὶ φράσας παρ' ὅτου καλοῖτο, ἐδέησα κινδύνῳ
10 περιπεσεῖν. ἀγνώμονος γάρ, ὡς ἔοικε, πειραθεῖσα τοῦ Γοργίου καὶ
μικροπρεποῦς περὶ τὰς ἀντιδόσεις, τὴν ὀργὴν ἔναυλον ἔχουσα,
πλήρη τὴν κακάβην ἀποσπάσασα τῶν χυτροπόδων ἐδέησέ μου κατὰ
τοῦ βρέγματος καταχέαι ζέοντος τοῦ ὕδατος, εἰ μὴ φθάσας
ἀπεπήδησα παρὰ βραχὺ φυγὼν τὸν κίνδυνον. οὕτως ἡμεῖς ἐλπίσιν
15 ἀπατηλαῖς βουκολούμενοι πλείους τῶν ἡδονῶν τοὺς προπηλακισμοὺς
ὑπομένομεν.

3.11

Ὡρολόγιος Λαχανοθαυμάσῳ

Ἑρμῆ κερδῷε καὶ ἀλεξίκακε Ἡράκλεις, ἀπεσώθην. οὐδὲν ἂν δεινὸν
ἔτι γένοιτο. προχόην ὑφελόμενος ἀργυρᾶν Φανίου τοῦ πλουσίου
δρόμῳ δοὺς φέρεσθαι (ἦν γὰρ ἀωρία τῆς νυκτὸς) κατηπειγόμην[a]
σώζειν ἑαυτόν. κύνες δὲ ἐξαίφνης οἰκουροὶ περιχυθέντες ἄλλος
5 ἀλλαχόθεν χαλεποὶ καὶ βαρεῖς τὴν ὑλακὴν ἐπήεσαν Μολοττοὶ καὶ
Κνώσιοι, ὑφ' ὧν οὐδὲν ἐκώλυσέ με ὡς ἠδικηκότα τὴν Ἄρτεμιν
διεσπάσθαι μέσον, ὡς μηδὲ τὰ ἀκρωτήρια[b] εἰς τὴν ὑστεραίαν περι-
λειφθῆναι πρὸς ταφὴν τοῖς ἑτοίμοις εἰς ἔλεον καὶ συμπάθειαν. εὑρὼν
οὖν ὑδορρόον ἀνεῳγότα οὐκ εἰς βάθος ἀλλ' ἐπιπολῆς καὶ ὑποδὺς εἰς
10 τοῦτον, κατεκρύβην. ἔτι σοι ταῦτα τρέμων καὶ παλλόμενος λέγω.
ἑωσφόρου δὲ ἀνασχόντος τῶν μὲν οὐκ ἠσθόμην οὐκέθ' ὑλακτούντων
(οἴκοι γὰρ πάντως ἐδέδεντο) αὐτὸς δὲ εἰς Πειραιᾶ δραμὼν νηὶ
Σικελικῇ λύειν μελλούσῃ τὰ πρυμνήσια περιτυχὼν ἀπεδόμην τῷ
ναυκλήρῳ τὴν προχόην. καὶ νυνὶ τὸ τίμημα ἔχων νένασμαι τοῖς
15 κέρμασι καὶ νεόπλουτος ἐπανελήλυθα, καὶ τοσοῦτον ῥιπίζομαι ταῖς
ἐλπίσιν ὡς ἐπιθυμεῖν κόλακας τρέφειν καὶ κεχρῆσθαι παρασίτοις, οὐ

Benner and Fobes   Schepers
[a] κατηπειγόμην *Meineke*: ἠπειγόμην x[1]: καὶ ἠπειγόμην x *Neap.*[a]
[b] ἀκρωτήρια *Bergler*: ἀκροθίνια *codd.*

Zeus, my fine fellow, off you go, and a bit later, after your
bath, come to see me and bring along Aëdonion the courtesan.
She's a pretty good friend of mine, and she lodges, as you
very well know, not far from the Leocorium. I have a noble
dinner prepared for us—sliced fish and jars filled with what
might be called Mendesian nectar.' So saying he went his way,
and I ran to Aëdonion's place, told her who had invited her—
and just missed running into danger. It seems she had found
Gorgias inconsiderate, and stingy in his payments to her; so
with her irritation still fresh in mind, she took a pot full of
water from its stand and narrowly missed pouring some of the
boiling water over my head. But I was quick enough to jump
back and just escaped the danger. And so we deceive ourselves
with false hopes, and find ourselves with more abuse than
pleasures.

3.11

HOROLOGIUS TO LACHANOTHAUMASUS
('CLOCK-WATCHER' TO
'VEGETABLE-WORSHIPPER')

O Hermes, giver of gain, and Hercules, averter of evil, I managed to get away safely. There can be no more trouble ahead. I
stole a silver jug belonging to rich Phanias, and took to my
heels—it was the very dead of night—and rushed off to save
myself. Suddenly I was surrounded on all sides and attacked
by watchdogs, savage deep-baying Molossians and Cretans;
and nothing could prevent my being torn apart by them, as
though I had offended Artemis, with not even my hands and
feet surviving next day to be buried by anyone who could feel
pity and sympathy for me. Well, I found an open water-channel,
not dug deep but near the surface, and diving into it I hid
myself—I'm trembling and quivering even as I tell you this.
When the dawn-star rose I was no longer aware of the dogs
howling (no doubt they had been tied up at home); so I ran to
the Peiraeus, found a Sicilian ship just about to cast off, and
sold the jug to the skipper. And now I've got my price for it
I've come back, newly rich with my load of cash; and so
fanned by hopes that I'm eager to keep flatterers and make

παρασιτεῖν αὐτός. ἀλλ' ἢν τουτὶ τὸ πορισθὲν ἀργύριον ἀπαναλώσω,
πάλιν ἐπὶ τὴν ἀρχαίαν ἐπιτήδευσιν τρέψομαι· οὐδὲ γὰρ κύων σκυτο-
τραγεῖν μαθοῦσα τῆς τέχνης ἐπιλήσεται.

3.17

Ἀκρατολύμας Χωνοκράτει

Χθὲς Καρίωνος περὶ τὸ φρέαρ ἀσχολουμένου εἰσέφρησα εἰς
τοὐπτάνιον. ἔπειτα εὑρὼν λοπάδα εὖ μάλα κεκαρυκευμένην καὶ
ἀλεκτρυόνα ὀπτὸν χύτραν τε μεμβράδας ἔχουσαν καὶ ἀφύας
Μεγαρικὰς ἐξήρπασα, καὶ ἀποπηδήσας ποῖ καταχθείην ἐζήτουν καὶ
5 εὐκαίρως[a] ἐμφάγοιμι μόνος. ἀπορίᾳ δὲ τόπου δραμὼν ἐπὶ τὴν
Ποικίλην (καὶ γὰρ οὐκ ἠνώχλει ταύτην οὐδὲ εἷς τῶν ἀδολέσχων
τουτωνὶ φιλοσόφων) κεῖθι τῶν πόνων ἀπέλαυον. ἀνανεύσας δὲ τῆς
λοπάδος ὁρῶ προσιόντας τῶν ἀπὸ τῆς τηλίας τινὰς νεανίσκων, καὶ
δείσας τὰ μὲν βρώματα ὄπισθεν ἀπεθέμην, αὐτὸς δὲ εἰς τοὔδαφος
10 ἐκείμην κρύπτων τὰ κλέμματα εὐχόμενός τε τοῖς Ἀποτροπαίοις τὸ
νέφος παρελθεῖν, χόνδρους ὑποσχόμενος λιβανωτοῦ ἱκανούς, οὓς
οἴκοι ἀναλεξάμενος τῶν ἱερῶν ἔχω εὖ μάλα εὐρωτιῶντας. καὶ οὐκ
ἠστόχησα· οἱ θεοὶ γὰρ αὐτοὺς ἄλλην ὁδὸν ἔτρεψαν. κἀγὼ σπουδῇ
καταβροχθίσας πάνθ' ὅσα ἐνέκειτο τοῖς σκεύεσι φίλῳ πανδοκεῖ τὴν
15 χύτραν καὶ τὸ λοπάδιον, τὰ λείψανα τῶν κλεμμάτων, χάρισμα δοὺς
ἔχειν ἀπεχώρησα ἐπιεικής τις καὶ δεξιὸς ἐκ τῶν δωρημάτων
ἀναφανείς.

Benner and Fobes　Schepers
[a] εὐκήλως *Meiser: fort. recte*

3.23

Λιμέντερος Ἀμασήτῳ

Παρ' ἕνα τινὰ τῶν τὰ πινάκια παρὰ τὸ Ἴακχεῖον προτιθέντων καὶ
τοὺς ὀνείρους ὑποκρίνεσθαι ὑπισχνουμένων βούλομαι ἐλθὼν τὰς δύο
ταύτας δραχμάς, ἃς οἶσθά με ἐν χεροῖν ἔχοντα, καταβαλὼν τὴν

use of parasites, and no longer be a parasite myself. But if I
do spend all this money I've got, I'll go back to my old pursuits: a dog that has learnt to chew leather will never forget
the habit.

3.17

ACRATOLYMAS TO CHONOCRATES
('NEATWINE-DESTROYER' TO 'FUNNEL-MASTER')

Yesterday, when Carion was occupied at the well, I went into
the kitchen. Then, finding a dish dressed with a rich sauce, a
roast fowl, and a pot full of sprats and Megarian anchovies,
I grabbed them and made off, looking round for a spot where
I could drop anchor and eat it up on my own at leisure. For
want of anywhere better I ran to the Painted Portico (for
indeed not one of those babbling philosophers was being a
nuisance there), and there I began to enjoy the fruit of my
efforts. But looking up from my dish I saw approaching me
some of the youths from the gaming-table, and in my alarm I
put the food behind me and lay down on the ground, hiding
my pickings and praying to the Averting Gods that the storm
would pass me by. I vowed them a fine amount of grains of
frankincense, which I've collected from sacrifices and have at
home, well and truly mouldy. And I scored a hit, for the gods
diverted the men another way. Meanwhile, I quickly gulped
down all that remained on the dishes, gave the pot and the
plate, all that was left of my plunder, as a free gift to an
innkeeper pal of mine, and took my departure, showing
myself to be not just clever but decent in my generosity.

3.23

LIMENTERUS TO AMASETUS
('HUNGRY-GUT' TO 'NON-CHEWER')

I want to visit one of those people who put up their notices by
the temple of Iacchus professing to interpret dreams, and
paying these two drachmas you know I have in my hands, to

φανεῖσαν ὄψιν μοι κατὰ τοὺς ὕπνους διηγήσασθαι. οὐ χεῖρον δὲ καὶ
5 πρὸς σὲ ὡς φίλον ἀναθέσθαι τὸ καινὸν τοῦτο καὶ πέρα πάσης
πίστεως φάσμα.

Ἐδόκουν γὰρ κατ᾽ ὄναρ εὐπρεπὴς εἶναι νεανίσκος καὶ οὐχ ὁ
τυχών, ἀλλ᾽ ἐκεῖνος εἶναι ὁ Ἰλιεὺς ὁ περίψηκτος[a] καὶ περικαλλής,
ὁ τοῦ Τρωὸς παῖς Γανυμήδης, καὶ καλαύροπα ἔχειν καὶ σύριγγα,
10 καὶ τιάρᾳ Φρυγίῳ σκέπειν τὴν κεφαλὴν ποιμαίνειν τε καὶ εἶναι κατὰ
τὴν Ἴδην. ἐξαίφνης δὲ ἐπιπτάντα μοι γαμψώνυχα καὶ μέγαν ἀετόν,
γοργὸν τὸ βλέμμα καὶ ἀγκυλοχείλην τὸ στόμα, κουφίσαντά με τοῖς
ὄνυξιν ἀφ᾽ οὗπερ ἐκαθήμην πέτρου μετεωρίζειν εἰς τὸν ἀέρα καὶ
πελάζειν τοῖς οὐρανίοις τόποις ἐπειγόμενον· εἶτα μέλλοντα ψαύειν
15 τῶν πυλῶν αἷς αἱ Ὧραι ἐφεστᾶσι, κεραυνῷ βληθέντα πεσεῖν, καὶ τὸ
ὄρνεον οὐκέτι εἶναι τὸν διπετῆ καὶ μέγαν ἀετόν, γῦπα δὲ πικρὸν[b]
ὀδωδότα, ἐμὲ δὲ τοῦτον ὅς εἰμι Λιμέντερον, γυμνὸν πάσης ἐσθῆτος,
οἷα πρὸς λουτρὸν ἢ παλαίστραν ηὐτρεπισμένον.

Ἐκταραχθεὶς οὖν ὡς εἰκὸς ἐπὶ τοσούτῳ πτώματι διηγειρόμην,
20 καὶ πρὸς τὸ παράδοξον τῆς ὄψεως ἀγωνιῶ καὶ δέομαι οἷ φέρει τὸ
ὄναρ μαθεῖν παρὰ τῶν τὰ τοιαῦτα ἀκριβούντων, εἰ μέλλει τις
ἀπλανῶς εἰδέναι καὶ εἰδὼς ἀληθίζεσθαι.

Benner and Fobes   Schepers
[a] περίπυστος *Harl.*: περίψυκτος *Bergler*   [b] πικρὸν *Bergler*: μικρὸν *codd.*

3.28
Τουρδοσύναγος Ἐφαλλοκύθρῃ

Ὁ μὲν Κρίτων ὑπ᾽ ἀνοίας καὶ ἀρχαιότητος τρόπου τὸν υἱὸν εἰς
φιλοσόφου φοιτᾶν ἐπέτρεψε, τὸν αὐστηρὸν πρεσβύτην καὶ ἀμειδῆ,
τὸν ἐκ τῆς Ποικίλης, ἐξ ἁπάντων τῶν φιλοσόφων καθηγεῖσθαι τοῦ
παιδὸς ἀξιώτερον ἡγησάμενος, ὡς ἂν παρ᾽ αὐτῷ λόγων τινὰς σκιν-
5 δαλμοὺς ἐκμαθὼν ἐριστικὸς καὶ ἀγκύλος τὴν γλῶσσαν γένηται. ὁ δὲ
παῖς ἐς τὸ ἀκριβέστατον ἐξεμάξατο τὸν διδάσκαλον· οὐ πρότερον
γὰρ λόγων γενέσθαι μαθητὴς ἀλλὰ τοῦ βίου καὶ τῆς ἀγωγῆς ἐσπού-
δασε. θεασάμενος γὰρ τὸν διδάσκαλον τῇ ἡμέρᾳ σεμνὸν καὶ
σκυθρωπὸν καὶ τοῖς νέοις ἐπιτιμῶντα, νύκτωρ δὲ περικαλύπτοντα
10 τὴν κεφαλὴν τριβωνίῳ καὶ περὶ χαμαιτυπεῖα εἰλούμενον, ἐζήλωσεν ἐν

describe the dream which came to me in my sleep. But it's not a bad idea to tell you too, as my friend, about this odd and utterly incredible apparition.

In my dream I seemed to be a fine-looking young man, no ordinary person, but that very sleek, handsome Ilian, Ganymede, the son of Tros, with shepherd's crook and pan pipe, my head covered with a Phrygian cap, and shepherding my flock on Mount Ida. Suddenly a large eagle with crooked talons, fierce eyes, and hooked beak, flew down on me, lifted me in his talons from the rock I was sitting on, carried me up into the sky, and arrived at a rush near the heavenly regions. Then, just as I was about to touch the gates where the Hours stand guard, I was struck by a thunderbolt and fell; and the bird was no longer the great divine eagle, but a foul-smelling vulture; and I was my usual self, Limenterus, without a stitch of clothing, as if prepared for a bath or a wrestling-match.

You can imagine that I was thoroughly shaken up by a fall like that, and I woke up; and I'm very anxious about this extraordinary vision. I want to find out from the experts in such things what the dream means, if there is somebody with accurate knowledge which he can pass on truthfully.

3.28

TURDOSYNAGUS TO EPHALLOCYTHRES ('THRUSH-COLLECTOR' TO 'POT-ATTACKER')

In his stupidity and old-fashioned simplicity Crito has let his son go to school to a philosopher. He considered that, out of all the philosophers, that harsh unsmiling old man from the Painted Portico was the most suitable to teach the boy, since he might learn from him some logic-chopping arguments and so become captious and devious in speech. The boy modelled himself on his teacher in every detail: he was an eager student not so much of his doctrines as of his life-style and behaviour. He noticed that by day his teacher was solemn and severe and highly critical of the young; but that at night he covered his head in an old cloak and frequented the brothels—and the boy

καλῷ. καὶ πέμπτην ταύτην ἡμέραν εἰς ἔρωτα Ἀκαλανθίδος τῆς ἐκ
Κεραμεικοῦ κατολισθήσας φλέγεται· αὕτη δὲ ἐπιεικῶς ἔχει πρὸς ἐμὲ
καὶ ἐρᾶν ὁμολογεῖ, τῷ μειρακίῳ δὲ ᵃ ἔτι ἀντιτείνεταιᵃ ἠσθημένη τῷ
πόθῳ τυφόμενον, καὶ οὐ πρότερόν φησιν ἐπιδώσειν ἑαυτὴν πρὶν ἂν
15 ἐγὼ τοῦτο ἐπιτρέψω· ἐμὲ γὰρ κύριον τοῦ τὰ τοιαῦτα προστάττειν
ἐποιήσατο. πολλὰ καὶ ἀγαθὰ δοίης, Ἀφροδίτη πάνδημε, τῇ φιλτάτῃ
γυναικί· ἑταίρου γάρ, οὐχ ἑταίρας, ἔργον διεπράξατο. ἐξ ἐκείνου
γὰρ θεραπεύομαι λιπαρῶς ἄλλοτε ἄλλαις δωροφορίαις· καὶ ἤνᵇ μοι
ῥεύσειε τοῦ χρόνου προϊόντος δαψιλέστερος ὁ πόρος,ᶜ οὐδὲν κωλύσει
20 με τούτου γαμοῦντος ἐπίκληρον γυναῖκα ἐν γαμετῆς σχήματι τὴν
Ἀκαλανθίδα λυσάμενον ἀναλαβεῖν. ἡ γὰρ τοῦ ζῆν αἰτία κοινωνὸς
τοῦ ζῆν δικαίως ἂν κατασταίη.

Benner and Fobes   Schepers
ᵃ⁻ᵃ ἔτι ἀντιτείνεται *Arnaud*: ἐπανατείνεται *codd*.
ᵇ ἤν *codd*.: εἰ *Jacobs*   ᶜ ὁ πόρος *add. Meiser*

4.7
Θαῒς Εὐθυδήμῳ

Ἐξ οὗ φιλοσοφεῖν ἐπενόησας, σεμνός τις ἐγένου καὶ τὰς ὀφρῦς ὑπὲρ
τοὺς κροτάφους ἐπῆρας. εἶτα σχῆμα ἔχων καὶ βιβλίδιον μετὰ χεῖρας
εἰς τὴν Ἀκαδημίαν σοβεῖς, τὴν δὲ ἡμετέραν οἰκίαν ὡς οὐδὲ ἰδὼν
πρότερον παρέρχῃ. ἐμάνης, Εὐθύδημε· οὐκ οἶδας οἷός ἐστιν ὁ
5 σοφιστὴς οὗτος ὁ ἐσκυθρωπακὼς καὶ τοὺς θαυμαστοὺς τούτους
διεξιὼν πρὸς ὑμᾶς λόγους; ἀλλ᾽ ἐμοὶ μὲν πράγματα πόσος ἐστὶν οἴει
χρόνος ἐξ οὗ παρέχει βουλόμενος ἐντυχεῖν; προσφθείρεται δὲ
Ἑρπυλλίδι τῇ Μεγάρας ἄβρᾳ. τότε μὲν οὖν αὐτὸν οὐ προσιέμην,
σὲ γὰρ περιβάλλουσα κοιμᾶσθαι μᾶλλον ἐβουλόμην ἢ τὸ παρὰ
10 πάντων σοφιστῶν χρυσίον. ἐπεὶ δέ σε ἀποτρέπειν ἔοικε τῆς μεθ᾽
ἡμῶν συνηθείας, ὑποδέξομαι αὐτὸν καί, εἰ βούλει, τὸν διδάσκαλον
τουτονὶ τὸν μισογύναιον ἐπιδείξω σοι νυκτὸς οὐκ ἀρκούμενον ταῖς
συνήθεσιν ἡδοναῖς. λῆρος ταῦτά εἰσι καὶ τῦφος καὶ ἐργολάβεια
μειρακίων, ὦ ἀνόητε. οἴει δὲ διαφέρειν ἑταίρας σοφιστήν; τοσοῦτον
15 ἴσως ὅσον οὐ διὰ τῶν αὐτῶν ἑκάτεροι πείθειν, ἐπεὶ ἔν γε ἀμφοτέροις
τέλος πρόκειται τὸ λαβεῖν. πόσῳ δὲ ἀμείνους ἡμεῖς καὶ
εὐσεβέστεραι· οὐ λέγομεν θεοὺς οὐκ εἶναι, ἀλλὰ πιστεύομεν

emulated him in fine style. Four days ago he fell passionately in love with Acalanthis from the Cerameicus. Now, she's on pretty good terms with me and admits that she loves me; but realizing that the boy is on fire with desire, she is still resisting him, and says she won't yield herself to him until I give permission. For she considered that I was the authority to make decisions in such cases. O Aphrodite Pandemus, grant many blessings to such a dear girl: she has acted like a man-friend, not a girl-friend. For I am being earnestly cultivated by him with a constant supply of gifts; and if as time passes these resources flow even more abundantly to me, when he marries a rich heiress there'll be nothing to stop me buying out Acalanthis and making her formally my wife. For as she has been the cause of my livelihood, she deserves to share my life.

4.7

THAÏS TO EUTHYDEMUS

Ever since you decided to take up philosophy you have become pompous and raised your eyebrows above your temples. Then, with a stately air and holding a book you strut along to the Academy, passing my house as though you had never even seen it before. You've lost your wits, Euthydemus: don't you realize what kind of a man your sophist is, delivering those marvellous lectures to you with his gloomy look? How long do you think he has made himself a nuisance to me, wishing me to make an appointment with him? And he's randy over Megara's maid Herpyllis too. Once upon a time I wouldn't have let him come near me, and would rather have hugged you in bed than the gold of all the sophists. But since he seems to be distracting you from going with me, I'll welcome him and, if you like, I'll show you that this misogynist teacher is not satisfied with the usual pleasures at night. You idiot, these pretensions are just nonsense and humbug and making a profit out of boys. Do you suppose a sophist is different from a courtesan? Perhaps their means of persuasion are different; but they both have one end in view—profit. But how much better and more righteous we are! We don't say there are no gods: rather we believe our lovers when they

ὀμνύουσι τοῖς ἐρασταῖς ὅτι φιλοῦσιν ἡμᾶς· οὐδ' ἀξιοῦμεν ἀδελφαῖς
καὶ μητράσι μίγνυσθαι τοὺς ἄνδρας, ἀλλ' οὐδὲ γυναιξὶν ἀλλοτρίαις.
20 εἰ μὴ ὅτι τὰς νεφέλας ὁπόθεν εἶεν καὶ τὰς ἀτόμους ὁποῖαι ἀγνοοῦ-
μεν, διὰ τοῦτο ἥττους δοκοῦμέν σοι τῶν σοφιστῶν. καὶ αὐτὴ παρὰ
τούτοις ἐσχόλακα καὶ πολλοῖς διείλεγμαι. οὐδὲ εἷς ἑταίρᾳ ὁμιλῶν
τυραννίδας ὀνειροπολεῖ καὶ στασιάζει τά κοινά, ἀλλὰ σπάσας τὸν
ἑωθινὸν καὶ μεθυσθεὶς εἰς ὥραν τρίτην ἢ τετάρτην ἠρεμεῖ. παιδεύομεν
25 δὲ οὐ χεῖρον ἡμεῖς τοὺς νέους. ἐπεὶ σύγκρινον, εἰ βούλει, Ἀσπασίαν
τὴν ἑταίραν καὶ Σωκράτην τὸν σοφιστήν, καὶ πότερος ἀμείνους
αὐτῶν ἐπαίδευσεν ἄνδρας λόγισαι· τῆς μὲν γὰρ ὄψει μαθητὴν
Περικλέα, τοῦ δὲ Κριτίαν. κατάβαλλε τὴν μωρίαν ταύτην καὶ ἀηδίαν,
ὁ ἐμὸς ἔρως Εὐθύδημε—οὐ πρέπει σκυθρωποῖς εἶναι τοιούτοις
30 ὄμμασι—καὶ πρὸς τὴν ἐρωμένην ἧκε τὴν ἑαυτοῦ οἷος ἐπανελθὼν ἀπὸ
Λυκείου πολλάκις τὸν ἱδρῶτα ἀποψώμενος, ἵνα μικρὰ κραιπαλήσαν-
τες ἐπιδειξώμεθα ἀλλήλοις τὸ καλὸν τέλος τῆς ἡδονῆς. καὶ σοὶ νῦν
μάλιστα φανοῦμαι σοφή. οὐ μακρὸν δίδωσιν ὁ δαίμων χρόνον τοῦ
ζῆν· μὴ λάθῃς τοῦτον εἰς αἰνίγματα καὶ λήρους ἀναλώσας. ἔρρωσο.

4.8

Σιμαλίων Πετάλῃ

Εἰ μὲν ἡδονήν σοί τινα φέρειν ἢ φιλοτιμίαν πρός τινας τῶν
διαλεγομένων οἴει τὸ πολλάκις ἡμᾶς ἐπὶ τὰς θύρας φοιτᾶν καὶ τοῖς
πεμπομένοις πρὸς τοὺς εὐτυχεστέρους ἡμῶν θεραπαινιδίοις
ἀποδύρεσθαι, οὐκ ἀλόγως ἡμῖν ἐντρυφᾷς. ἴσθι μέντοι, καίτοι ποιῶν
5 οἶδα πρᾶγμα ἀσύμφορον ἐμαυτῷ, οὕτω με διακείμενον ὡς ὀλίγοι
τῶν ἐντυγχανόντων σοι νῦν ἀμεληθέντες ἂν διατεθεῖεν. καίτοι γε
ᾤμην τὸν ἄκρατον ἔσεσθαί μοι παρηγόρημα[a] ὃν παρ' Εὐφρονίῳ
τρίτην ἑσπέραν πολύν τινα ἐνεφορησάμην, ὡς δὴ τὰς παρὰ τὴν νύκτα
φροντίδας διωσόμενος· τὸ δὲ ἄρα ἐναντίως ἔσχεν. ἀνερρίπισε γάρ
10 μου τὴν ἐπιθυμίαν ὥστε κλαίοντά με καὶ βρυχώμενον ἐλεεῖσθαι μὲν
παρὰ τοῖς ἐπιεικεστέροις, γέλωτα δὲ τοῖς ἄλλοις παρέχειν. μικρὰ δ'
ἔπεστί μοι παραψυχὴ καὶ μαραινόμενον ἤδη παραμύθιον ὁ στέφανος[b]

Benner and Fobes   Schepers
[a] παρηγόρημα *Bergler*: κατηγόρημα   [b] ὁ στέφανος *add. Schepers*

swear they love us. Nor do we think it right for men to have
sex with their sisters and mothers—or even with other men's
wives. Maybe you think us inferior to the sophists because we
don't know where the clouds come from and what atoms are.
Well, I too have attended their lectures and talked to many of
them. No man, when he is in a courtesan's company, dreams of
being a tyrant or a revolutionary. No—he downs his morning
tipple and stays quietly drunk until the third or fourth hour.
We are just as good educators of young men. Come, judge, if
you will, between the courtesan Aspasia and the sophist
Socrates, and decide which of them educated better men. You
will see Pericles the pupil of the one and Critias of the other.
Give up this silly, disagreeable attitude, Euthydemus my
love—eyes like yours should not be scowling—and come to
your beloved just as you have often done, when you return
from the Lyceum wiping off the sweat; so we can have a bit of
a revel ourselves, and show each other how to achieve that
noble end, pleasure. To you too I shall now appear a
supremely wise woman. The gods give us no long span of life:
don't waste yours unawares on riddles and nonsense.

Farewell

4.8

SIMALION TO PETALE

If you think that it gives you pleasure or gains you credit in
the eyes of any of the men who consort with you, that I am
constantly coming to your door, and complaining bitterly to
the maids who are sent to greet more fortunate visitors than
myself, then you have some reason to treat me with contempt.
But let me remind you, though I realize that I'm doing myself
a disservice, that few of your present lovers would feel as I do
towards you if they were neglected. And yet I thought I
would get some consolation from the wine which two evenings
ago I put away neat in large quantities at Euphronius' house.
My idea was that it would banish my night-time worries; but
as it turned out the opposite happened. For it so fanned my
desire that my weeping and howling, while occasioning pity
among the more decent of the party, raised a laugh among all
the others. Nor is there much consolation for me—the comfort

ὅν μοι ὑπὸ τὴν λυπρὰν ἐν^c τῷ συμποσίῳ μέμψιν προσέρριψας ἀπ'
αὐτῶν περισπάσασα τῶν πλοκάμων, ὡς δὴ πᾶσι τοῖς ὑφ' ἡμῶν
15 πεμφθεῖσιν ἀχθομένη. εἰ δή σοι ταῦτα ἡδονὴν φέρει, ἀπόλαυε τῆς
ἡμετέρας μερίμνης, κἂν ᾖ σοι φίλον διηγοῦ τοῖς νῦν μὲν
μακαριωτέροις ἡμῶν, οὐκ εἰς μακρὰν δέ, ἄνπερ ὡς ἡμεῖς ἔχωσιν,
ἀνιασομένοις. εὔχου μέντοι μηδέν σοι νεμεσῆσαι ταύτης τῆς
ὑπεροψίας τὴν Ἀφροδίτην. ἕτερος ἂν λοιδορούμενος ἔγραφε καὶ
20 ἀπειλῶν, ἀλλ' ἐγὼ δεόμενος καὶ ἀντιβολῶν· ἐρῶ γάρ, ὦ Πετάλη,
κακῶς. φοβοῦμαι δὲ μὴ κάκιον ἔχων μιμήσωμαί τινα τῶν περὶ τὰς
ἐρωτικὰς μέμψεις ἀτυχεστέρων.

^c ἐν add. Bergler

4.9

Πετάλη Σιμαλίωνι

Ἐβουλόμην μὲν ὑπὸ δακρύων οἰκίαν ἑταίρας τρέφεσθαι· λαμπρῶς
γὰρ ἂν ἔπραττον ἀφθόνων τούτων ἀπολαύουσα παρὰ σοῦ· νῦν δὲ δεῖ
χρυσίου ἡμῖν, ἱματίων, κόσμου, θεραπαινιδίων. ἡ τοῦ βίου διοίκησις
ἅπασα ἐντεῦθεν. οὐκ ἔστιν ἐν Μυρρινοῦντι πατρῷον ἐμοὶ κτημάτιον,
5 οὐδ' ἐν τοῖς ἀργυρείοις ἐμοὶ μέταλλον, ἀλλὰ μισθωμάτια καὶ αἱ
δυστυχεῖς αὗται καὶ κατεστεναγμέναι τῶν ἀνοήτων ἐραστῶν
χάριτες. σοὶ δὲ ἐνιαυτὸν ἐντυγχάνουσα ἀδημονῶ, καὶ αὐχμηρὰν μὲν
ἔχω τὴν κεφαλὴν μηδὲ ἰδοῦσα τοῦ χρόνου τούτου μύρον, τὰ δὲ
ἀρχαῖα καὶ τρύχινα περιβαλλομένη ταραντινίδια αἰσχύνομαι τὰς
10 φίλας, οὕτως ἀγαθόν τί μοι γένοιτο. εἶτα οἴει μέ σοι παρακαθημένην
πόθεν ζήσειν; ἀλλὰ δακρύεις; πεπαύσῃ μετὰ μικρόν. ἐγὼ δὲ ἂν μή
τις ὁ διδοὺς ᾖ, πεινήσω τὸ καλόν. θαυμάζω δέ σου καὶ τὰ δάκρυα
ὡς ἐστιν ἀπίθανα. δέσποινα Ἀφροδίτη, φιλεῖς, ἄνθρωπε, φής, καὶ
βούλει σοι τὴν ἐρωμένην διαλέγεσθαι· ζῆν γὰρ χωρὶς ἐκείνης μὴ
15 δύνασθαι. τί οὖν; οὐ ποτήριά ἐστιν ἐπὶ τῆς οἰκίας ὑμῖν;...^a μὴ
χρυσία τῆς μητρός, μὴ δάνεια τοῦ πατρὸς κομιούμενος.^b μακαρία
Φιλῶτις· εὐμενεστέροις ὄμμασιν εἶδον ἐκείνην αἱ Χάριτες· οἷον

Benner and Fobes   Schepers
^a lacunam indic. edd. plerique: ἔρρε suppl. Meiser, alii alia
^b κομιουμένοις; Hercher

is already fading—from the garland which you tore from your hair and threw at me during that wretched quarrel we had at the party—just to show your displeasure with everything I sent you. Well, if this gives you pleasure, enjoy my distress; and if you like, tell the story to those who are now more fortunate than me, but who will soon be grieving if they share my fate. But you'd better offer a prayer to Aphrodite that you don't suffer her resentment for this show of disdain. Another man would have written to you with threats and abuses, but I write with prayers and entreaties. For I'm desperately in love with you, Petale; and I'm afraid that if things get worse I may follow the example of one of those who have come to an unfortunate end through lovers' quarrels.

4.9

PETALE TO SIMALION

I wish that a courtesan's house could be maintained on tears, for I would be doing marvellously, with the endless supply I have of them from you. But, as it is, I must have money, clothes, finery, maids: running my life depends entirely on these. I have no inherited estate in Myrrhinus, nor a share in the silver mines—just my paltry fees and these wretched thank-offerings I get from my stupid lovers, covered in their sighs. I've been your mistress for a year and I'm fed up. My hair is all dry and horrible, as I've not seen any unguent for it all that year, and I'm wearing tatty old Tarentine cloaks that—so help me!—make me ashamed to meet my girl friends. Where then do you think I'm going to find a living if I only stay by your side? So you're weeping? You'll soon get over it. But if I can't find a generous man, I'll well and truly starve. As for your tears, I do wonder: they're not convincing. By our lady Aphrodite, you say you're in love, sir, and you want your mistress to take you to bed, for you can't live without her. Well—haven't you men got any goblets at home? Don't come near me unless you are bringing me your mother's jewels or money borrowed from your father. Lucky Philotis! The Graces looked on her with kindlier eyes. What a lover she has

ἐραστὴν ἔχει Μενεκλείδην, ὃς καθ᾿ ἡμέραν δίδωσί τι. ἄμεινον γὰρ ἢ
κλάειν. ἐγὼ δὲ ἡ τάλαινα θρηνῳδόν, οὐκ ἐραστὴν ἔχω· στεφάνιά μοι
20 καὶ ῥόδα ὥσπερ ἀώρῳ τάφῳ πέμπει καὶ κλάειν δι᾿ ὅλης φησὶ τῆς
νυκτός. ἐὰν φέρῃς τι, ἧκε μὴ κλάων, εἰ δέ μή, σεαυτὸν οὐχ ἡμᾶς
ἀνιάσεις.

4.18

Μένανδρος Γλυκέρᾳ

Ἐγὼ μὰ τὰς Ἐλευσινίας θεάς, μὰ τὰ μυστήρια αὐτῶν, ἅ σοι καὶ
ἐναντίον ἐκείνων ὤμοσα πολλάκις, Γλυκέρα, μόνος μόνῃ, ὡς οὐδὲν
ἐπαίρων τἀμά, οὐδὲ βουλόμενός σου χωρίζεσθαι ταῦτα καὶ λέγω καὶ
γράφω. 2. τί γὰρ ἐμοὶ χωρὶς σοῦ γένοιτ᾿ ἂν ἥδιον; τί δ᾿ ἐπαρθῆναι
5 μεῖζον δυναίμην τῆς σῆς φιλίας εἰ καὶ τὸ ἔσχατον ἡμῶν γῆρας διὰ
τοὺς σοὺς τρόπους καὶ τὰ σὰ ἤθη νεότης ἀεὶ φανεῖταί μοι; 3. καὶ
συννεάσαιμεν ἀλλήλοις καὶ συγγηράσαιμεν, καὶ νὴ τοὺς θεοὺς
συναποθάνοιμεν, ἀλλ᾿ αἰσθανόμενοι, Γλυκέρα, ὅτι συναποθνήσκομεν,
ἵνα μηδετέρῳ ἡμῶν ἐν Ἅιδου συγκαταβαίη τις ζῆλος, εἴ τινων
10 ἄλλων ὁ σωθεὶς πειράσεται ἀγαθῶν. μὴ δὴ γένοιτό μοι πειραθῆναι
σοῦ μηκέτ᾿ οὔσης· τί γὰρ ἂν ἔτι καταλείποιτο ἀγαθόν;
4. Ἃ δὲ νῦν ἤπειξέ με ἐν Πειραιεῖ μαλακιζόμενον (οἶσθα γὰρ
μου τὰς συνήθεις ἀσθενείας, ἃς οἱ μὴ φιλοῦντές με τρυφὰς καὶ
σαλακωνίας καλεῖν εἰώθασιν) ἐπιστεῖλαί σοι ἐν ἄστει μενούσῃ διὰ
15 τὰ Ἁλῷα τῆς θεοῦ, ταῦτ᾿ ἐστίν· 5. ἐδεξάμην ἀπὸ Πτολεμαίου
τοῦ βασιλέως Αἰγύπτου γράμματα, ἐν οἷς δεῖταί μου πάσας δεήσεις,
καὶ προτρέπεται βασιλικῶς ὑπισχνούμενος τὸ δὴ λεγόμενον τοῦτο
τὰ τῆς γῆς ἀγαθὰ καὶ ἐμὲ καὶ Φιλήμονα· καὶ γὰρ ἐκείνῳ γράμματα
κεκομίσθαι φησί· καὶ αὐτὸς δὲ ὁ Φιλήμων ἐπέστειλέ μοι τὰ ἴδια
20 δηλῶν ἐλαφρότερα καὶ ὡς οὐ Μενάνδρῳ γεγραμμένα ἧττον λαμπρά·
6. ἀλλ᾿ ὄψεται καὶ βουλεύσεται τὰ ἴδια οὗτος.
Ἐγὼ δὲ οὐ περιμενῶ βουλάς, ἀλλὰ σύ μοι, Γλυκέρα, καὶ γνώμη
καὶ Ἀρεοπαγῖτις βουλὴ καὶ Ἡλιαία, ἅπαντα νὴ τὴν Ἀθηνᾶν, ἀεὶ

in Menecleides, who brings her a gift every day. That's better than weeping and wailing. Poor me: I have a dirge-singer, not a lover. He sends wreaths and roses as if to the grave of some-one untimely dead, and says he cries all night long. If you are bringing me something, then come without crying, or else you'll cause not me but yourself to suffer.

4.18

MENANDER TO GLYCERA

By the Eleusinian goddesses, and by their mysteries by which I have often sworn to you in their presence when we were alone together, Glycera, I assure you that I am not exalting myself, nor wishing to be away from you, when I both tell you and give you this news by letter. **2.** For what pleasure is there for me in your absence? What greater exaltation could I have than your love, since because of your habits and your ways even our extreme old age will always seem as youth to me? **3.** May we be young together and grow old together, and, by the gods, die together—so long as we are aware, Glycera, that we are dying together, to prevent either of us going down to Hades with a feeling of resentment that the other survives to experience fur-ther pleasures. **6.** May I not experience them when you're no longer alive: for what pleasure could I have left?

4. What I'm anxious to write to you about, while I am ill at the Peiraeus (you know my bouts of weakness, which people who don't like me generally call self-indulgence and affectation), and you are staying in the city for the goddess's Haloa, is this: **5.** I have had a letter from Ptolemy, the king of Egypt, in which he uses every entreaty and persuasion, and promises me in his lordly way all the world's goods, as they say. He includes Philemon as well as me, for he says that Philemon has also received a letter. And Philemon himself has written to me, telling me of his own invitation, which is expressed in a lighter style and (as it's not addressed to Menander) uses less brilliant diction. **6.** But he will see about it and decide for himself.

I do not have to wait to make up my mind. No, Glycera, you have always been and shall now be my judgement, my

γέγονας καὶ νῦν ἔσῃ. 7. τὰς μὲν οὖν ἐπιστολὰς τοῦ βασιλέως σοι
25 διεπεμψάμην, ἵνα δὴ[a] κόπτω σε δὶς καὶ τοῖς ἐμοῖς καὶ τοῖς ἐκείνου
γράμμασιν ἐντυγχάνουσαν· ἃ δὲ ἐπιστέλλειν αὐτῷ ἔγνωκα, βούλομαί
σε εἰδέναι. πλεῖν μὲν καὶ εἰς Αἴγυπτον ἀπιέναι μακρὰν οὕτως καὶ
ἀπῳκισμένην βασιλείαν οὖσαν, μὰ τοὺς δώδεκα θεούς, οὐδὲ
ἐνθυμοῦμαι. 8. ἀλλ' οὐδὲ εἰ ἐν Αἰγίνῃ ταύτῃ γε τῇ πλησίον ἔκειτο
30 Αἴγυπτος, οὐδ' οὕτως ἐν νῷ ἂν ἔσχον ἀφεὶς τὴν ἐμὴν βασιλείαν τῆς
σῆς φιλίας μόνος ἐν τοσούτῳ ὄχλῳ Αἰγυπτίων χωρὶς Γλυκέρας
ἐρημίαν πολυάνθρωπον ὁρᾶν. 9. ἥδιον γὰρ καὶ ἀκινδυνότερον τὰς
σὰς θεραπεύω μᾶλλον ἀγκάλας ἢ τὰς αὐλὰς[b] ἁπάντων τῶν
σατραπῶν καὶ βασιλέων, ἵνα[c] ἐπικίνδυνον μὲν τὸ λίαν ἐλεύθερον,[d]
35 εὐκαταφρόνητον δὲ τὸ κολακεῦον, ἄπιστον δὲ τὸ εὐτυχούμενον.
10. ἐγὼ δὲ καὶ τὰς θηρικλείους[e] καὶ τὰ καρχήσια καὶ τὰς χρυσίδας
καὶ πάντα τὰ ἐν ταῖς αὐλαῖς ἐπίφθονα παρὰ τούτοις ἀγαθὰ φυόμενα,
τῶν κατ' ἔτος Χοῶν καὶ τῶν ἐν τοῖς θεάτροις Ληναίων καὶ τῆς
χθιζῆς Ἀμαλλολογίας[f] καὶ τῶν τοῦ Λυκείου γυμνασίων καὶ τῆς
40 ἱερᾶς Ἀκαδημίας οὐκ ἀλλάττομαι, μὰ τὸν Διόνυσον καὶ τοὺς βακ-
χικοὺς αὐτοῦ κισσούς, οἷς στεφανωθῆναι μᾶλλον ἢ τοῖς Πτολεμαίου
βούλομαι διαδήμασιν, ὁρώσης καὶ καθημένης ἐν τῷ θεάτρῳ
Γλυκέρας. ποῦ γὰρ ἐν Αἰγύπτῳ ὄψομαι ἐκκλησίαν καὶ ψῆφον
ἀναδιδομένην; 11. ποῦ δὲ δημοκρατικὸν ὄχλον οὕτως
45 ἐλευθεριάζοντα; ποῦ δὲ θεσμοθέτας ἐν[g] τοῖς ἱεροῖς κώμοις[g]
κεκισσωμένους; ποῖον περισχοίνισμα; ποίαν αἵρεσιν; ποίους
Χύτρους; Κεραμεικόν, ἀγοράν, δικαστήρια, τὴν καλὴν ἀκρόπολιν,
τὰς σεμνὰς θεάς, τὰ μυστήρια, τὴν γειτνιῶσαν Σαλαμῖνα, τὰ στενά,
τὴν Ψυτταλίαν, τὸν Μαραθῶνα, ὅλην ἐν ταῖς Ἀθήναις τὴν
50 Ἑλλάδα, ὅλην τὴν Ἰωνίαν, τὰς Κυκλάδας πάσας;
12. Ἀφεὶς ταῦτα καὶ Γλυκέραν μετ' αὐτῶν εἰς Αἴγυπτον ἀπέλθω[h]
χρυσὸν λαβεῖν καὶ ἄργυρον καὶ πλοῦτον; ᾧ μετὰ τίνος χρήσομαι;
μετὰ Γλυκέρας τοσοῦτον διατεθαλασσευμένης; 13. οὐ πενία δέ μοι
ἔσται χωρὶς αὐτῆς ταῦτα; ἐὰν δὲ ἀκούσω τοὺς σεμνοὺς ἔρωτας εἰς
55 ἄλλον αὐτὴν μετατεθεικέναι, οὐ σποδός μοι πάντες οἱ θησαυροὶ
γενήσονται; καὶ ἀποθνήσκων τὰς μὲν λύπας ἐμαυτῷ συναποίσω, τὰ
δὲ χρήματα τοῖς ἰσχύουσιν ἀδικεῖν ἐν μέσῳ κείσεται; ἢ μέγα τὸ

Benner and Fobes   Schepers
[a] δὴ *Meineke:* μὴ *codd.*
[b] αὐλὰς *add. Bergler*   [c] ἵνα *add. Cobet*
[d] λίαν ἐλεύθερον *Maehly:* ἀνελεύθερον *codd.*
[e] θηρικλείους *Bergler:* ἡρακλείους *codd.*
[f] Ἀμαλλολογίας *Wilamowitz:* ἀμαλογίας *Vat2 Flor.* Π: ἀνολογίας Δ: ὁμολογίας Φ
[g] τοῖς ἱεροῖς κώμοις *Reiske:* ταῖς ἱεραῖς κώμαις Φ: ταῖς ἱεραῖς κόμαις x²
[h] ἀπέλθω *Schepers:* διέλθω *codd.*

Council of Areopagus, my Heliaea—my everything, I swear by Athena. **7.** So I am enclosing the king's letter, so that indeed I shall weary you twice over, presenting you with both my letter and the king's; and I wish you to know the reply I have decided to send to him. To go off by sea to Egypt, a kingdom so far away and remote—by the twelve gods, I can't begin to think of it. **8.** But even if Egypt were just over in Aegina nearby, even so I wouldn't have thought of giving up my own kingdom, which is your love, and alone without Glycera in all that throng of Egyptians, gazing upon a crowded emptiness. **9.** It is sweeter and less perilous for me to cultivate your embraces than the courts of all the satraps and kings, where too much frankness is dangerous, flattery is contemptible, success is unreliable. **10.** As for the Thericlean pottery, the goblets, the gold plate, and all the treasures you find in abundance and stirring up envy in their courts, I wouldn't have them in exchange for the annual Feast of Pitchers, the theatre at the Lenaea, yesterday's gathering of the sheaves, the exercises in the Lyceum, the inspiration of the Academy—no, I would not, by Dionysus and his Bacchic ivy, with which I'd much rather be crowned, with Glycera sitting in the theatre and looking on, than with the diadems of Ptolemy. For where shall I see a people's assembly in Egypt, or a vote being taken? **11.** Where shall I see a democratic multitude exercising such freedom? Or lawgivers wreathed with ivy at the sacred festivals? What roped enclosure, or election of magistrates, or Feast of Pots? Where shall I find a Cerameicus, a market place, law courts, a lovely Acropolis, the Awesome Goddesses, the Mysteries, Salamis nearby, the straits, Psyttalia, Marathon, the whole of Greece in Athens, the whole of Ionia, all the Cyclades?

12. Am I to desert these and Glycera along with them, and go off to Egypt to acquire gold and silver and wealth? With whom shall I spend that wealth? With Glycera, so far parted from me by the sea? **13.** Without her won't all this be but poverty to me? And if I hear that she has transferred her noble love to another man, won't all my treasures turn to ashes? Furthermore, when I die shall I take my sorrows with me, and leave my property as a prize for any who have the power to do me wrong? Or is it so important to consort with

συμβιοῦν Πτολεμαίῳ καὶ σατράπαις καὶ τοιούτοις ψόφοις, ὧν οὔτε τὸ
φιλικὸν βέβαιον οὔτε τὸ διεχθρεῦον ἀκίνδυνον; 14. ἐὰν δὲ διοργισθῇ
60 τί μοι Γλυκέρα, ἅπαξ αὐτὴν ἁρπάσας κατεφίλησα· ἂν ἔτι
ὀργίζηται, μᾶλλον αὐτὴν ἐβιασάμην· κἂν βαρυθύμως ἔχῃ,
δεδάκρυκα· καὶ πρὸς ταῦτ' οὐκέθ' ὑπομείνασα τὰς ἐμὰς λύπας,
δεῖται λοιπὸν οὔτε στρατιώτας ἔχουσα οὔτε δορυφόρους οὔτε
φύλακας· ἐγὼ γὰρ αὐτῇ εἰμι πάντα.
65 15. Ἦ μέγα καὶ θαυμαστὸν ἰδεῖν τὸν καλὸν Νεῖλον· οὐ μέγα δὲ
καὶ τὸν Εὐφράτην ἰδεῖν; οὐ μέγα δὲ καὶ τὸν Ἴστρον; οὐ τῶν
μεγάλων καὶ ὁ Θερμώδων, ὁ Τίγρις, ὁ Ἅλυς, ὁ Ῥῆνος; εἰ μέλλω
πάντας τοὺς ποταμοὺς ὁρᾶν, καταβαπτισθήσεταί μοι τὸ ζῆν μὴ
βλέποντι Γλυκέραν. 16. ὁ δὲ Νεῖλος οὗτος, καίπερ ὢν καλός, ἀλλ'
70 ἀποτεθηρίωται, καὶ οὐκ ἔστιν οὐδὲ προσελθεῖν αὐτοῦ ταῖς δίναις
ἐλλοχωμένου τοσούτοις κακοῖς. ἐμοὶ γένοιτο χώματος καὶ τάφου
πατρῴου τυχεῖν. ἐμοὶ γένοιτο, βασιλεῦ Πτολεμαῖε, τὸν Ἀττικὸν ἀεὶ
στέφεσθαι κισσὸν καὶ τὸν ἐπ' ἐσχάρας ὑμνῆσαι κατ' ἔτος Διόνυσον,
τὰς μυστηριώτιδας ἄγειν τελετάς, δραματουργεῖν τι καινὸν ταῖς
75 ἐτησίοις θυμέλαις δρᾶμα, γελῶντα καὶ χαίροντα καὶ ἀγωνιῶντα καὶ
φοβούμενον καὶ νικῶντα. 17. Φιλήμων δὲ εὐτυχείτω καὶ τἀμὰ
ἀγαθὰ γενόμενος ἐν Αἰγύπτῳ· οὐκ ἔχει Φιλήμων Γλυκέραν τινά,
οὐδὲ ἄξιος ἦν ἴσως τοιούτου ἀγαθοῦ. σὺ δὲ ἐκ τῶν Ἁλώων
δέομαι, Γλυκέριον, εὐθὺς πετομένη πρὸς ἡμᾶς ἐπὶ τῆς ἀστράβης
80 φέρου. μακροτέραν ἑορτὴν οὐδέποτε ἔγνων οὐδὲ ἀκαιροτέραν.
Δήμητερ, ἵλεως γενοῦ.

4.19

Γλυκέρα Μενάνδρῳ

Ἃς διεπέμψω μοι τοῦ βασιλέως ἐπιστολὰς εὐθὺς ἀνέγνων. μὰ τὴν
Καλλιγένειαν, ἐν ἧς νῦν εἰμι, κατέχαιρον, Μένανδρε, ἐκπαθὴς ὑπὸ
ἡδονῆς γινομένη, καὶ τὰς παρούσας οὐκ ἐλάνθανον. ἦν δὲ ἥ τε
μήτηρ μου καὶ ἡ ἑτέρα ἀδελφὴ Εὐφρόνιον καὶ τῶν φίλων ἣν οἶσθα·
5 καὶ παρὰ σοὶ ἐδείπνησε πολλάκις, καὶ ἐπῄνεις αὐτῆς τὸν ἐπιχώριον
ἀττικισμόν, ἀλλ' ὡς φοβούμενος αὐτὴν ἐπαινεῖν—ὅτε καὶ μειδιάσασα

Ptolemy and satraps and empty titles like that, whose friendship is not steadfast, and whose enmity brings danger?
14. Now, if Glycera gets angry with me she just needs one
embrace and a kiss; if she continues to be cross, I hold her
more tightly; and if she's really sullen, I burst into tears.
Against these weapons she no longer resists my grief, and she
finally begs my pardon, not having soldiers or bodyguards or
watchmen: for I am everything to her.

15. It is indeed a great and marvellous experience to see the
beautiful Nile; but is it not also great to see the Euphrates? Is
it not great to see the Ister? Do not the Thermodon, the
Tigris, the Halys, and the Rhine count among great rivers? If
I'm going to see all the rivers, my life will be utterly swamped
without the sight of Glycera. **16.** This Nile, beautiful
though it is, is infested with wild creatures, and you can't even
go near its eddies, it has such lurking dangers. May I find a
mound and a grave in my own land! May I, King Ptolemy, be
garlanded always with Attic ivy, and every year honour in
song Dionysus at his altar, celebrate the rites of the Mysteries,
and produce a new play at the annual stage shows, laughing,
rejoicing, agonizing, fearing the outcome—and winning!
17. Philemon can enjoy his good fortune in Egypt, and have
mine too there. He doesn't have a Glycera, and maybe he
wasn't worthy of such a blessing. And as soon as the Haloa
is over, I beg you, dear Glycera, to get in your saddle and
come flying to me. I've never known a longer or more
ill-timed festival—forgive me, Demeter!

4.19

GLYCERA TO MENANDER

The letter from the king which you sent me I read straight
away. By Calligeneia, in whose temple I am now, Menander, I was
absolutely delighted, and so beside myself with pleasure that it
was obvious to the women I was with. There was my mother,
and one of my two sisters, Euphronion, and a girl friend of
mine whom you know. She has often dined at your house, and
you praised her real Attic speech, though you seemed afraid to
praise her—don't you remember, Menander, when I smiled and

θερμότερόν σε κατεφίλησα—οὐ μέμνησαι, Μένανδρε; **2.** θεασάμεναι δέ
με παρὰ τὸ εἰωθὸς καὶ τῷ προσώπῳ καὶ τοῖς ὀφθαλμοῖς χαίρουσαν,
"ὦ Γλυκέριον," ἤροντο, "τί σοι τηλικοῦτον γέγονεν ἀγαθόν, ὅτι καὶ
10 ψυχῇ καὶ σώματι καὶ πᾶσιν ἀλλοιοτέρα νῦν ἡμῖν πέφηνας; καὶ τὸ
σῶμα γεγάνωσαι καὶ διαλάμπεις ἐπιχάριτόν τι καὶ εὐκταῖον."
κἀγώ, "Μένανδρον," ἔφην, "τὸν ἐμὸν ὁ Αἰγύπτου βασιλεὺς
Πτολεμαῖος ἐπὶ τῷ ἡμίσει τῆς βασιλείας τρόπον τινὰ
μεταπέμπεται," μείζονι τῇ φωνῇ φθεγξαμένη καὶ σφοδροτέρᾳ ὅπως
15 πᾶσαι ἀκούσωσιν αἱ παροῦσαι. καὶ ταῦτα ἔλεγον ἐγὼ διατινάσσουσα
καὶ σοβοῦσα ταῖς χερσὶν ἐμαυτῆς τὴν ἐπιστολὴν σὺν τῇ βασιλικῇ
σφραγῖδι. **3.** "χαίρεις οὖν ἀπολειπομένη;" ἔφασαν. τὸ δὲ οὐκ ἦν,
Μένανδρε. ἀλλὰ τοῦτο μὲν οὐδενὶ τρόπῳ μὰ τὰς θεάς, οὐδ᾽ εἰ βοῦς
μοι τὸ λεγόμενον φθέγξαιτο, πεισθείην ἂν ὅτι βουλήσεταί μέ ποτε ἢ
20 δυνήσεται Μένανδρος ἀπολιπὼν ἐν Ἀθήναις Γλυκέραν τὴν ἑαυτοῦ
μόνος ἐν Αἰγύπτῳ βασιλεύειν μετὰ πάντων τῶν ἀγαθῶν. **4.** ἀλλὰ
καὶ τοῦτό γε δῆλος ἐκ τῶν ἐπιστολῶν, ὧν ἀνέγνων, ἣν ὁ βασιλεὺς
τἀμὰ πεπυσμένος ὡς ἔοικε περὶ σοῦ, καὶ ἀτρέμα δι᾽ ὑπονοιῶν
Αἰγυπτίοις θέλων ἀττικισμοῖς σε διατωθάζειν. χαίρω διὰ τοῦτο, ὅτι
25 πεπλεύκασι καὶ εἰς Αἴγυπτον πρὸς αὐτὸν οἱ ἡμέτεροι ἔρωτες· καὶ
πείθεται πάντως ἐξ ὧν ἤκουσεν ἀδύνατα σπουδάζειν ἐπιθυμῶν
Ἀθήνας πρὸς αὐτὸν διαβῆναι. **5.** τί γὰρ Ἀθῆναι χωρὶς
Μενάνδρου; τί δὲ Μένανδρος χωρὶς Γλυκέρας; ἥτις αὐτῷ καὶ τὰ
προσωπεῖα διασκευάζω καὶ τὰς ἐσθῆτας ἐνδύω, κἂν τοῖς
30 παρασκηνίοις ἕστηκα τοὺς δακτύλους ἐμαυτῆς πιέζουσα ἕως ἂν
κροταλίσῃ τὸ θέατρον καὶ τρέμουσα. τότε νὴ τὴν Ἄρτεμιν ἀναψύχω
καὶ περιβάλλουσά σε τὴν ἱερὰν[a] ἐκείνην κεφαλὴν ἐναγκαλίζομαι. **6.**
ἀλλ᾽ ὅ γε ταῖς φίλαις τότε χαίρειν ἔφην, τοῦτ᾽ ἦν, Μένανδρε, ὅτι
οὐκ ἄρα Γλυκέρα μόνον ἀλλὰ καὶ βασιλεῖς ὑπερθάλασσοι ἐρῶσί σου
35 καὶ διαπόντιοι φῆμαι τὰς σὰς ἀρετὰς κατηγγέλκασι. καὶ Αἴγυπτος
καὶ Νεῖλος καὶ Πρωτέως ἀκρωτήρια καὶ αἱ Φάριαι σκοπιαὶ πάντα
μετέωρα νῦν ἐστι, βουλόμενα ἰδεῖν Μένανδρον καὶ ἀκοῦσαι
φιλαργύρων καὶ ἐρώντων καὶ δεισιδαιμόνων καὶ ἀπίστων καὶ
πατέρων καὶ υἱῶν καὶ θεραπόντων καὶ παντὸς ἐνσκηνοβατουμένου·
40 ὧν ἀκούσονται μέν, οὐκ ὄψονται δὲ Μένανδρον εἰ μὴ ἐν ἄστει παρὰ
Γλυκέρᾳ γένοιτο καὶ τὴν ἐμὴν εὐδαιμονίαν ἴδοιεν, τὸν πάντῃ διὰ τὸ
κλέος αἰτούμενον[b] Μένανδρον καὶ νύκτωρ καὶ μεθ᾽ ἡμέραν ἐμοὶ
περικείμενον.
7. Οὐ μὴν ἀλλ᾽ εἴγε ἄρα πόθος αἱρεῖ σέ τις καὶ τῶν ἐκεῖ ἀγαθῶν

Benner and Fobes   Schepers
[a] (post ἱερὰν) τῶν δραμάτων del. Hercher
[b] αἰτούμενον conj. Russell: αὐτοῦ codd.

gave you a specially warm kiss? **2.** Well, when they saw my
face and eyes beaming more than usual, they said, 'Glycera,
dear, what tremendous blessing has happened to you, to make
you seem so transformed in body and soul and everything? You
look happy all over, and you're glowing with delight and wishes
come true.' I told them, 'Ptolemy, king of Egypt, is sending for
my Menander, offering him half his kingdom, as it were';
speaking quite loudly and vehemently, so that all the women
present could hear. And as I said this, I waved and flaunted in
my hands the letter with the royal seal. **3.** 'Then are you
pleased to be left behind?' they said. But that wasn't the reason,
Menander. By the two goddesses, I just couldn't be persuaded,
even if the proverbial ox should tell me, that Menander would
ever be able or willing to leave me, his Glycera, in Athens and
lord it on his own in Egypt with all its treasures. **4.** Indeed, it
was clear from my reading of his letter that the king seemed to
be aware of my relationship with you, and wanted to tease you
gently with insinuations in his Egyptian style of Attic wit. My
joy is due to this, that the news of our love has crossed the sea
to the king in Egypt; and he certainly believes, from what he
has heard, that he is urging the impossible in his desire for
Athens to cross over to him. **5.** For what is Athens without
Menander? And what is Menander without Glycera? It is I who
prepare the masks for him, and dress the actors; and I stand in
the wings, clenching my hands, even trembling, until the audi-
ence gives its applause. Then, by Artemis, I recover, and throw-
ing my arms around you, embrace that inspired head of yours.
6. Yes, that was why I was joyful then, as I explained to my
friends, that not only Glycera loves you but kings overseas as
well, and that fame has proclaimed your virtues across the sea.
Egypt and the Nile and the promontory of Proteus and the
watch-tower of Pharos are all agog to see Menander and to lis-
ten to his characters—the miserly, the lovers, the superstitious,
the treacherous, fathers, sons, servants, every type he brought
on the stage. All these they will hear, but they won't see
Menander unless they visit Glycera's house in the city and
observe my happiness there—Menander, who is everywhere
asked for through his fame and lies night and day in my arms.
7. Yet, supposing you are indeed seized by some longing for
the delights over there, even if for nothing else but Egypt

καὶ εἰ μηδενὸς ἄλλου τῆς γε Αἰγύπτου, χρήματος μεγάλου,
45 καὶ τῶν αὐτόθι πυραμίδων καὶ τῶν ἠχούντων ἀγαλμάτων καὶ τοῦ
περιβοήτου λαβυρίνθου καὶ τῶν ἄλλων ὅσα ὑπὸ χρόνου ἢ τέχνης
παρ᾽ αὐτοῖς τίμια, δέομαί σου, Μένανδρε, μὴ ποιήσῃ με πρόφασιν·
8. μηδέ με Ἀθηναῖοι διὰ ταῦτα μισησάτωσαν ἤδη τοὺς μεδίμνους
ἀριθμοῦντες οὓς αὐτοῖς ὁ βασιλεὺς πέμψει διὰ σέ. ἀλλ᾽ ἄπιθι
50 πᾶσι θεοῖς, ἀγαθῇ τύχῃ, δεξιοῖς πνεύμασι, Διὶ οὐρίῳ. ἐγὼ γάρ σε
οὐκ ἀπολείψω· μὴ τοῦτο δόξῃς με λέγειν, οὐδ᾽ αὐτὴ δύναμαι
κἂν θέλω. 9. ἀλλὰ παρεῖσα τὴν μητέρα καὶ τὰς ἀδελφὰς ναυτὶς
ἔσομαι συμπλέουσά σοι. καὶ σφόδρα τῶν εὐθαλάσσων γεγένημαι, εὖ
οἶδα, κἂν ἐκκλωμένης κώπης ναυτιᾷς ἐγὼ θεραπεύσω. θάλψω σου
55 τὸ ἀσθενοῦν τῶν πελαγισμῶν, ἄξω δέ σε ἄτερ μίτων[c] Ἀριάδνη εἰς
Αἴγυπτον, οὐ Διόνυσον ἀλλὰ Διονύσου θεράποντα καὶ προφήτην.
10. οὐδὲ ἐν Νάξῳ καὶ ἐρημίαις ναυτικαῖς ἀπολειφθήσομαι τὰς σὰς
ἀπιστίας κλαίουσα καὶ ποτνιωμένη. χαιρέτωσαν οἱ Θησεῖς ἐκεῖνοι
καὶ τὰ ἄπιστα τῶν πρεσβυτέρων ἀμπλακήματα. ἡμῖν δὲ βέβαια
60 πάντα, καὶ τὸ ἄστυ καὶ ὁ Πειραιεὺς καὶ ἡ Αἴγυπτος. οὐδὲν χωρίον
ἡμῶν τοὺς ἔρωτας οὐχὶ δέξεται πλήρεις· κἂν πέτραν οἰκῶμεν, εὖ
οἶδα ἀφροδίσιον αὐτὴν τὸ εὔνουν ποιήσει. 11. πέπεισμαι μήτε
χρημάτων σε μήτε περιουσίας μήτε πλούτου τὸ καθάπαξ ἐπιθυμεῖν,
ἐν ἐμοὶ καὶ τοῖς δράμασι τὴν εὐδαιμονίαν κατατιθέμενον· ἀλλ᾽ οἱ
65 συγγενεῖς, ἀλλ᾽ ἡ πατρίς, ἀλλ᾽ οἱ φίλοι, σχεδὸν οἶσθα πάντῃ πάντες
πολλῶν δέονται, πλουτεῖν θέλουσι καὶ χρηματίζεσθαι. 12. σὺ μὲν
οὐδέποτε περὶ οὐδενὸς αἰτιάσῃ με οὔτε μικροῦ οὔτε μεγάλου. τοῦτο
εὖ οἶδα, πάλαι μὲν ἡττημένος μου πάθει καὶ ἔρωτι, νῦν δὲ ἤδη καὶ
κρίσιν προσθεικὼς αὐτοῖς, ἧς μᾶλλον περιέχομαι, Μένανδρε,
70 φοβουμένη τῆς ἐμπαθοῦς φιλίας τὸ ὀλιγοχρόνιον· ἔστι γὰρ ὡς βίαιος
ἡ ἐμπαθὴς φιλία οὕτω καὶ εὐδιάλυτος· οἷς δὲ[d] παραβέβληται καί τι
βουλῆς,[d] ἀρραγέστερον ἐν τούτοις ἤδη τὸ ἔργον οὔτε ἀμιγὲς ἡδονῆς
οὔτε περιδεές. 13. λύσεις[e] δὲ τὴν γνώμην, ὥς με πολλάκις περὶ
τούτων αὐτὸς νουθετῶν διδάσκεις.
75 Ἀλλ᾽ εἰ καὶ σὺ μή μέ τι μέμψῃ μηδὲ αἰτιάσῃ, δέδοικα τοὺς
Ἀττικοὺς σφῆκας, οἵτινες ἄρξονται πάντῃ με περιβομβεῖν ἐξιοῦσαν
ὡς αὐτὸν ἀφῃρημένην τῆς Ἀθηναίων πόλεως τὸν πλοῦτον.
14. ὥστε δέομαί σου, Μένανδρε, ἐπίσχες, μηδέ πω τῷ βασιλεῖ μηδὲν

---

[c] μίτων *Bergler*: μύθων *codd.*
[d-d] παραβέβληται καί τι βουλῆς *Meineke*: παραβέβληνται καὶ βουλῆς Π
(*superscr.*) Δ: παραβέβληνται καὶ βουλαὶ *Ald.*
[e] λύσεις *Ald.*: λύσει *codd.*: θήσει *Meineke*

itself, a tremendous marvel, with its pyramids, its echoing statues, its famous labyrinth, and everything else which they value
for antiquity or art, I beg you, Menander, don't make me an
excuse and so cause the Athenians to hate me.   **8.** They are
already counting up the bushels of corn which the king will
send them because of you. Go, with the blessing of all the
gods, and good luck to you, with favouring winds, and Zeus
prospering you! For I shall not be parted from you: don't suppose I mean that—I could not even if I wanted to.   **9.** I shall
abandon my mother and sisters and become a sailor-girl to
share your voyage. I know I am a very good sailor, and if an
oar breaks and you get seasick I will look after you. I'll cherish
you in any affliction brought on by the sea-voyage; and like
Ariadne, but without her thread, I'll bring you to Egypt—not
Dionysus himself, but his servant and spokesman.   **10.** Nor
shall I be abandoned on Naxos or any other deserted shore, to
lament and bewail your treachery. Good-bye to Theseus and
his like, and the incredible crimes of the men of old. All that
we have is steadfast—the city, the Peiraeus, Egypt. There is
no place that will not welcome our love in all its fullness: even
if we live on a rock, I'm sure our affection will make it a
shrine to Aphrodite.   **11.** I am convinced that you are not for
a moment striving for money or superfluous goods or wealth,
because you stake your happiness on me and your plays. But
your relatives, your country, your friends, almost everybody
everywhere, as you know, want lots of things, and long to
make money and get rich.   **12.** I'm well aware that you will
never find fault with me for anything great or small. Long ago
you were overcome by passionate love for me. To this you
have now added judgement, and that is what I prefer to rely
on, Menander, as I fear that love based on passion may be
short-lived. Its very violence makes it prone to dissolve; but
where it is joined by counsel the resulting bond is much less
fragile, since it both has an element of pleasure and is free
from too much anxiety.   **13.** But you shall make the decision:
on these matters you yourself often teach and advise me.

But even if you don't blame or find fault with me, I'm
afraid of those Attic wasps, who will start buzzing around me
everywhere when I go out, alleging that I have deprived the
city of Athens of its wealth.   **14.** I beg you, Menander, wait a

ἀντεπιστείλῃς. ἔτι βούλευσαι, περίμεινον ἕως κοινῇ γενώμεθα καὶ
80 μετὰ τῶν φίλων καὶ Θεοφράστου καὶ Ἐπικούρου. τάχα γὰρ
ἀλλοιότερα κἀκείνοις καὶ σοὶ φανεῖται ταῦτα. μᾶλλον δὲ καὶ
θυσώμεθα καὶ εἰδῶμεν τί λέγει τὰ ἱερά, εἴτε λῷον εἰς Αἴγυπτον
ἡμᾶς ἀπιέναι εἴτε μένειν. καὶ χρηστηριασθῶμεν εἰς Δελφοὺς
πέμψαντες· πάτριος ἡμῶν ἐστι θεός· ἀπολογίαν ἕξομεν καὶ
85 πορευόμενοι καὶ μένοντες πρὸς ἀμφότερα τοὺς θεούς. **15.** μᾶλλον
δὲ ἐγὼ τοῦτο ποιήσω· καὶ γὰρ ἔχω τινὰ νεωστὶ γυναῖκα ἀπὸ
Φρυγίας ἥκουσαν εὖ μάλα τούτων ἔμπειρον, γαστρομαντεύεσθαι
δεινὴν τῇ τῶν *ᶠσπαρτῶν διατάσειᶠ* νύκτωρ καὶ τῇ τῶν θεῶν δείξει·
καὶ οὐ δεῖ λεγούσῃ πιστεύειν, ἀλλ᾽ ἰδεῖν, ὥς φασι. διαπέμψομαι
90 πρὸς αὐτήν. **16.** καὶ γάρ, ὡς ἔφη, καὶ κάθαρσίν τινα δεῖ
προτελέσαι τὴν γυναῖκα καὶ παρασκευάσαι τινὰ ζῷα ἱερεῦσαι καὶ
λιβανωτὸν ἄρρενα καὶ στύρακα μακρὸν καὶ πέμματα σελήνης καὶ
ἄγρια φύλλα τῶν ἄγνων. **17.** οἶμαι δὲ καὶ σὲ φθήσεσθαι Πειραιόθεν
ἐλθεῖν. ἢ δήλωσόν μοι σαφῶς μέχρι τίνος οὐ δύνασαι Γλυκέραν
95 ἰδεῖν, ἵν᾽ ἐγὼ μὲν καταδράμω πρὸς σέ, τὴν δὲ Φρυγίαν ταύτην
ἑτοιμάσωμαι ἤδη. καὶ εἰ*ᵍ* μελετᾶν πειράζεις ἀπὸ σαυτοῦ ἐμὲ καὶ τὸν
Πειραιᾶ καὶ τὸ ἀγρίδιον καὶ τὴν Μουνυχίαν καὶ πάντα*ʰ* κατ᾽
ὀλίγον ὅπως ἐκπέσωσι τῆς ψυχῆς—οὐ δύναμαι ταῦτα*ⁱ* ποιεῖν μὰ
τοὺς θεούς, σὺ δὲ οὐ δύνασαι διαπεπλεγμένος ὅλως ἤδη μοι.
100 **18.** κἂν οἱ βασιλεῖς ἐπιστείλωσι πάντες, ἐγὼ πάντων εἰμὶ παρὰ σοὶ
βασιλικωτέρα καὶ εὐσεβεῖ σοι κέχρημαι ἐραστῇ καὶ ὅρκων ἱερῶν
μνήμονι.
   19. Ὥστε πειρῶ μᾶλλον ἐμοί, φιλότης, θᾶσσον εἰς ἄστυ
παραγενέσθαι, ὅπως εἴ γε μεταβουλεύσαιο τῆς πρὸς βασιλέα ἀφίξεως,
105 ἔχῃς εὐτρεπισμένα τὰ δράματα καὶ ἐξ αὐτῶν ἃ μάλιστα ὀνῆσαι
δύναται Πτολεμαῖον καὶ τὸν αὐτοῦ*ʲ* Διόνυσον (οὐ δημοκρατικόν, ὡς
οἶσθα), εἴτε Θαΐδα εἴτε Μισούμενον εἴτε Θρασυλέοντα εἴτε
Ἐπιτρέποντας εἴτε Ῥαπιζομένην εἴτε Σικυώνιον, εἴθ᾽ ὁτιοῦν ἄλλο.
τί δέ; ἐγὼ θρασεῖα καὶ τολμηρά τίς εἰμι τὰ Μενάνδρου διακρίνειν
110 ἰδιῶτις οὖσα; ἀλλὰ σοφὸν ἔχω σου τὸν ἔρωτα καὶ ταῦτ᾽ εἰδέναι
δύνασθαι. **20.** σὺ γάρ με ἐδίδαξας εὐφυᾶ γυναῖκα ταχέως παρ᾽
ἐρώντων μανθάνειν· ἀλλ᾽ *ᵏεἰ κοινωσοῦσινᵏ* οἱ*ˡ* ἔρωτες σπεύδοντες,
αἰδούμεθα μὰ τὴν Ἄρτεμιν ἀνάξιοι ὑμῶν εἶναι μὴ θᾶττον μανθάνουσαι.

ᶠ⁻ᶠ σπαρτῶν διατάσει codd.: ἄστρων διαθέσει *Arnaud*
ᵍ εἰ *Jacobs*: ἂ codd.   *ʰ* πάντα add. *Jacobs*
ⁱ ταῦτα *Seiler*: πάντα codd.   *ʲ* αὐτοῦ codd.: σαυτοῦ *Hercher*
ᵏ⁻ᵏ εἰ κοινωσοῦσιν *Hermann*: οἰκονομοῦσιν codd.   *ˡ* οἱ add. *Metropulos*

bit, and don't answer the king's letter yet. Consider it further, wait till we are together and with our friends Theophrastus and Epicurus. Maybe you and they together will look at the situation differently. Even better, let us sacrifice and learn what the omens say, whether it is better for us to go to Egypt or to remain here. And let us send to Delphi to consult the oracle: the god there is our ancestral god. In either event, whether we go or stay, we shall have the gods to justify us. **15.** Better still, I shall do this. I have a woman, recently arrived from Phrygia, who has much experience in these matters. She is clever at belly-divination, which she does by noting the tension of the strings at night and by calling up the gods. We need not trust what she says, but see for ourselves, as they say. I'll send her a message. **16.** In fact, so she said, the woman has to perform some purification first, and to prepare some animals for sacrifice, as well as strong frankincense, a long stalk of styrax, crescent cakes, and leaves of the wild chaste tree. **17.** But I think that you will get here first from the Peiraeus. Otherwise, tell me clearly how long it will be before you can see Glycera, so I can hasten down to you and have this Phrygian woman already prepared. And if you are trying on your part to practise banishing me and the Peiraeus and the little farm and Munychia and gradually everything from your mind—well, I can't do this, by the gods, and you can't either, as you are now totally involved with me. **18.** Even if all the kings in the world should write to you, I am more royal to you than all of them; and I know you for a dutiful lover, mindful of sacred promises.

19. So do try instead, my love, to come speedily to Athens, so that if you change your mind about going to the king, you will have your plays prepared, especially those most likely to delight Ptolemy and his Dionysus (who, as you know, is not democratic)—*Thaïs*, or *The Hated Man*, or *The Swashbuckler*, or *The Arbitrants*, or *The Girl Who Gets Slapped*, or *The Sicyonian*, or whatever. But what am I saying? Am I, an unprofessional woman, so rash and daring as to distinguish among Menander's works? Well, my love for you is clever at understanding these things too. **20.** For you taught me that a woman who is naturally bright learns quickly from her lovers. But if eager lovers share their knowledge with us, we women

πάντως δέομαι, Μένανδρε, κἀκεῖνο παρασκευάσασθαι τὸ δρᾶμα
115 ἐν ᾧ με γέγραφας, ἵνα κἂν μὴ παραγένωμαι σὺν σοί, δι' ἄλλου
πλεύσω πρὸς Πτολεμαῖον, καὶ μᾶλλον αἴσθηται ὁ βασιλεὺς ὅσον
ἰσχύει καὶ παρὰ σοὶ γεγραμμένους φέρειν ἑαυτοῦ τοὺς ἔρωτας ἀφεὶς
ἐν ἄστει τοὺς ἀληθινούς.

21. Ἀλλ' οὐδὲ τούτους ἀφήσεις, εὖ ἴσθι· κυβερνᾶν ἢ πρωρατεύειν,
120 ἕως δεῦρο παραγίνῃ πρὸς ἡμᾶς Πειραιόθεν, μυηθήσομαι, ἵνα σε ταῖς
ἐμαῖς χερσὶν ἀκύμονα ναυστολήσω πλέουσα, εἰ τοῦτο ἄμεινον εἶναι
φαίνοιτο. φανείη δέ, ὦ θεοὶ πάντες, ὃ κοινῇ λυσιτελήσει, καὶ μαν-
τεύσαιτο ἡ Φρυγία τὰ συμφέροντα κρεῖσσον τῆς Θεοφορουμένης σου
κόρης. ἔρρωσο.

are ashamed, by Artemis, to be unworthy of you in being slow
to learn. Especially, Menander, I beg you to get ready that
play too in which you have portrayed me, so that even if I am
not by your side I can in another's guise sail over to Ptolemy;
and so that the king can have a better idea how much
influence he has with you, inducing you to bring over your
own darling in writing, while leaving the real one in Athens.

21. But you won't leave her, make no mistake. Until you
come to me here from the Peiraeus, I shall be initiating myself
into the mysteries of steering a ship or commanding at the
bow, so that I can pilot you with my own hands over a calm
sea, if that is your decision. And by all the gods I pray that
your decision will turn out well for both of us, and that the
Phrygian woman may be a better prophetess of what is good
than your *Girl Possessed of a God*.

Farewell

PHILOSTRATUS

12

Γυναικί

Πόθεν μου τὴν ψυχὴν κατέλαβες; ἢ δῆλον ὅτι ἀπὸ τῶν ὀμμάτων,
ἀφ᾿ ὧν μόνων κάλλος ἐσέρχεται; ὥσπερ γὰρ τὰς ἀκροπόλεις οἱ
τύραννοι καὶ τὰ ἐρυμνὰ οἱ βασιλεῖς καὶ τὰ ὑψηλὰ οἱ θεοὶ
καταλαμβάνουσιν, οὕτω καὶ ὁ ἔρως τὴν τῶν ὀφθαλμῶν ἀκρόπολιν,
5 ἦν οὐ ξύλοις οὐδὲ πλίνθοις ἀλλὰ μόνοις βλεφάροις τειχίσας ἡσυχῇ
καὶ κατὰ μικρὸν τὴν ψυχὴν ἐσδύεται, ταχέως μέν, ὡς πτηνός,
ἐλεύθερος δέ, ὡς γυμνός, ἄμαχος δέ, ὡς τοξότης. τὰ δὲ ὄμματα,
ἐπεὶ πρῶτα συνίησι κάλλους, διὰ τοῦτο μάλιστα καὶ καίεται, θεοῦ
τινος, οἶμαι, θελήσαντος αὐτοῖς τὴν αὐτὴν ὁδὸν καὶ τῆς ἐς τὸ
10 βλέπειν ἡδονῆς εἶναι καὶ τῆς ἐς τὸ λυπεῖσθαι προφάσεως. τί γάρ, ὦ
κακοὶ δᾳδοῦχοι ἔρωτος καὶ τῆς σωμάτων ὥρας περίεργοι μάρτυρες,
πρῶτοι μὲν τὸ κάλλος ἡμῖν ἐπυρσεύσατε, πρῶτοι δὲ μεμνῆσθαι τὴν
ψυχὴν ἐδιδάξατε τῆς ἔξωθεν ἐπιρροῆς, πρῶτοι δὲ ἐβιάσασθε τὸν
ἥλιον καταλιποῦσαν[a] πῦρ ἀλλότριον ἐπαινεῖν; τοιγαροῦν ἀγρυπνεῖτε
15 καὶ καίεσθε καὶ φλογίζεσθε, ἀπαλλαγὴν ὧν εἵλεσθε εὑρεῖν μὴ
δυνάμενοι. μακαρίων, ὦ θεοί, τῶν ἐκ γενετῆς τυφλῶν, ἐφ᾿ οὓς ἔρως
ὁδὸν οὐκ ἔχει.

Benner and Fobes
[a] καταλιποῦσαν *Hercher*: καταλιπόντα *vel* καταλιποῦσι *codd.*

18

Μειρακίῳ ἀνυποδέτῳ

Μαλακώτερον διετέθης ὑπὸ τοῦ σανδαλίου θλιβείς, ὡς πέπεισμαι,
δειναὶ γὰρ δακεῖν σάρκας ἁπαλὰς αἱ τῶν δερμάτων καινότητες. διὰ
τοῦτο ὁ Ἀσκληπιὸς τὰ μὲν ἐκ πολέμου καὶ θήρας τραύματα καὶ
πάσης τῆς τοιαύτης τύχης ἰᾶται ῥᾳδίως, ταῦτα δὲ ἐᾷ διὰ τὸ ἑκού-
5 σιον, ὡς ἀνοίᾳ μᾶλλον ἢ ἐπηρείᾳ δαίμονος γενόμενα. τί οὖν οὐκ
ἀνυπόδητος βαδίζεις; τί δὲ τῇ γῇ φθονεῖς; βλαυτία καὶ σανδάλια καὶ
κρηπῖδες καὶ πέδιλα νοσούντων εἰσὶ φορήματα ἢ γερόντων. τὸν γοῦν
Φιλοκτήτην ἐν τούτοις γράφουσι τοῖς ἐρύμασιν ὡς χωλὸν καὶ
νοσοῦντα, τὸν δὲ ἐκ Σινώπης φιλόσοφον καὶ τὸν Θηβαῖον Κράτητα

PHILOSTRATUS

12
To a Woman

From what point did you seize my soul? Clearly from the eyes, whereby alone beauty makes its entrance? For just as tyrants seize citadels, and kings strongholds, and gods lofty sites, so too Love seizes the citadel of the eyes. He fortifies it not with wooden palisades or brick walls, but only with the eyelids, and then quietly and insidiously he enters the soul—swiftly as he has wings, unimpeded as he is naked, irresistible as he is an archer. So the eyes, as soon as they observe beauty, catch fire in very truth from it: I suppose that some god has decided that they should have the same route that gives them both the pleasure of seeing and the cause of suffering. O you wicked torch-bearers of love, you prying observers of bodily charm, why did you first light the beacon of beauty for us, first teach our souls to remember influences from outside, and first forced them to desert the sun and praise an alien flame? Very well, then, pass sleepless nights consumed with fire and flame, unable to gain relief from what you chose yourselves! O gods, how blessed are those who are blind from birth: love has no access to them!

18
To a Barefoot Boy

You are rather unwell, and I'm sure it's because your sandal is pinching you: new leather is terribly apt to cut into delicate skin. For that reason Asclepius is willing to heal wounds received in fighting and hunting and all that sort of mishap; but he ignores those arising from voluntary acts, since they are due to folly rather than God's abusive treatment. So why don't you walk barefoot? Do you bear the earth some ill will? Slippers and sandals and boots and shoes are for invalids and old people to wear. At any rate, Philoctetes is described having

10 καὶ τὸν Αἴαντα καὶ τὸν Ἀχιλλέα ἀνυποδέτους καὶ τὸν Ἰάσονα ἐξ
ἡμισείας. λέγεται γὰρ ὡς τὸν Ἄναυρον διαβαίνοντος αὐτοῦ τὸν
ποταμὸν ἐνεσχέθη ἡ κρηπὶς τῷ ῥεύματι ἐς ἀντίληψιν τῆς ἰλύος
γενομένης, καὶ ὁ Ἰάσων οὕτως ἠλευθέρωτο τῶν ποδῶν τὸν ἕτερον
τύχῃ τὸ δέον διδαχθείς, οὐ γνώμῃ ἑλόμενος, καὶ ἀπῄει καλῶς
15 σεσυλημένος. μηδὲν ἤτω σοι μεταξὺ τῆς γῆς καὶ τοῦ ποδός. μὴ
φοβηθῇς· δέξεται τὴν βάσιν ἡ κόνις ὡς πόαν, καὶ τὸ ἴχνος
προσκυνήσομεν πάντες. ὦ ῥυθμοὶ ποδῶν φιλτάτων, ὦ καινὰ ἄνθη, ὦ
γῆς φυτά, ὦ φίλημα ἐρριμμένον.

20

Γυναικί

Καὶ τῷ Διί, ὅτε ἐκοιμᾶτο ἐν τῇ Ἴδῃ τῷ ὄρει, ἄνθη ἡ γῆ ἀνῆκεν
λωτὸν καὶ ὑάκινθον καὶ κρόκον· ῥόδα δὲ οὐ παρῆν, πότερον ὡς μόνης
Ἀφροδίτης κτήματα, παρ' ἧς καὶ ταῦτα ἔδει τὴν Ἥραν
δανείσασθαι, καθάπερ καὶ τὸν κεστὸν ἐδανείσατο, ἢ ὡς οὐκ ἂν
5 κοιμηθέντος τοῦ Διὸς εἰ καὶ ταῦτα παρῆν, οἱ δὲ ἐδέοντο καθεύδειν
τὸν Δία. ὅταν δὲ πνέῃ ῥόδα, ἀνάγκη πᾶσα δήπου καὶ ἀνθρώποις καὶ
θεοῖς ἀγρυπνεῖν ἡδέως, ἡ γὰρ εὐωδία δεινὴ πᾶσαν ἡσυχίαν ἐξοικίσαι.
ταῦτα μὲν οὖν ἀφείσθω Ὁμήρῳ καὶ τῇ τῶν ποιητῶν ἐξουσίᾳ, σὺ δὲ
ἀγροίκως ἐποίησας μόνη κοιμηθεῖσα ἐν ῥόδοις καὶ σωφρονήσασα ἐν
10 οὐ σώφροσιν. ἢ γὰρ τῶν ἐραστῶν ἐχρῆν σοι παρεῖναί τινα ἢ ἐμὲ[a] ἢ
τὸν Δία,[a] πλὴν εἰ μὴ προενεθυμήθης, ὦ καλή, τὸν στέφανον τοῖς
στέρνοις προσαγαγοῦσα καινῷ μοιχῷ συμπλακῆναι.

Benner and Fobes
   [a–a] ἢ τὸν Δία: νὴ τὸν Δία Huet

25

Γυναικί

Ἐχθές σε ὀργιζομένην κατέλαβον καὶ ἔδοξα ἄλλην βλέπειν· τούτου
δὲ αἴτιον ἡ τοῦ θυμοῦ ἔκστασις ἀκριβῶς σοι συγχέασα τὴν τοῦ

such protective wear, as he was lame and diseased; whereas the philosopher from Sinope and Theban Crates and Ajax and Achilles are barefoot, and Jason has only one shoe. According to the legend, when Jason was crossing the river Anaurus one of his boots was caught by the stream when it stuck fast in the mud; so he had one bare foot, not through his own choice, but the accident taught him what he had to do; and he continued on his way most luckily stripped of his shoe. Let there be nothing between the earth and your foot. Don't be afraid: the dust will receive your step as it would grass, and we shall all kiss your footprint. O beautifully formed beloved feet! O exotic flowers, sprung from the earth! O kiss cast upon the ground!

20

To a Woman

For Zeus too the earth bore flowers when he was sleeping on Mount Ida—clover, larkspur, and crocus. But there were no roses, whether because they belong to Aphrodite alone, and Hera would have had to borrow them too from her as she borrowed her girdle, or because Zeus would not have gone to sleep if there had been roses too—and they wanted him to sleep. For when roses give off their scent, I imagine both men and gods absolutely must stay awake with pleasure: for their fragrance has a marvellous capacity to banish all repose.

Anyway, let us leave these things to Homer and the licence of the poets. But it was ill-mannered of you to go to sleep alone among roses, acting chastely in unchaste company. Surely you should have had one of your lovers beside you, or me, or Zeus—unless, my beauty, you had already decided that with your garland on your breast you were in the arms of a novel kind of adulterer.

25

To a Woman

I caught you yesterday in a temper and thought I was seeing another woman. The reason for this was the frenzy of passion

προσώπου χάριν. νῦν δὴ μεταποίει σεαυτὴν μηδὲ ἄγριον βλέπε. οὐδὲ
γὰρ τὴν σελήνην ἔτι λαμπρὰν δοκοῦμεν ὅταν ᾖ συννεφής, οὐδὲ τὴν
5 Ἀφροδίτην καλὴν ὅταν ὀργίζηται ἢ δακρύῃ, οὐδὲ τὴν Ἥραν
βοῶπιν ὅταν χαλεπαίνῃ τῷ Διί, οὐδὲ τὴν^a ἄλα δῖαν^a ὅταν ταράττη-
ται. ἡ δὲ Ἀθηνᾶ καὶ τοὺς αὐλοὺς ἔρριψε ὡς τὸ πρόσωπον αὐτῆς
συγχέοντας. ἤδη καὶ τὰς Ἐρινῦς Εὐμενίδας καλοῦμεν, ὡς τὸ
σκυθρωπὸν ἀρνουμένας, καὶ ταῖς ἀκάνθαις τῶν ῥόδων χαίρομεν, ὅτι
10 ἐξ ἀγρίου θάμνου καί λυπεῖν καὶ κεντεῖν εἰδότος γελῶσιν ἐν τοῖς
ῥόδοις. ἄνθος ἐστὶ καὶ γυναικὸς ἡ τοῦ προσώπου γαλήνη. μὴ
τραχεῖα γίγνου μηδὲ φοβερά, μηδὲ ἀποστεροῦ τὸ κάλλος, μηδὲ
ἀφαιροῦ ῥόδων σεαυτήν, ἃ ταῖς καλαῖς ὑμῖν ἐν τοῖς ὄμμασι φύεται.
εἰ δὲ ἀπιστεῖς οἷς λέγω, τὸ κάτοπτρον λαβοῦσα ἴδε σου τὸ
15 πρόσωπον ἠλλαγμένον· εὖγ᾽ ὅτι ἐπεστράφης^b ἢ γὰρ ἐμίσησας ἢ
ἐφοβήθης ἢ οὐκ ἐγνώρισας ἢ μετενόησας.

Benner and Fobes
  $^{a-a}$ ἄλα δῖαν Cobet: θάλατταν vel θάλαττα ἡδεῖαν codd.
  ^{b} ἐπεστράφης: ἀπεστράφης codd. pauci

32
Γυναικὶ καπηλίδι

Τὰ μὲν ὄμματά σου διαυγέστερα τῶν ἐκπωμάτων, ὡς δύνασθαι δι᾽
αὐτῶν καὶ τὴν ψυχὴν ἰδεῖν, τὸ δὲ τῶν παρειῶν ἐρύθημα εὔχρουν
ὑπὲρ αὐτὸν τὸν οἶνον, τὸ δὲ λινοῦν τοῦτο χιτώνιον ἀντιλάμπει ταῖς
παρειαῖς, τὰ δὲ χείλη βέβαπται τῷ τῶν ῥόδων αἵματι, καί μοι
5 δοκεῖς τὸ ὕδωρ φέρειν ὡς ἀπὸ πηγῶν τῶν ὀμμάτων καὶ διὰ τοῦτο
εἶναι νυμφῶν μία. πόσους ἱστᾷς ἐπειγομένους; πόσους κατέχεις
παρατρέχοντας; πόσους φθεγξαμένη καλεῖς; ἐγὼ πρῶτος, ἐπειδὰν
ἴδω σε, διψῶ καὶ ἴσταμαι μὴ θέλων. καὶ τὸ ἔκπωμα κατέχων
[καὶ]^{a}τὸ μὲν οὐ προσάγω τοῖς χείλεσι, σοῦ δ᾽ οἶδα πίνων.

Benner and Fobes
  ^{a} καὶ om. codd. primae familiae

which utterly distorted the charm of your features. You must now change yourself and stop looking so savage. We don't think even the moon is still shining when it is covered by clouds, or that Aphrodite is beautiful when she is angry or tearful, or Hera 'large-eyed' when she is enraged with Zeus, or the sea bright when it is stirred up. Athena even threw away her pipes because they distorted her features. Furthermore we even call the Furies the Eumenides to mark their disowning of their sullen nature; and we take delight in rose thorns since, though they grow on a wild bush that knows how to give us painful pricks, they break out with smiling roses. With a woman her flower is a calm and peaceful countenance. Don't be harsh or threatening: don't steal away your own beauty, or deprive yourself of the roses which grow in the eyes of you lovely women. If you don't believe what I'm saying, take your mirror and look at your altered features. Good! You've taken heed. You must have loathed or feared what you saw, or didn't recognize yourself, or repented of your ways.

32

To a Woman Innkeeper

Your eyes gleam more brightly than your drinking-cups, so that through them even your soul is visible; and the blush in your cheeks is a better colour than the wine itself; this linen dress reflects the glow in your cheeks; your lips are dyed in the blood of roses; and it seems to me it's from the springs in your eyes that you bring the water, and so you must be one of the nymphs. How many men hurrying on do you stop in their tracks? How many of those rushing past do you detain? How many does your clear call summon to you? I am the first to feel thirsty when I see you, and yet stand still against my will; and holding my cup, I don't bring it to my lips, but I know I am drinking you in.

51

Κλεονίδῃ

Ἡ Σαπφὼ τοῦ ῥόδου ἐρᾷ καὶ στεφανοῖ αὐτὸ ἀεί τινι ἐγκωμίῳ τὰς καλὰς τῶν παρθένων ἐκείνῳ ὁμοιοῦσα, ὁμοιοῖ δὲ αὐτὸ καὶ τοῖς τῶν Χαρίτων πήχεσιν ἐπειδὰν ἀποδύσῃ σφῶν τὰς ὠλένας. ἐκεῖνο μὲν οὖν, εἰ καὶ[a] κάλλιστον ἀνθέων, βραχὺ τὴν ὥραν, παρέπεται γὰρ τοῖς
5 ἄλλοις[b] ἐννεάσαν τῷ ἦρι. τὸ δὲ σὸν εἶδος ἀεὶ τέθηλεν· ὅθεν ὀφθαλμοῖς ἐμμειδιᾷ καὶ παρειαῖς οἷόν τι ἔαρ τὸ μετόπωρον τοῦ κάλλους.

Benner and Fobes
  [a] καὶ *add. Kayser* [b] ἄλλοις *Kayser:* ἄνοις *codd.*

71

Πλεισταιρετιανῷ

Τὸ ποιητικὸν ἔθνος πολλοὶ καὶ πλείους ἢ οἱ τῶν μελιττῶν ἐσμοί, βόσκουσι δὲ τὰς μὲν λειμῶνες, τοὺς δὲ οἰκίαι καὶ πόλεις· ἀνθεστιῶσί τε αἷ[a] μὲν κηρίοις, οἱ δὲ ὀψοποιίᾳ λαμπρᾷ. εἰσὶ δὲ τῶν ποιητῶν οἱ καὶ τραγήμασιν ἑστιῶντες· τούτους δὲ ἡγώμεθα τοὺς
5 τῶν ἐρωτικῶν ποιητάς, ὧν εἷς καὶ Κέλσος οὗτος ᾠδαῖς παραδεδωκὼς τὸν ἑαυτοῦ βίον, ὥσπερ οἱ χρηστοὶ τέττιγες. ὡς δ' ἂν μὴ δρόσῳ ἀλλὰ σιτίοις ἀληθινοῖς τραφείη, πεπίστευκά σοι μελήσειν.

Benner and Fobes
  [a] αἱ *Kayser:* οἱ *codd.*

73

Ἰουλίᾳ Σεβαστῇ

Οὐδὲ ὁ θεσπέσιος Πλάτων τοῖς σοφισταῖς ἐβάσκηνεν, εἰ καὶ σφόδρα ἐνίοις δοκεῖ τοῦτο, ἀλλὰ φιλοτίμως πρὸς αὐτοὺς εἶχεν, ἐπειδὴ διεφοίτων θέλγοντες μικράς τε καὶ μείζους πόλεις τὸν Ὀρφέως καὶ Θαμύρου τρόπον, τοῦ δὲ βασκαίνειν ἀπεῖχε τοσοῦτον ὅσον φιλοτιμία
5 φθόνου· φθόνος μὲν γὰρ τρέφει τὰς μοχθηρὰς φύσεις, φιλοτιμία δὲ τὰς λαμπρὰς ἐγείρει, καὶ βασκαίνει μέν τις τὰ μὴ ἑαυτῷ ἐφικτά, ἃ δὲ ἄμεινον ἢ μὴ χεῖρον διαθήσεται, φιλοτιμεῖται πρὸς ταῦτα. ὁ γοῦν Πλάτων καὶ ἐς τὰς ἰδέας τῶν σοφιστῶν ἵεται καὶ οὔτε τῷ Γοργίᾳ

51

To Cleonide

Sappho loves the rose and always crowns it with praise, comparing lovely girls to it; and she also compares it to the arms of the Graces, when she describes their bare forearms. Now the rose, though indeed the most beautiful of flowers, has a short season of perfection; for in common with other flowers it has its youth in the spring. But your beauty is a perpetual bloom, so that the autumn of your loveliness, as if it were still spring, goes on smiling in your eyes and your cheeks.

71

To Pleistaeretianus

The tribe of poets is numerous, and they even outnumber the swarms of bees. But the bees are nurtured by meadows, and the poets by houses and cities. The bees return the hospitality with honey, the poets with sumptuous banquets. There are also poets who give us a dinner of sweetmeats. Let us consider the erotic poets in this class, one of whom is Celsus here, who has devoted his own life to songs, as do the excellent cicadas. I trust to you to make sure he is fed not on dew but on real food.

73

To Julia Augusta

Not even the inspired Plato was envious of the sophists, though some people strongly believe that he was, but he was emulous of them, because they travelled around beguiling cities large and small in the manner of Orpheus and Thamyras. He was as far removed from envy as emulation is from jealousy. For jealousy nurtures mean natures but emulation stimulates brilliant ones; and a man envies what he cannot achieve himself, but he emulates whatever he can outdo or equal. Now Plato is eager to employ the styles of the

παρίησι τὸ ἑαυτοῦ ἄμεινον γοργιάζειν πολλά τε κατὰ τὴν Ἱππίου
10 καὶ Πρωταγόρου ἠχὼ φθέγγεται. ζηλωταὶ δὲ ἐγένοντο ἄλλοι μὲν
ἄλλων, καὶ γὰρ δὴ καὶ ὁ τοῦ Γρύλλου φιλοτιμεῖται πρὸς τὸν τοῦ
Προδίκου Ἡρακλέα, ὁπότε ὁ Πρόδικος τὴν Κακίαν καὶ τὴν Ἀρετὴν
ἄγει παρὰ τὸν Ἡρακλέα καλούσας αὐτὸν ἐς βίου αἵρεσιν, Γοργίου
δὲ θαυμασταὶ ἦσαν ἄριστοί τε καὶ πλεῖστοι· πρῶτον μὲν οἱ κατὰ
15 Θετταλίαν Ἕλληνες, παρ' οἷς τὸ ῥητορεύειν γοργιάζειν ἐπωνυμίαν
ἔσχεν, εἶτα τὸ ξύμπαν Ἑλληνικόν, ἐν οἷς Ὀλυμπίασι διελέχθη
κατὰ τῶν βαρβάρων ἀπὸ τῆς τοῦ νεὼ βαλβῖδος. λέγεται δὲ καὶ
Ἀσπασία ἡ Μιλησία τὴν τοῦ Περικλέους γλῶτταν κατὰ Γοργίαν
θῆξαι, Κριτίας δὲ καὶ Θουκυδίδης οὐκ ἀγνοοῦνται τὸ μεγαλόγνωμον
20 καὶ τὴν ὀφρὺν παρ' αὐτοῦ κεκτημένοι, μεταποιοῦντες δὲ αὐτὸ ἐς τὸ
οἰκεῖον ὁ μὲν ὑπ' εὐγλωττίας ὁ δὲ ὑπὸ ῥώμης. καὶ Αἰσχίνης δὲ ὁ
ἀπὸ τοῦ Σωκράτους, ὑπὲρ οὗ πρώην ἐσπούδαζες ὡς οὐκ ἀφανῶς
τοὺς διαλόγους κολάζοντος, οὐκ ὤκνει γοργιάζειν ἐν τῷ περὶ τῆς
Θαργηλίας λόγῳ, φησὶ γάρ που ὧδε· Θαργηλία Μιλησία ἐλθοῦσα
25 εἰς Θετταλίαν ξυνῆν Ἀντιόχῳ Θετταλῷ βασιλεύοντι πάντων
Θετταλῶν." αἱ δὲ ἀποστάσεις αἵ τε προσβολαὶ τῶν λόγων Γοργίου
ἐπεχωρίαζον πολλαχοῦ μέν, μάλιστα δὲ ἐν τῷ τῶν ἐποποιῶν κύκλῳ.
πεῖθε δὴ καὶ σύ, ὦ βασίλεια, τὸν θαρσαλεώτερον τοῦ Ἑλληνικοῦ
Πλούταρχον μὴ ἄχθεσθαι τοῖς σοφισταῖς μηδὲ ἐς διαβολὰς
30 καθίστασθαι τοῦ Γοργίου. εἰ δὲ οὐ πείθεις, σὺ μέν, οἷά σου σοφία
καὶ μῆτις, οἶσθα τί χρὴ ὄνομα θέσθαι τῷ τοιῷδε· ἐγὼ δὲ εἰπεῖν
ἔχων οὐκ ἔχω.[a]

Benner and Fobes
  [a] οὐκ ἔχω vel οὐ λέγω codd.

sophists: he does not admit inferiority to Gorgias in using Gorgias' own mannerisms, and many of his utterances have the ring of Hippias and Protagoras.

Different writers have admired different sophists: see, for example, how the son of Gryllus emulates the *Heracles* of Prodicus, where Prodicus brings Virtue and Vice to Heracles and they invite him to choose his kind of life. There were very many excellent admirers of Gorgias: firstly, the Thessalian Greeks, among whom oratory acquired the nickname 'Gorgianizing'; thereafter, the whole of the Greek people, among whom at Olympia he made a speech against the barbarians at the entrance to the temple. The Milesian Aspasia is also said to have sharpened Pericles' tongue to imitate Gorgias; and it is well known that Critias and Thucydides acquired their grandeur and hauteur from him, adapting his style to their own talents, the one through fluency, the other through vigour. Aeschines, too, the Socratic, whom you recently discussed earnestly as one who composed his dialogues in an obviously restrained style, did not hesitate to imitate Gorgias in his speech about Thargelia. In one place he says: 'Thargelia the Milesian, coming to Thessaly, associated with Antiochus the Thessalian, ruler of all the Thessalians'. Moreover, Gorgias' figures of 'sharp break' and 'sudden transition' were widely used, especially among the poets of the epic cycle. You must then, O Empress, persuade Plutarch, the most audacious of the Greeks, not to be offended with the sophists and not to quarrel with Gorgias. If you can't persuade him, such is your wit and wisdom that at least you know what name to call a man like that: though I could tell you, I can't.

ARISTAENETUS

1.13

Εὐτυχόβουλος Ἀκεστοδώρῳ

Τῷ μακρῷ καὶ τοῦτο, φίλτατε, κατέμαθον χρόνῳ, ὡς καὶ τέχναι
πᾶσαι προσδέονται τύχης, καὶ τύχη διακοσμεῖται ταῖς ἐπιστήμαις.
αἳ μὲν γὰρ ἀτελεῖς μὴ συνεργοῦντος τοῦ θείου, ἢ δὲ μᾶλλον
εὐδοκιμεῖ τὰς ἑαυτῆς ἀφορμὰς τοῖς ἐπιστήμοσι δωρουμένη. ἐπεὶ
5 τοίνυν μακρόν γε τὸ προοίμιον, εὖ οἶδα, τῷ ποθοῦντι θᾶττον ἀκοῦσαι, ἤδη λέξω τὸ συμβάν, μηδὲν ἔτι μελλήσας.
   Χαρικλῆς ὁ τοῦ βελτίστου Πολυκλέους υἱὸς παλλακίδος τοῦ
τεκόντος πόθῳ κλινοπετὴς ἦν, σώματος μὲν ἀφανῆ πλαττόμενος
ἀλγηδόνα, ψυχῆς δὲ ταῖς ἀληθείαις αἰτιώμενος νόσον. ὁ γοῦν πατήρ,
10 οἷα πατὴρ ἀγαθὸς καὶ σφόδρα φιλόπαις, αὐτίκα Πανάκειον
μεταπέμπεται τὸν ὄντως ἐπώνυμον ἰατρόν, ὃς τοὺς μὲν δακτύλους
τῷ σφυγμῷ προσαρμόζων, τὸν δὲ νοῦν μετάρσιον ἄγων τῇ τέχνῃ,
καὶ τοῖς ὄμμασι τὸ διαγνωστικὸν ὑποφαίνων κίνημα τῆς διανοίας
οὐδὲν ὅλως ἀρρώστημα κατενόει γνώριμον ἰατροῖς. ἐπὶ πολὺ μὲν οὖν
15 ὁ τοιοῦτος ἰατρὸς ἀμήχανος ἦν· τῆς δὲ ποθουμένης ἐκ ταὐτομάτου
παριούσης διὰ τοῦ μειρακίου, ἀθρόον ὁ σφυγμὸς ἄτακτον ἤλατο, καὶ
τὸ βλέμμα ταραχῶδες ἐδόκει, καὶ οὐδὲν ἄμεινον τὸ πρόσωπον
διέκειτο τῆς χειρός. καὶ διχόθεν ὁ Πανάκειος διέγνω τὸ πάθος, καὶ
ὅπερ ἁπλῶς ἐκ τέχνης οὐχ εἷλεν, ἐκ τύχης μᾶλλον εἶχε λαβών, καὶ
20 τὸ δῶρον τῆς προνοίας εἰς καιρὸν ἐταμιεύετο τῇ σιωπῇ. καὶ πρῶτος
ἦν αὐτῷ τῆς ἐπισκέψεως ἡγούμενος ὅδε ὁ τρόπος. αὖθις δὲ[a] παρα-
γενόμενος διεκελεύετο πᾶσαν τῆς οἰκίας κόρην τε καὶ γυναῖκα διὰ
τοῦ κάμνοντος παριέναι, καὶ μὴ χύδην, ἀλλὰ κατὰ μίαν, ἐκ
διαστήματος βραχέος διακρινομένας ἀλλήλων. καὶ τούτου
25 γιγνομένου αὐτὸς μὲν τὴν ὑποκάρπιον ἀρτηρίαν τοῖς δακτύλοις
ἡρμοκὼς ἐπεσκόπει, τὸν ἀκριβῆ γνώμονα τῶν Ἀσκληπιαδῶν καὶ
μάντιν ἀψευδῆ τῶν ἐμφυομένων ἡμῖν διαθέσεων· ὁ δὲ τῷ πόθῳ
κλινήρης πρὸς μὲν τὰς ἄλλας ἀτάραχος ἦν, τῆς δὲ παλλακῆς, ἧς
εἶχεν ἐρωτικῶς, ἐκφανείσης, εὐθὺς καὶ τὸ βλέμμα πάλιν καὶ τὸν
30 σφυγμὸν ἀλλοιότερος ἦν. ὁ δὲ σοφὸς καὶ λίαν εὐτυχὴς ἰατρὸς ἔτι
μᾶλλον τὴν ἀπόδειξιν τῆς νόσου παρ᾽ ἑαυτῷ βεβαιότερον ἐπιστοῦτο,
τὸ τρίτον τῷ σωτῆρι φάσκων. προφασισάμενος γὰρ κατασκευῆς

Mazal   [a] δὲ *Mercier*: τε V

ARISTAENETUS

1.13
EUTYCHOBULUS TO ACESTODORUS

Over a long time, my good friend, I have learnt also that all skills have need of fortune, and fortune is improved upon by skills. For these do not achieve their ends without divine assistance, while she wins greater esteem by giving the experts opportunities to use her. Well, then, since I'm quite aware that a preamble is tedious if you are impatient to hear more, without further ado I'll tell you what happened.

Charicles, noble Polycles' son, took to his bed because of a passion for his father's mistress, making out that he had some obscure physical pain, but knowing that the real cause was a sickness in his heart. So his father, as you'd expect of a good father who dotes on his child, at once sent for the rightly named doctor Panaceus. He put his fingers on the pulse, raised his mind to its greatest heights by his art, let his eyes reveal how his mind was moving to a diagnosis—but he completely failed to detect any sickness known to doctors. So for a long time even so good a doctor was at a loss, when the girl he loved happened to walk by the young man. At once his pulse began to beat wildly, his gaze seemed confused, and his features were no more settled than his pulse. Then Panaceus recognized the ailment from two sources, and what he had not grasped solely through his skill he now fully understood by the help of fortune. For the time being, however, he silently stored up this gift of providence.

This first examination had led the way; and the next time he came he ordered every woman and girl in the household to walk past the patient, not in a group but one by one, with a short distance between them. Meanwhile, with his fingers on the wrist pulse he continued to observe the medical profession's sure indicator and unerring presage of our inward states. The love-lorn patient was unmoved at sight of the other women, but when the object of his passion, the mistress, appeared, at once his gaze and his pulse completely altered. By his skill and remarkable good fortune the doctor sought to

αὐτῷ φαρμάκων δεῖσθαι τὸ πάθος, ἀπεχώρει τέως ὑπισχνούμενος
τῇ ὑστεραίᾳ ταῦτα κομίζειν, ἅμα τε τὸν νοσοῦντα χρησταῖς
35 παραθαρρύνων ἐλπίσι καὶ δυσφοροῦντα ψυχαγωγῶν τὸν πατέρα. ὡς
δὲ κατὰ καιρὸν ἐπηγγελμένον παρῆν, ὁ μὲν πατὴρ καὶ πάντες οἱ
λοιποὶ σωτῆρα τὸν ἄνδρα προσεῖπον, καὶ φιλοφρόνως ἠσπάζοντο
προσιόντες· ὁ δὲ χαλεπαίνων ἐβόα, καὶ δυσανασχετῶν αὐστηρῶς τὴν
θεραπείαν ἀπέγνω. τοῦ δὲ Πολυκλέους λιπαροῦντος ἅμα καὶ πυν-
40 θανομένου τῆς ἀπογνώσεως τὴν αἰτίαν, ἠγανάκτει σφοδρότερον
κεκραγώς, καὶ ἀπαλλάττεσθαι τὴν ταχίστην ἠξίου. ἀλλ’ ὁ πατὴρ
ἔτι μᾶλλον ἱκέτευε, τά τε στήθη φιλῶν καὶ τῶν γονάτων ἁπτόμενος.
τότε δῆθεν πρὸς ἀνάγκης ὧδε σὺν ὀργῇ τὴν αἰτίαν ἐξεῖπε· "τῆς
ἐμῆς γαμετῆς οὗτος ἐκτόπως ἐρᾷ καὶ παρανόμῳ τήκεται πόθῳ, καὶ
45 ζηλοτυπῶ τὸν ἄνθρωπον ἤδη καὶ οὐ φέρω θέαν ἀπειλουμένου
μοιχοῦ." ὁ τοίνυν Πολυκλῆς τοῦ παιδὸς ᾐσχύνθη τὴν νόσον ἀκούων,
καὶ τὸν Πανάκειον ἠρυθρία, πλὴν ὅλως τῆς φύσεως γεγονὼς οὐκ
ἀπώκνησε περὶ τῆς αὐτοῦ γυναικὸς τὸν ἰατρὸν ἱκετεύειν, ἀναγκαίαν
τινὰ σωτηρίαν οὐ μοιχείαν τὸ πρᾶγμα καλῶν. ἔτι δὲ τοιαῦτα
50 δεομένου τοῦ Πολυκλέους ὁ Πανάκειος διωλύγιον κατεβόα φάσκων
οἷάπερ εἰκὸς ἦν φθέγγεσθαι δεινοπαθοῦντα τὸν αἰτούμενον ἐξ ἰατροῦ
μεταβαλεῖν εἰς μαστροπὸν καὶ μοιχείας τῆς ἑαυτοῦ γαμετῆς
⟨συλλαβεῖν⟩,[b] εἰ μὴ φανερῶς οὕτως τοῖς ῥήμασιν. ἐπεὶ δὲ πάλιν
ἐνέκειτο[c] Πολυκλῆς ἀντιβολῶν τὸν ἄνδρα, καὶ πάλιν σωτηρίαν οὐ
55 μοιχείαν ἐκάλει τὸ πρᾶγμα, ὁ συλλογιστικὸς ἰατρὸς ὡς ἐν ὑποθέσει[d]
τὸ συμβὰν ἀληθῶς ἀντεπάγων ἤρετο Πολυκλέα· "τί οὖν, πρὸς Διός,
οὐδ’ ἂν ὁ παῖς τῆς σῆς ἤρα παλλακίδος, ἐκαρτέρεις αὐτῷ ποθοῦντι
ταύτην ἐκδοῦναι;" ἐκείνου δὲ φήσαντος "πάνυ γε, νὴ τὸν Δία", ὁ
σοφὸς ἔφη Πανάκειος·"οὐκοῦν σαυτόν, ὦ Πολύκλεις, ἱκέτευε, καὶ
60 παραμυθοῦ τὰ εἰκότα. τῆς σῆς γὰρ οὗτος παλλακίδος ἐρᾷ. εἰ δὲ
δίκαιον ἐμὲ τὴν ὁμόζυγα παραδιδόναι τῷ τυχόντι διὰ σωτηρίαν, ὡς
ἔφης, πολύ γε μᾶλλον δικαιότερόν σε τῷ παιδὶ κινδυνεύοντι
παραχωρῆσαι τῆς παλλακίδος." εἶπεν εὐμεθόδως, συνελογίσατο
δυνατῶς, καὶ πέπεικε τὸν τεκόντα τοῖς οἰκείοις πειθαρχῆσαι
65 δικαίοις. πρότερον μέντοι Πολυκλῆς ἑαυτῷ προσεφθέγγετο λέγων·

[b] ⟨συλλαβεῖν⟩ suppl. Lesky   [c] ἐνέκειτο Hercher: ἐπέκειτο V
[d] ὑποθέσει Boissonade: ἐπιθέσει V

make the demonstration of the disease still more convincing to himself—'third time lucky', he thought. He went away for a while, on the pretext that he had to prepare drugs for the disease, promising that he would bring them with him the next day. At the same time he encouraged the patient with good hopes and gave consolation to the afflicted father.

When he appeared at the promised time, the father and all the others greeted him as their saviour and gave him a most affectionate welcome. But he shouted at them harshly, and in an angry tone he told them curtly that he was abandoning the treatment. Polycles kept pleading with him and asking him why he was giving up, at which he grew still more irritated and noisy and declared his intention to depart immediately. The father renewed his pleas, kissing his chest and clasping his knees. Then he let himself give way to pressure and angrily told them the reason: 'This lad is wildly in love with my wife, wasting away through an unlawful passion. I'm now jealous of the fellow and can't bear the sight of an adulterer threatening me.' Polycles felt ashamed at hearing what ailed his son, and blushed before Panaceus; but yielding entirely to his own natural feelings he did not hesitate to beg the doctor to give up his wife, saying that this would not be a case of adultery but an essential cure. Polycles kept on making this request, while Panaceus replied with loud shouts and complaints, saying what you would expect from a man who was asked to change from a doctor to a pimp and to cooperate in an adultery with his own wife—even if not stated in so many words. But when Polycles pressed him again with entreaties, and again called it cure, not adultery, the doctor, acting the logician, offered as a hypothesis what had actually happened, and asked Polycles: 'Come, tell me truly, if your son was in love with your mistress could you bear to give her up to satisfy his passion?' The other replied, 'Indeed I could'; and the crafty Panaceus went on: 'Then make your appeals to yourself, Polycles, and offer the consolations that fit the case. For it is your mistress that he loves. And if it is right for me to offer my wife to anybody to cure him, as you say, it is far more right for you to yield up your mistress to your own son when his life is in danger'. His argument was sound, his conclusion compelling, and he persuaded the father to follow his own

"χαλεπὴ μὲν ἡ αἴτησις· δύο κακῶν εἰς αἴρεσιν προκειμένων τὸ
μετριώτερον αἱρετέον."

2.3

Γλυκέρα Φιλίννη

Οὐκ εὐτυχῶς, Φίλιννα, Στρεψιάδῃ τῷ σοφῷ ῥήτορι συνεζύγην·
οὗτος γὰρ ἑκάστοτε παρὰ τὸν καιρὸν τῆς εὐνῆς πόρρω τῶν νυκτῶν
πλάττεται περὶ πραγμάτων σκοπεῖσθαι, καὶ, ἃς ἐδιδάχθη δίκας
τηνικαῦτα προφασίζεται μελετᾶν, σχηματιζόμενος δὲ ὑπόκρισιν
5 ἠρέμα τὼ χεῖρε^a κινεῖ καὶ ἄττα δήπου πρὸς ἑαυτὸν ψιθυρίζει. τί οὖν
οὗτος ἔγημε κόρην καὶ λίαν ἀκμάζουσαν, μηδὲν δεόμενος γυναικός;
ἢ ἵνα μοι τῶν πραγμάτων μεταδοίη, καὶ νύκτωρ αὐτῷ συνεπιζητήσω
τοὺς νόμους; ἀλλ' εἴγε δικῶν γυμναστήριον τὴν ἡμῶν ποιεῖται
παστάδα, ἐγὼ καὶ νεόνυμφος οὖσα ἀποκοιτήσω λοιπὸν καὶ
10 καθευδήσω χωρίς. κἂν ἐπιμείνῃ πρὸς μὲν ἀλλότρια πράγματα
κεχηνώς, μόνης δὲ τῆς κοινῆς ὑποθέσεως ἀμελῶν, ἕτερος ῥήτωρ τῆς
ἐμῆς ἐπιμελήσεται δίκης. ἆρα κατάδηλον ὃ βούλομαι λέγειν; πάντως
δήπου, ἐπεὶ ταῦτα γράφω συντόμως ἐκ τούτων συνιέναι καὶ τὰ
λείποντα δυναμένῃ. ταῦτά μοι νόει καλῶς, ὦ γύναιον δηλαδὴ
15 συμπαθὲς γυναικί, κἂν αἰδουμένη τὴν χρείαν οὐ μάλα σαφῶς
ἐπιστέλλω, καὶ πειρῶ τὸ λυποῦν^b εἰς δύναμιν θεραπεύειν. σὲ γὰρ
τὴν καλὴν προμνήστριαν χρή, καὶ ἄλλως ^cἐμὴν αὐτανεψιὰν^c οὖσαν,
μὴ μόνον τὴν ἀρχὴν ἐσπουδακέναι τῷ γάμῳ, ἀλλὰ καὶ νῦν αὐτὸν
σαλεύοντα διορθοῦσθαι. ἐγὼ γὰρ τὸν λύκον τῶν ὤτων ἔχω, ὃν οὔτε
20 κατέχειν ἐπὶ πολὺ δυνατόν, οὔτε μὴν ἀκίνδυνον ἀφεῖναι, μή με
δικορράφος ὢν ἀναίτιον αἰτιάσηται.

Mazal
   ^a τὼ χεῖρε *Boissonade*: τὼ χεῖλε V
   ^b λυποῦν *Mercier*: λοιποῦν V
   ^c−c ἐμὴν αὐτανεψιὰν *Hercher*: αὐτὴν ἐμὴν ἀνεψιὰν V

2.15

Χρυσὶς Μυρρίνῃ

Τοὺς ἀλλήλων, ὦ φιλτάτη, συνεπιστάμεθα πόθους. σὺ μὲν τὸν ἐμὸν
ἄνδρα ποθεῖς, ἐγὼ δὲ τοῦ σοῦ θεράποντος ἐκθύμως ἐρῶ. τί οὖν
πρακτέον; πῶς ἂν εὐμηχάνως ἑκάστη τὸν ἑαυτῆς ἔρωτα θεραπεύσῃ;

principles—but not before Polycles remarked to himself, 'It's indeed a harsh demand; but given a choice of two evils, one must choose the lesser.'

2.3

GLYCERA TO PHILINNA

It was an unlucky day for me, Philinna, when I married that sophist. Far into the night, long past bedtime, he is always claiming he must think about his law-suits and making the excuse that that is the time he has to practise the speeches for the cases in which he has been instructed—working at his delivery, gesturing solemnly with his hands, and even muttering to himself. Why did a man like this marry a girl, especially one in the bloom of youth, when he doesn't need a wife? Was it in order to share his cases with me, and have me examine the laws with him every night? Well, if he's going to make our bedroom a training ground for his law-suits, even though I'm a new bride I'm going to desert his bed from now on and sleep apart. And if he continues to devote himself to other people's cases, with no thought of our common cause, I'll find another sophist to look after *my* interests. You get my meaning? Of course you do: I'm writing concisely to one who can understand what I leave out from what I say. Please think this over carefully, with your woman's natural sympathy for another woman, even if I am too modest to make my request explicitly, and try your best to find a cure for my problem. For you were my good matchmaker, and indeed you are my own cousin, so you should be concerned not only in having started my marriage, but in putting it to rights now it is storm-tossed. I've got the wolf by the ears, which I can neither hold on to for long nor safely let go, for fear the pettifogger brings a false charge against me.

2.15

CHRYSIS TO MYRRHINA

My dear, we understand each other's desires. You desire my husband and I have a burning passion for your servant. What

ἐδεήθην ⟨τῆς Ἀφροδίτης⟩ᵃ, εὖ ἴσθι, τῆς θεραπείας τὴν ἔννοιαν
5 ἐμβαλεῖν, καὶ ταύτην ἐξ ἀφανοῦς ἡ δαίμων προσέπνευσέ μοι τὴν
γνώμην, ἣν οὕτω πράττειν παρεγγυῶ σοι, Μυρρίνη. τὸν σὸν μὲν
οἰκέτην, ἐμὸν ⟨δὲ⟩ᵇ δεσπότην ἐρωτικὸν δόκει οὖν θυμουμένη ἅμα
καὶ τύπτουσα τῆς οἰκίας ἐκπέμπειν, ἀλλὰ πρὸς θεῶν πεφεισμένως
καὶ τῷ παρόντι μοι πόθῳ τὴν μάστιγα συμμετροῦσα· ὁ δ' οὖν
10 οἰκέτης, Εὔκτιτος ὁ καλός, πάντως ἅτε πρὸς φίλην τῆς κεκτημένης
φεύξεται παρ' ἐμέ, κἀγὼ τὸν ἄνδρα ὡς ὑπὲρ τοῦ θεράποντος τὴν
δέσποιναν ἱκετεύσοντα τὴν ταχίστην ἐξαποστέλλω πρὸς σέ, οἷον
μετὰ δεήσεως αὐτὸν ἐξωθοῦσα. τοῦτον δὴ τὸν τρόπον ἑκατέρα τὸν
ἑαυτῆς δεξαμένη ἐρώμενον οὐκ ἀμελήσει τοῦ Ἔρωτος ὑφηγουμένου
15 ἐπὶ σχολῆς ἅμα καὶ ῥᾳστώνης χρήσασθαι τῷ παραπεπτωκότι
καιρῷ. ἀλλ' ἐπὶ μήκιστον ἐμφοροῦ τῆς ἐπιθυμίας τῇ συγκοιμήσει,
καί μοι συνεπεκτείνουσα τῶν ἀφροδισίων τὴν τέρψιν. ἔρρωσο, καὶ
πέπαυσό μοι θρηνοῦσα τοῦ συζύγου τὴν ἄωρον τελευτήν, φίλον ἀντ'
ἐκείνου τὸν ἐμὸν σύνοικον εὐτυχοῦσα.

Mazal
ᵃ τῆς Ἀφροδίτης suppl. Hercher   ᵇ δὲ suppl. Abresch

can we do about it? How can we each contrive to indulge our love successfully? Let me tell you that I begged Aphrodite to suggest a cure, and the goddess out of the blue inspired me with this thought which I commend to you, Myrrhina, to put into action like this. You pretend to be angry with your slave, the lord of my heart, and beat him out of your house—but sparingly, for God's sake, and curbing your whip for the sake of my current passion. Then the slave, gorgeous Euctitus, will be sure to come running to me as a friend of his mistress, and I'll send my husband full speed to you to plead with mistress for slave, making out that I'm despatching him with a petition to you. In this way each of us will receive her favourite, and not neglect to use the opportunity that presents itself, at leisure and in comfort, under love's guidance. But mind you indulge your appetite in bed for as long as possible, so you can prolong my sexual delights as well. Farewell, and do stop mourning your husband's untimely death: take mine as a lover in a happy exchange for yours.

ANACHARSIS

1

Ἀνάχαρσις Ἀθηναίοις

Γελᾶτε ἐμὴν φωνήν, διότι οὐ τρανῶς Ἑλληνικὰ γράμματα λέγει. Ἀνάχαρσις παρ' Ἀθηναίοις σολοικίζει, Ἀθηναῖοι δὲ παρὰ Σκύθαις. οὐ φωναῖς διήνεγκαν ἄνθρωποι ἀνθρώπων εἰς τὸ εἶναι ἀξιόλογοι, ἀλλὰ γνώμαις, αἷσπερ καὶ Ἕλληνες Ἑλλήνων. Σπαρτιᾶται οὐ τρανοὶ 5 ἀττικίζειν, ἀλλ' ἔργοις λαμπροὶ καὶ εὐδόκιμοι. οὐ ψέγουσι Σκύθαι λόγον, ὃς ἂν ἐμφανίζῃ τὰ δέοντα, οὐδ' ἐπαινοῦσιν, ὅταν μὴ ἐφικνῆται τοῦ δέοντος. πολλὰ καὶ ὑμεῖς οἰκονομεῖτε οὐ προσέχοντες φωνῇ ἄρθρα οὐκ ἐχούσῃ. εἰσάγεσθε ἰατροὺς Αἰγυπτίους, κυβερνήταις χρῆσθε Φοίνιξιν, ὠνεῖσθε ἐν ἀγορᾷ οὐ διδόντες πλεῖον τῆς ἀξίας τοῖς 10 ἑλληνιστὶ λαλοῦσιν. οὐδὲ ὀκνηρῶς λαμβάνετε παρὰ βαρβάρων, ἐὰν πρὸς τρόπου πωλῶσι. βασιλεῖς Περσῶν κἀκείνων φίλοι μέγα φρονοῦντες, ὅταν βούλωνται πρὸς Ἑλλήνων πρεσβευτὰς Ἑλληνικῇ φωνῇ φθέγγεσθαι, ἀναγκάζονται σολοικίζειν, ὧν ὑμεῖς οὔτε βουλὰς οὔτε ἔργα καταμέμφεσθε. λόγος δὲ κακὸς οὐ γίνεται, ὅταν βουλαὶ 15 ἀγαθαὶ ὦσι καὶ ἔργα καλὰ λόγοις παρακολουθῇ. Σκύθαι δὲ κρίνουσι λόγον φαῦλον, ὅταν διαλογισμοὶ φαῦλοι γίνωνται. πολλῶν καθυστερήσετε, ἂν δυσχεραίνητε φωναῖς βαρβάροις καὶ μετὰ τοῦτο μὴ ἀποδεχόμενοι τὰ λεγόμενα. πολλοὺς γὰρ ποιήσετε ὀκνηροὺς εἰσηγεῖσθαι ὑμῖν τὰ συμφέροντα. διὰ τί βαρβαρικὰ τιμᾶτε ὑφάσματα, 20 φωνὴν δὲ βάρβαρον οὐ δοκιμάζετε; αὐλούντων καὶ ᾀδόντων φωνὰς ζητεῖτε ἐμμελεῖς, καὶ ποιητῶν ἔμμετρα ποιούντων ἐπιλαμβάνεσθε, εἰ μὴ ἀναπληροῦσι γράμμασιν Ἑλληνικοῖς τὰ μέτρα. λεγόντων δὲ θεωρεῖτε αὐτὰ τὰ λεγόμενα. τὸ γὰρ τέλος τούτων εἰς ὄνησιν. καὶ βαρβάροις πειθόμενοι οὐκ ἐπιτρέψετε γυναιξὶ καὶ τέκνοις μὴ 25 προσέχουσιν ὑμῖν, ἐὰν σολοικίζητε. κρεῖσσον γὰρ σολοικίζουσι πειθαρχοῦντας σώζεσθαι ἢ τρανῶς ἀττικίζουσιν ἐπακολουθοῦντας μέγα βλάπτεσθαι. ἀπαιδεύτων ταῦτά ἐστι καὶ ἀπειροκάλων, ἄνδρες Ἀθηναῖοι. σώφρων γὰρ οὐδεὶς ἂν διανοηθείη ταῦτα.

ANACHARSIS

I

ANACHARSIS TO THE ATHENIANS

You laugh at my speech because it doesn't utter Greek sounds clearly. Anacharsis makes mistakes in his speech among the Athenians: but so do the Athenians among the Scythians. It is not in speech that men differ from one another in worthiness, but in their judgement—just as Greeks differ from Greeks. Spartans do not speak Attic clearly, but they are distinguished and famous for their deeds. The Scythians don't find fault with any speech which makes clear what is necessary, nor do they approve of any speech which falls short of this. You people too manage most of your affairs without worrying about speech that is not clearly articulated. You call in Egyptian doctors; you employ Phoenician skippers; you buy things in the market, not paying over the odds to those who prattle away in Greek, and not hesitating to take from foreigners if they are selling at a reasonable price. Whenever the Persian kings and their grand friends want to talk in Greek to Greek envoys, they inevitably make mistakes, but you don't thereby blame their intentions or their acts. Speech is not bad when intentions are good and fine actions follow upon the words. The Scythians judge a speech to be poor when the arguments are poor. You will lack many things if you are annoyed at barbarian ways of speaking and consequently do not take in the sense of what is being said—that is the way to make many people reluctant to offer you advantageous proposals. Why do you value barbarian woven cloths, yet disapprove of barbarian speech? You can require harmonious notes from pipe-players and singers, and criticize poets if they do not fill their verse with Greek syllables. But when people make speeches keep a watchful eye on what they actually say: for that in the end is what benefits you. And if you take barbarian advice, you will not allow your women and children to ignore you if you happen to speak badly. It is better to be kept safe by obeying faulty speakers than to come to grief by attending just to those who speak pure Attic. That is a sign of stupid and ill-bred people, Athenians: no reasonable man would take that attitude.

2

Ἀνάχαρσις Σόλωνι

Ἕλληνες σοφοὶ ἄνδρες, οὐδέν γε σοφώτεροι βαρβάρων. τὸ γὰρ
ἐπίστασθαι καλὸν εἰδέναι οὐκ ἀφείλοντο θεοὶ βαρβάρων. πεῖραν δ᾽
ἔξεστι λαμβάνειν ἐξετάζοντας λόγοις, εἰ καλὰ φρονοῦμεν, καὶ
βασανίζειν εἰ συμφωνοῦμεν λόγοις πρὸς ἔργα, εἰ ὅμοιοί ἐσμεν τοῖς
5 ἀγαθῶς ζῶσι. στῆλαι δὲ καὶ κόσμος σώματος μὴ γινέσθωσαν
ἐμπόδια ὀρθῆς κρίσεως. ἄλλοι γὰρ ἄλλως κατὰ νόμους πατέρων
κεκοσμήκασι τὰ σώματα. σημεῖα δὲ ἀσυνεσίας τὰ αὐτὰ βαρβάροις
καὶ Ἕλλησιν, ὁμοίως δὲ καὶ συνέσεως. σὺ δέ, διότι Ἀνάχαρσις
ἐλθὼν ἐπὶ σὰς θύρας ἠβούλετό σοι ξένος γενέσθαι, ἀπηξίωσας καὶ
10 ἀπεκρίνω ἐν οἰκείᾳ χώρᾳ[a] με δεῖν[a] ξενίαν συνάπτειν. εἰ δέ τίς σοι
κύνα Σπαρτιάτην ἐδωρεῖτο, οὐκ ἂν προσέτασσες ἐκείνῳ ἀνδρὶ κύνα
τοῦτον εἰς Σπάρτην ἀγαγόντα δοῦναί σοι. πότε δὲ καὶ ἐσόμεθα
ἑτέροις ξένοι, ἐπειδὰν ἕκαστος τοῦτον τὸν λόγον λέγῃ; ἐμοὶ μὲν οὐ
καλῶς ἔχειν ταῦτα δοκεῖ, Σόλων, Ἀθηναῖε σοφέ. καί με κελεύει
15 θυμὸς πορεύεσθαι πάλιν ἐπὶ σὰς θύρας οὐκ ἀξιώσοντα ἃ καὶ
πρότερον, ἀλλὰ πευσόμενον πῶς ἔχει, ἅπερ ἀπεφήνω ὑπὲρ ξενίας.

Reuters
[a-a] με δεῖν *Reuters:* με δεῖ Ω: μὴ δεῖν θ

2

ANACHARSIS TO SOLON

The Greeks are wise men, yet in no way are they wiser than barbarians. For the gods have not deprived barbarians of knowing how to recognize the good. You can prove this by examining us with words to see if we have noble thoughts, and putting us to the test, whether our words harmonize with our deeds and whether we are like those who live good lives. But do not let monumental columns and bodily adornment impede correct judgement. For different people adorn their bodies differently according to their ancestral customs. The symptoms of stupidity—and likewise of good sense—are the same for barbarians and for Greeks. Now, because Anacharsis came to your door wishing to become your friend, you declined, replying that I should form friendship in my own land. But if someone offered you a Spartan dog, you wouldn't tell that man to take the dog first to Sparta and give it to you there. When shall we ever be friends with each other if everyone speaks like this? This does not seem to me the right attitude, Solon, you wise Athenian. I have a strong urge to come back to your door, not with the same request as before, but to find out what your theory about friendship really means.

DIOGENES

30

Ἰκεσίᾳ

Ἧκον, ὦ πάτερ, Ἀθήναζε, καὶ πυθόμενος τὸν Σωκράτους ἑταῖρον
εὐδαιμονίαν διδάσκειν, εἰσῆλθον παρ᾽ αὐτόν. ὃ δὲ ἐτύγχανε τότε
σχολάζων περὶ ταῖν ὁδοῖν ταῖν φερούσαιν, ἔλεγε δὲ αὐτὰς εἶναι δύο
καὶ οὐ πολλάς, καὶ τὴν μὲν σύντομον, τὴν δὲ πολλήν. ἐξεῖναι οὖν
5 ἑκάστῳ ὁποτέραν βούλοιτο βαδίζειν. κἀγὼ ταῦτα ἀκούσας τότε μὲν
κατεσίγησα, τῇ δὲ ἑξῆς, ἐπειδὴ πάλιν εἰσιόντων ἡμῶν παρ᾽ αὐτὸν
περὶ ταῖν ὁδοῖν παρεκάλεσα αὐτὸν ἐπιδεῖξαι ἡμῖν, καὶ ὃς μάλ᾽
ἑτοίμως ἀπαναστὰς τῶν θάκων ἦγεν ἡμᾶς εἰς ἄστυ καὶ δι᾽ αὐτοῦ
εὐθὺς εἰς τὴν ἀκρόπολιν. **2.** καὶ ἐπεὶ ἀγχοῦ ἐγενόμεθα,
10 ἐπιδείκνυσιν ἡμῖν δύο τινὲ ὁδὼ ἀναφερούσα, τὴν μὲν ὀλίγην
προσάντη τε καὶ δύσκολον, τὴν δὲ πολλὴν λείαν τε καὶ ᵃῥᾳδίαν.
καθιστας ἅμα γάρᵃ "αἱ μὲν εἰς τὴν ἀκρόπολιν" εἶπε "φέρουσαι ὁδοί
εἰσιν αὗται, αἱ δὲ ἐπὶ τὴν εὐδαιμονίαν τοιαῦται· αἱρεῖσθε δὲ ἕκαστος
ἣν ἐθέλετε, ξεναγήσω δ᾽ ἐγώ." τότε οἱ μὲν ἄλλοι τῆς ὁδοῦ τὸ
15 δύσκολον καὶ πρόσαντες καταπλαγέντες ὑποκατεκλίνησαν καὶ τὴν
μακρὰν καὶ λείαν παρεκάλουν αὐτὸν διάγειν, ἐγὼ δὲ κρείττων
γενόμενος τῶν χαλεπῶν τὴν προσάντη καὶ δύσκολον· ἐπὶ γὰρ εὐδαιμονίαν ἐπειγομένῳ κἂν διὰ πυρὸς ἢ ξιφῶν βαδιστέον εἶναι. **3.** ἐπεὶ
δὲ ταύτην εἱλόμην τὴν ὁδόν, ἀφαιρεῖταί μου τὸ ἱμάτιον καὶ τὸν
20 χιτῶνα καὶ περιβάλλει μοι τρίβωνα διπλοῦν καὶ ἀποκρήμνησί μου
τοῦ ὤμου πήραν, ἐμβαλὼν εἰς αὐτὴν ἄρτον καὶ τρίμμα καὶ ποτήριον
καὶ τρυβλίον, ἔξωθεν δὲ αὐτῇ παρήρτησε λήκυθον καὶ στλεγγίδα,
δίδωσι δέ μοι καὶ βακτηρίαν. καὶ ἐγὼ τούτοις ἐκοσμήθην, ἠρόμην
δὲ αὐτόν, διὰ τί με τρίβωνα περιέβαλε διπλοῦν. ὃ δὲ ἔφη "ἵνα σε
25 πρὸς ἄμφω συνασκήσω, καὶ καῦμα τὸ ἀπὸ θερείας καὶ ψῦχος τὸ
ἀπὸ χειμῶνος." "τί γάρ" ἔφην, "ὁ ἁπλοῦς τοῦτο οὐκ ἐποίει; **4.**
"οὐ μὲν οὖν" εἶπεν, "ἀλλὰ θέρους μὲν ῥᾳστώνην, χειμῶνος δὲ
πλείονα ἢ κατ᾽ ἄνθρωπον ταλαιπωρίαν." "τὴν δὲ πήραν διὰ τί μοι
περιτέθεικας;" "ἵνα πάντῃ τὴν οἰκίαν" εἶπε "περιφέρῃς." "τὸ δὲ
30 ποτήριον καὶ τὸ τρυβλίον διὰ τί ἐνέβαλες;" "ὅτι δεῖ σε" εἶπε "καὶ
πίνειν καὶ ὄψῳ χρῆσθαι, ὄψῳ ἑτέρῳ" ἔφη, "κάρδαμον μὴᵇ ἔχοντα."

Capelle   Malherbe
ᵃ⁻ᵃ καθιστάς. ἅμα γάρ *alii interpungunt*
ᵇ μὴ *add. Westermann*

DIOGENES

30

To Hicesias

I came to Athens, father, and having learnt that the companion of Socrates was giving lessons on happiness, I went to hear him. At the time he happened to be lecturing on the two roads that lead to it, saying that there are two and not many, one a short cut and one a long path: so that everyone is free to take the one he wants. At the time I listened to this in silence, but the next day when we went back to hear him, I urged him to explain to us about the two roads. He very readily got up from his seat and took us to the city, right through it to the Acropolis. **2.** And when we were near to it, he showed us two roads leading uphill, one short, steep, and difficult, and the other long, smooth, and easy. As he brought us back together he said 'These are the roads leading to the Acropolis, and such are the roads to happiness. Each of you choose the one you want and I will guide you.' Then the others, panic-stricken at the difficulty and steepness of one road, gave in and urged him to take them on the long smooth one. But since I can conquer hardships, I chose the steep and difficult one; for if you are pressing eagerly on to happiness you must make your way even through fire and sword.

3. When I had chosen this road, he took off my mantle and tunic, and putting on me a double cloak, he hung a pouch from my shoulder, filling it with bread, porridge, a cup and a bowl, attached an oil flask and scraper to the outside of it, and gave me a staff as well. With these trappings on, I asked him why he put a double cloak on me. He replied, 'So I can help you to cope with both the heat of summer and the cold of winter.'

'Well,' I said, 'didn't the single one do that?'

4. 'Certainly not,' he said, 'it gives relief in summer, but causes more distress in winter than a man can bear.'

'And why did you furnish me with a pouch?'

"τὴν δὲ λήκυθον καὶ τὴν στλεγγίδα πρὸς τί ἀπήρτησας;" "τὴν
μὲν ἀρωγόν" ἔφη "πόνων, τὴν δὲ γλοιοῦ." "ἡ δὲ βακτηρία πρὸς τί;"
ἔφην. "πρὸς τὴν ἀσφάλειαν" εἶπε. "ποίαν τήνδε;" "πρὸς ἣν οἱ θεοὶ
35 αὐτῇ ἐχρήσαντο, πρὸς τοὺς ποιητάς."

'So you can take your house with you everywhere', he said.

'And why add the cup and bowl?'

'Because you have to drink and use a relish', he replied; 'some other sort if you don't have cress.'

'And why attach the oil flask and scraper?'

'The one is to help you in physical toil,' he said, 'and the other for oil and dirt.'

'And what's the staff for?' I asked.

'As a precaution', he said.

'What sort of precaution?'

'The sort the gods use it for—against the poets.'

CRATES

34

Μητροκλεῖ

Ἴσθι με συμφορᾷ κεχρῆσθαι πυθόμενον Διογένη ἐς ληστρικὰ
ἁλῶναι, καὶ εἰ μή τις τῶν αἰχμαλώτων λυτρωθεὶς ἦλθεν Ἀθήναζε,
ἔτι ἂν ἦν καὶ νῦν ἐν τοῖς ὁμοίοις. νῦν δ' ἀφικόμενος οὗτος ἰάσατό
με, διηγησάμενος ὡς "ἤνεγκε τὴν συμφορὰν πράως, ὥστε ποτὲ καὶ
5 εἶπε τοῖς λησταῖς ὀλιγωροῦσιν ἡμῶν, ὦ οὗτοι, τί δήποτε; εἰ μὲν σῦς
ἤγετε εἰς ἐμπορίαν, ἐπεμελεῖσθε ἂν αὐτῶν, ἵνα ὑμῖν πλεῖον ἀργύριον
πωλούμενοι ἐνέγκωσιν· ἡμῶν δέ, οὓς καὶ αὐτοὺς μέλλετε ὥσπερ σῦς
πιπράσκειν, καταμελεῖτε. 2. ἢ οὐ δοκεῖτε καὶ ἡμᾶς πλεῖον
εὑρίσκειν, ἐὰν παχεῖς ὁρώμεθα, ἔλαττον δὲ ἐὰν λεπτοί; ἐπεὶ ἄνθρω-
10 ποι οὐκ ἐσθίονται, οὐκ οἴεσθε δεῖν καὶ ἀνθρώπων ἐπιμελεῖσθαι ὧδε;
ἀλλ' ἴστε γε ὡς πάντες οἱ ἀγοράζοντες τὰ ἀνδράποδα εἰς ἓν τοῦτο
βλέπουσιν, εἰ παχὺ τὸ σῶμα καὶ μέγα. ἐρῶ δὲ ὑμῖν καὶ αἰτίαν, ὅτι
καὶ ἄνθρωπον διὰ τὴν τοῦ σώματος χρείαν ἀγοράζουσι καὶ οὐ τῆς
ψυχῆς.' ἐξ ἐκείνου οἱ λησταὶ οὐκέτι ἠμέλουν ἡμῶν, ἐπὶ τούτῳ δὲ
15 καὶ ἡμεῖς αὐτῷ χάριν ἐγινώσκομεν.

3. Ὡς δὲ ἥκομεν ἔς τινα πόλιν, ἵνα ἠδυνάμεθα κέρμα γενέσθαι
αὐτοῖς, προήγαγον ἡμᾶς ἐς ἀγοράν, εἶτα ἡμεῖς μὲν ἑστῶτες
ἐδακρύομεν, ὃ δὲ ἄρτου ἐπιλαβόμενος ἤσθιε καὶ ἡμῖν προσώρεγεν.
ἀπονευόντων δὲ ἡμῶν προσδέξασθαι ἔφη

20   καὶ γάρ τ' ἠύκομος Νιόβη ἐμνήσατο σίτου

καὶ τοῦτο μετὰ παιδιᾶς καὶ γέλωτος εἰπών 'οὐ παύσεσθε' ἔφη
'εἰρωνευόμενοι καὶ κλαίοντες ἐπὶ τῷ μέλλειν δουλεύειν, ὥσπερ πρὶν
ἁλῶναι εἰς τοὺς λῃστὰς ἐλεύθεροι ὄντες καὶ οὐ δοῦλοι καὶ τῶν γε
φαύλων δεσποτῶν; νυνὶ μὲν γὰρ κληρώσεσθε ἴσως δεσπότας μετρίους,
25 οἳ ἐκκόψουσιν ὑμῶν τὴν τρυφήν, ὑφ' ἧς διεφθάρητε, ἐμποιήσουσι δὲ
καρτερίαν καὶ ἐγκράτειαν, τὰ τιμιώτατα ἀγαθά.' 4. ταῦτα οὖν
διεξιόντος οἱ ὠνηταὶ ἑστῶτες τῶν λόγων ἠκροῶντο καὶ αὐτὸν ἐθαύ-
μαζον τῆς ἀπαθείας, τινὲς δὲ καὶ ἠρώτων εἴ τι ἐπίσταται. ὃ δὲ ἔλεγεν
ἐπίστασθαι ἀνθρώπων ἄρχειν, ὥστε εἴ τις ὑμῶν κυρίου δεῖται,
30 συμφωνείτω προσιὼν τοῖς πωληταῖς.' κἀκεῖνοι ἀναγελάσαντες ἐπὶ
τουτῳ 'καὶ τίς' ἔφασαν 'ἔστίν, ὃς ἂν ἐλεύθερος κυρίου δεῖται;'

CRATES

34
To Metrocles

You must know how distressed I was to learn that Diogenes had been captured by pirates, and I would still be feeling the same way if one of the prisoners had not been ransomed and come to Athens. But as it is, this man on his arrival relieved me by his account of how Diogenes 'bore the disaster easily, so much so that once, when the pirates were neglecting us, he said to them, "Here, you, what are you up to? If you were taking pigs to market, you would look after them so they would fetch you a better price when sold; but you are ignoring us, though you intend to sell us too like pigs. **2.** Don't you think that we will also get you a better price if we look fat, and a worse price if skinny? Do you suppose you don't have to take such care of men because men are not eaten? But surely you realize that everyone who buys slaves at market looks for this one thing, whether they are physically big and strong. And I'll tell you why: they buy a man too because they want his body and not his soul." After that the pirates no longer neglected us, and we have him to thank for that.

3. 'When we arrived at a city where they could convert us into cash, they took us to market. Then the rest of us stood around weeping, while he seizing a loaf, ate some and offered it to us. As we refused to take it, he said,
"Even fair Niobe took thought for food",
and then he added, speaking light-heartedly and jokingly, "Can't you stop dissembling and wailing over your coming slavery?—as if you were free men before the pirates took you, and not slaves, and of bad masters at that. For now you'll perhaps be allotted to reasonable masters, who will eradicate the luxury which was corrupting you, and will instil in you those most valuable assets, endurance and self-control." **4.** As he was expounding all this, the purchasers stood listening to his words and marvelling at his lack of emotion, while some of them also asked him if he had any skills. He replied that he had the skill to rule men—"So if any of you needs a master,

'πάντες᾽ εἶπεν 'οἱ φαῦλοι καὶ τιμῶντες μὲν ἡδονήν, ἀτιμάζοντες δὲ πόνον, τὰ μέγιστα τῶν κακῶν δελέατα.'

5. "Διὰ ταῦτα περιμάχητος ἐγένετο ὁ Διογένης καὶ οὐκέτι
35 ἐπράθη, ἀλλ᾽ οἱ λησταὶ καθελόντες αὐτὸν ἀπὸ τοῦ λίθου ἦγον οἴκαδε παρ᾽ αὑτούς, ὑπισχνούμενοι, εἰ ἐπιδείξαι τι αὐτοῖς ὧν πωλούμενος ἔλεγεν εἰδέναι, ἀφήσειν."

Διὰ ταῦτα οὔτε αὐτὸς ἐπανελθὼν οἴκαδε τὸ λύτρον ἐπόρισα, οὔτε σοι ἐπέστειλα πορίζειν. ἀλλὰ χαῖρε καὶ σύ, ὅτι ζῇ ἁλοὺς εἰς τὰ
40 ληστρικὰ καὶ ὅτι ἃ μὴ ὑπὸ πολλῶν ἐπιστεύετο εἶναι ἐφάνη.

go and bargain with the sellers." They laughed at this, saying "What free man needs a master?" "All low types", he said, "who esteem pleasure and despise hard work, and so are most enticed into evil."

5. 'As a result of this Diogenes became much prized and was no longer for sale; but the pirates removed him from the platform and took him to their house, promising to let him go if he would reveal to them some of what he claimed to know when he was up for sale.'

Because of this I neither returned home myself and offered the ransom, nor wrote to you to offer it. Instead, you too should rejoice that he survives though captured by pirates, and that what many people did not believe appears to have happened.

SOCRATES

5

Σωκράτης Ξενοφῶντι

Σὲ μὲν ἐν Θήβαις ἡμῖν γενέσθαι ἀπηγγέλλετο, Πρόξενον δὲ κατα-
λαβεῖν εἰς τὴν Ἀσίαν ὡς Κῦρον ὡρμηκότα. εἰ μὲν οὖν εὐτυχῶν
ἐφίεσαι πραγμάτων, θεὸς οἶδεν, ὡς ἤδη γέ τινες τῶν ἐνταῦθα
καταμέμφεσθαι αὐτὰ ἐπιχειροῦσιν· οὐ γὰρ ἄξιόν^a φασιν εἶναι^a
5 Κύρῳ βοηθεῖν Ἀθηναίους, δι᾽ ὃν τὴν ἀρχὴν ὑπὸ Λακεδαιμονίων
ἀφῃρέθησαν, οὐδ᾽ αὐτοὺς ὑπὲρ ἐκείνου πολεμεῖν καταπολεμηθέντας
δι᾽ ἐκεῖνον. οὐκ ἂν οὖν θαυμάσαιμι, εἰ μεταπεσούσης τῆς πολιτείας
συκοφαντεῖν σέ τινες ἀφ᾽ ἑαυτῶν ἐπιχειρήσουσιν· ἀλλ᾽ ὅσῳ
λαμπρότερον τἀκεῖ χωρήσειν ὑπολαμβάνω, τοσούτῳ σφοδρότερον
10 ἐπικείσεσθαι τούτους ἡγοῦμαι· τὰς γὰρ ἐνίων φύσεις οὐκ ἀγνοῶ.
2. Ἡμεῖς δ᾽ ἐπείπερ ἅπαξ εἰς τοῦτο ἑαυτοὺς ἔδομεν, ἄνδρες
ἀγαθοὶ γενώμεθα, τῶν τε ἄλλων, ἃ περὶ ἀρετῆς εἰώθειμεν λέγειν
ἀναμιμνησκόμενοι καὶ τὸ "μηδὲ γένος πατέρων αἰσχυνέμεν" ἐν τοῖς
ἄριστα τῷ ποιητῇ εἰρῆσθαι τιθέντες. ἴσθι δέ, ὡς δυοῖν τούτοιν
15 μάλιστα προσδεῖται πόλεμος, καρτερίας τε καὶ ἀφιλοχρηματίας· δι᾽
ἐκείνην μὲν γὰρ τοῖς οἰκείοις φίλοι, διὰ καρτερίαν δὲ φοβεροὶ τοῖς
ἀντιπάλοις γινόμεθα· ὧν ἀμφοτέρων οἰκεῖα ἔχεις τὰ παραδείγματα.

Köhler
   $^{a-a}$ φασιν εἶναι Hercher: φανῆναι PG

SOCRATES

5
SOCRATES TO XENOPHON

I am told that you are in Thebes, and have caught up with Proxenus as he was setting off to Cyrus in Asia. Whether this venture of yours will turn out well God knows, as some people here are already trying to criticize it. They say it is not right for Athenians to help Cyrus, through whose support the Spartans deprived them of their power, nor should Athenians fight for the very man who subdued them in war. So as there has been a change in the political situation, I shouldn't be surprised if some people of their own accord try to denounce you. In fact, the more splendidly I see things going to turn out over there, the more vigorously I think these people will assail you: I know the nature of some of them all too well. **2.** But now we have set ourselves to do this, we must be true men, remembering all the other things we used to say about virtue, and in particular considering 'Shame not the race of your fathers' to be one of the finest utterances of the Poet. You must know that warfare has most need of these two qualities, endurance and indifference to riches. Through the latter we are dear to our own associates; through endurance we are formidable to our adversaries. You have your own examples of both qualities.

SOCRATICS

21

Αἰσχίνης Ξανθίππῃ τῇ Σωκράτους

1. Εὔφρονι τῷ Μεγαρεῖ ἔδωκα ἀλφίτων χοίνικας ἓξ καὶ δραχμὰς
ὀκτὼ καὶ ἐξωμίδα καινὴν τὸ χεῖμά σοι διαγαγεῖν. Ταῦτα οὖν
λάβε καὶ ἴσθι Εὐκλείδην καὶ Τερψίωνα πάνυ καλώ τε καὶ ἀγαθὼ
ἄνδρε καί σοί τε καὶ Σωκράτει εὔνω. ἡνίκα δ᾽ ἂν οἱ παῖδες
5 ἐθέλοιεν παρ᾽ ἡμᾶς ἰέναι, μὴ κώλυε· οὐ γὰρ πόρρω ἐστὶν ἰέναι εἰς
Μέγαρα. τῶν δὲ πολλῶν σοὶ δακρύων, ὦ ἀγαθή, ἅλις. Ὀνήσει γὰρ
οὐδέν, σχεδὸν δέ τι καὶ βλάψει. ἀναμιμνήσκου γὰρ ὧν ἔλεγε
Σωκράτης καὶ τοῖς ἤθεσιν αὐτοῦ καὶ τοῖς λόγοις πειρῶ ἀκολουθεῖν,
ἐπεὶ λυπουμένη παρ᾽ ἕκαστα καὶ σεαυτὴν ἀδικήσεις ὅτι μάλιστα καὶ
10 τοὺς παῖδας. 2. οὗτοι γὰρ οἱονεὶ νεοττοί εἰσι Σωκράτους, οὓς δεῖ οὐ
μόνον τρέφειν ἡμᾶς, ἀλλὰ καὶ ἡμᾶς αὐτοὺς αὐτοῖς πειρᾶσθαι
παραμένειν· ὡς εἰ σὺ ἢ ἐγὼ ἢ ἄλλος τις, ὅτῳ μέλει τελευτήσαντος
Σωκράτους τῶν παίδων, ἀποθάνοι, ἀδικήσονται οὗτοι, ἔρημοι
γενόμενοι τοῦ βοηθήσοντος καὶ θρέψοντος ὁμολογουμένως· ὅθεν πειρῶ
15 ζῆν αὐτοῖς. τοῦτο δὲ οὐκ ἂν ἄλλως γένοιτο, εἰ μὴ τὰ πρὸς τὸ ζῆν
αὐτὴ αὑτῇ παρέχοις. Λύπη δὲ δοκεῖ τῶν ἐναντίων ζωῇ εἶναι, ὅπου
βλάπτονται ὑπ᾽ αὐτῆς οἱ ζῶντες. 3. Ἀπολλόδωρος ὁ μαλακὸς
ἐπικαλούμενος καὶ Δίων ἐπαινοῦσί σε, διότι παρ᾽ οὐδενὸς οὐδὲν
λαμβάνεις, φῇς δὲ πλουτεῖν. καὶ εὖ ποιεῖς. εἰς ὅσον γὰρ ἐγώ τε καὶ οἱ
20 ἄλλοι φίλοι ἰσχύομεν ἐπικουρεῖν σοι, δεήσει οὐδενός. θάρρει οὖν, ὦ
Ξανθίππη, καὶ μηδὲν καταβάλῃς τῶν Σωκράτους καλῶν εἰδυῖα ὡς
μέγα τι ἡμῖν ἐγένετο οὗτος ὁ ἄνθρωπος· καὶ ἐπινόει αὐτὸν ὁποῖα ἔζησε
καὶ[a] ὁποῖα ἐτελεύτησε. Ἐγὼ μὲν γὰρ οἶμαι καὶ τὸν θάνατον αὐτοῦ
μέγα τε καὶ καλὸν γεγονέναι, εἰ δή[b] τις καθ᾽ ὃ χρὴ σκοπεῖν σκοποίη.
25 ἔρρωσο.

Köhler

[a] καὶ *Westermann:* μὴ PG [b] δή *Orelli:* δέ PG

SOCRATICS

21

AESCHINES TO XANTHIPPE, WIDOW OF SOCRATES

I have given Euphron the Megarian six measures of barley, eight drachmas, and a new tunic, to see you through the winter. Please accept them, and know that Euclides and Terpsion are eminently good and true men, and well-disposed to you as well as Socrates. And whenever the children want to come to us, don't stop them: it's not far to come to Megara. Enough of all your weeping, my good friend: it will do you no good, and maybe even some harm. Remember what Socrates used to say and try to be guided by his character and his words; for constant grieving will do the utmost damage both to yourself and to the children. For they are, as it were, nestlings of Socrates, and we must not only nurture them, but also try to preserve ourselves on their account. If you or I or anyone else, who is concerned for Socrates' children now he is dead, should die, they will suffer wrong being deprived of anyone to help and support them on a comparable basis. That is why you must try to live for their sakes, and you can't do this without allowing yourself the essentials for living. Grief seems to be one of the enemies of life, as it causes injury to the living. Apollodorus, nicknamed the Mild, and Dion commend you for accepting nothing from anyone and saying you are rich. That's the spirit. For so far as I and your other friends have the power to help you, you will lack nothing. So be of good courage, Xanthippe, and do not abandon any of the noble qualities of Socrates, knowing how remarkable a man he was for us. Keep in mind how he lived and how he died. For my part I regard even his death as great and noble, if you consider it in the right way.

Farewell

EURIPIDES

5

Εὐριπίδης Κηφισοφῶντι

Καὶ ἀφικόμεθα εἰς Μακεδονίαν, ὦ βέλτιστε Κηφισοφῶν, τό τε
σῶμα οὐ μοχθηρῶς διατεθέντες καὶ ὡς οἷόν τε μάλιστα ἦν ἐπιεικῶς
κομιζόμενοι συντόμως, καὶ ἀπεδέξατο ἡμᾶς Ἀρχέλαος, ὡς εἰκός τε
ἦν καὶ προσεδοκῶμεν ἡμεῖς, οὐ δωρεαῖς μόνον, ὧν οὐδὲν ἐχρήζομεν
5 ἡμεῖς, ἀλλὰ καὶ φιλοφροσύναις, ὧν οὐδ᾽ ἂν εὔξαιτό τις μείζους
παρὰ βασιλέων. καὶ κατελάβομεν Κλείτωνα ἐρρωμένον, καὶ ἔστιν
ἡμῖν σὺν ἐκείνῳ τὰ πολλὰ καί, ὅταν τύχῃ, σὺν Ἀρχελάῳ ἄμεμπτος
ἡ διαγωγή· πρός τε τοῖς ἔργοις οὐδὲν κωλυόμεθα τοῖς τούτων
γίγνεσθαι. ἀλλὰ καὶ πολὺς μὲν ἔγκειται ὁ Κλείτων, πολὺς δὲ ὁ
10 Ἀρχέλαος, ἑκάστοτε φροντίζειν ἀεί τι καὶ ποιεῖν τῶν εἰωθότων
ἀναγκάζοντες, ὥστ᾽ ἔμοιγε μισθὸν οὐκ ᵃἀηδῆ μέν, ἀλλ᾽ οὐδὲᵃ ἄπονον
δοκεῖ Ἀρχέλαος ἀναπράσσεσθαι τῶν τε δωρεῶν, ὧν ἔδωκέ μοι
εὐθέως ἀφικομένῳ, καὶ ὅτι εἱστία με λαμπρότερον ἢ ἐμοὶ φίλον
ἑκάστης ἡμέρας. 2. Περὶ δὲ ὧν ἐπέστειλας ἡμῖν σὺ μὲν εὖ ποιεῖς ἐπιστέλλων ἃ
15 δοκεῖς ἡμῖν εἰδέναι διαφέρειν· ἴσθι μέντοι μηδὲν μᾶλλον ἡμῖν ὧν
νῦν Ἀγάθων ἢ Μέσατος λέγει μέλον ἢ τῶν Ἀριστοφάνους φλη-
ναφημάτων οἶσθά ποτε μέλον. καὶ τούτοις γε ἂν ἀδικήσαις ἡμᾶς εἰς
τὰ μάλιστα ἀποκρινάμενός ποτε, κἂν ὅλως μὴ παυομένους
20 τῆς ἀναγωγίας αὐτοὺς ὁρᾷς. ἦν μέντοι τις τῶν ἀξίων περὶ
Εὐριπίδου λέγειν τι ἢ ἀκούειν αἰτιᾶται ἡμᾶς τῆς πρὸς Ἀρχέλαον
ὁδοῦ, ἃ μὲν τὸ πρόσθεν εἴπομεν περὶ τοῦ μὴ δεῖν εἰς Μακεδονίαν
ἡμᾶς ἀποδημεῖν ἐπιστάμενος, ἃ δὲ μετὰ ταῦτα ἡμᾶς ἀπηνάγκασε
βαδίσαι ἀγνοῶν, τοῦτον δὲ ἄξιον νόμιζε δηλοῦν αὐτῷ ἅπερ οἶσθα, ὦ
25 Κηφισοφῶν· καὶ οὕτως πεπαύσεται ἀγνοῶν τὰς αἰτίας καὶ ἅμα,
ὅπερ εἰκός ἐστι τὸν ἀγνοοῦντα πάσχειν, καταγινώσκων ἡμῶν ὡς
φιλοχρημάτων γενομένων. 3. Οὐ γάρ που δὴ πορφύραν καὶ σκῆπτρον φορεῖν ἢ φρούρια
λαβόντας ἐν Τριβαλλοῖς ἡγεῖσθαι ὑπάρχους καλουμένους ὀρεχθῆναί
30 τις ἂν φήσειεν ἡμᾶς καὶ διὰ τοῦτο δὴ στείλασθαι τὴν πρὸς
Ἀρχέλαον ὁδόν, ἀλλὰ δηλονότι πλούτου ἕνεκα. εἶτα πῶς ἄν, ὅτε

Gösswein
ᵃ⁻ᵃ οὖν delevi: ⟨ἀλλ᾽⟩ οὐδὲ Hercher: ἀηδῆ μὲν οὖν οὐδὲ codd.

EURIPIDES

5
EURIPIDES TO CEPHISOPHON

I have arrived in Macedonia, my good Cephisophon, in fine shape physically and as speedily as I conveniently could. Archelaus welcomed me appropriately and, as I expected, not only with gifts (which I didn't need), but with marks of friendly kindness such that you couldn't hope for greater from kings. And I found Clito in good health, and I spend a lot of my time contentedly with him, and, on occasion, with Archelaus: there is no hindrance to my taking part in their activities. On the contrary, both Clito and Archelaus are very pressing with me, and take every opportunity to urge me to be always thinking and writing on my usual themes. I think this is Archelaus' way of claiming repayment—not unpleasant but not unlaborious either—for his gifts to me on my arrival, and for entertaining me daily more sumptuously than I like.

2. Regarding what you wrote to tell me, you are right to let me know what you think it is important for me to be aware of; but you must realize that I care no more now what Agathon or Mesatus says than you know I used to care about Aristophanes' rubbish. You would actually do me serious harm if you replied to these men, even if you see them in no way giving up their coarse behaviour. However, if anyone who has a claim to say or hear something about Euripides censures me for my trip to Archelaus, because he knows that I said earlier that I did not have to travel to Macedonia, but is unaware of what subsequently forced me to make the journey, then, Cephisophon, you may consider that he deserves to be told what you know. He will then cease to be ignorant of my reasons and (a natural consequence of ignorance) to accuse me of having become greedy.

3. For no one, I suppose, would imagine that I long to don purple and a sceptre, or to take over a fortress among the Triballi and rule there with the title of governor, and that I made my journey to Archelaus for that reason. Of course I did it for riches! But then, how could anybody reasonably believe

νέοι τε καὶ ὅτε μέσοι τὴν ἡλικίαν ἦμεν, καὶ ὃν ἔτι ζώσης ἡμῖν τῆς
μητρός (ἧς ἕνεκα ἂν μόνης ἐβουλόμεθα πλουτεῖν, εἴπερ ἄλλως
ἐβουλόμεθα) οὐχ ὅπως ἐδιώξαμεν, ἀλλὰ καὶ ἀπεωσάμεθα
35 ἐγκείμενον, τὸν αὐτὸν τοῦτον πλοῦτον ἤδη τηλικοῖσδε οὖσιν ἡμῖν
ἱμερτὸν εἶναι εἰκότως ἄν τις νομίσειεν, εἰ μὴ διὰ τοῦτο ἄρα πολλὰ
λαβεῖν σὺν ἀδοξίᾳ τέ τινι ἡμετέρᾳ καὶ οὐδὲ ἀπολαύσει ἔτι οὐδεμιᾷ
ἐπεθυμήσαμεν, ἵνα ἐν βαρβάρῳ γῇ ἀποθάνωμεν καὶ ἵνα πλείονα
Ἀρχελάῳ καταλίποιμεν χρήματα;
40 **4.** Ἔτι δὲ δὴ καὶ προσθείης ὅτι, ἐπειδὴ τάχιστα ἀφικόμεθα εἰς
Μακεδονίαν, ὀλίγαις ὕστερον ἡμέραις τεσσαράκοντα τάλαντα
ἀργυρίου διδόντος Ἀρχελάου καὶ ἀγανακτοῦντος ὅτι οὐ
λαμβάνοιμεν, ἀντέσχομεν μὴ λαβεῖν· τῶντε ἄλλων δωρεῶν,
ὁπόσας ἢ Κλείτων ἔδωκεν ἡμῖν ἢ Ἀρχέλαος ἔπεισε λαβεῖν, οὐκ
45 ἔσθ' ὅτι ἐνθάδε ὑπολελείμμεθα, ἀλλ' οἴχονται αὐτὰ φέροντες, οἵπερ
καὶ ταύτην τὴν ἐπιστολὴν φέρουσιν, ὑμῖν τοῖς αὐτόθι ἑταίροις καὶ
ἐπιτηδείοις νεμήσοντες ἅπαντα. τίς ⟨οὖν⟩ᵇ ἂν οὕτω εὑρεθείη ἔτι
σκαιὸς καὶ βάσκανος τὸν τρόπον, ὅστις ἂν φιλοχρηματίᾳ με
θελχθέντα ταύτην ἀποδημῆσαι ὑπολάβοι τὴν ἀποδημίαν; ἀλλὰ
50 δήπου ἀλαζονείαν τινὰ ἢ τοῦ δύνασθαί τι μέγα ἐπιθυμίαν ἐροῦσιν.
5. Ἀλλ' ἡ μὲν δύναμις ἡμῖν καὶ μένουσιν Ἀθήνησιν ἡ παρὰ
Ἀρχελάου καὶ πάλαι ἦν (ἄλλως τε καὶ Κλείτων τοσοῦτον ἐδύνατο
μέγα) τοῦ μηδέ⟨ν'⟩ᶜ ἄλλον ἢ ὃν προῃρούμην ἐξ ἀρχῆς τρόπον
βιοῦν ἐμέ, μηδ' ὅπου μὴ ἐθέλοιμι ἀποθανεῖν, τελευταῖον δὲ μὴ
55 παρέχειν λόγους εἰσαεὶ τοῖς κακῶς βουλομένοις ἡμᾶς λέγειν. εἰ δὲ
δὴ καὶ δυνάμεώς τινος ὠρέχθημεν, τί ἄλλο ταύτῃ τῇ δυνάμει ἢ
πρῶτον μὲν εἰς τὰ τῆς πόλεως, ἔπειτα εἰς τὰ τῶν φίλων χρήσασθαι
ἐμέλλομεν; ἀλαζονείας τε ἕνεκα πολὺ ἂν μᾶλλον ἐν ὄψει τῶν τε
φίλων καὶ οὐχ ἥκιστα τῶν ἐχθρῶν δύνασθαί τι ἐβουλόμεθα. καὶ μὴν
60 εὐμετάβολόν γέ με οὔτε εἰς τὰ ἐπιτηδεύματα οὔτε εἰς ὑμᾶς τοὺς
φίλους καὶ οὐχ ἧσσον εἰς τοὺς ἐχθροὺς σκοπῶν εἴποι τις ἄν, οἷς
ἅπασιν ἐκ νέου μέχρι τοῦ νῦν τοῖς αὐτοῖς κέχρημαι πλὴν ἑνὸς
ἀνδρός, Σοφοκλέους· πρὸς γὰρ δὴ τοῦτον μόνον ἴσασί με τάχα οὐχ
ὁμοίως ἀεὶ τὴν γνώμην ἔχοντα.
65 **6.** Ὃν ἐγὼ ἐμίσησα μὲν οὐδέποτε, ἐθαύμασα δὲ ἀεί, ἔστερξα δὲ
οὐχ ὁμοίως ἀεί, ἀλλὰ φιλοτιμότερον μέν τινα εἶναίᵈ ποτε δόξας
ὑπεῖδον, βουληθέντα δὲ ἐκλύσασθαι τὰ νείκη προθυμότατα

ᵇ οὖν add. *Gösswein*   ᶜ μηδέν' *Gösswein:* μὴ δὲ *plerique*
ᵈ εἶναί *Barnes:* εἰδέναι ω

that I would find riches attractive at my time of life, when as a youth, and in my middle age, and when my mother was still alive (for whose sake alone, if ever, I would have wished for wealth), I not only did not pursue it but rejected it when it was readily available? Unless, of course, I was eager to gain riches at the cost of my own reputation and, without enjoying it myself, simply to die in a foreign land and leave even more wealth to Archelaus.

4. Indeed you might also add this fact, that a few days after I first arrived in Macedonia, Archelaus offered me a gift of forty silver talents and was annoyed at my refusing them, but I persisted in my refusal. And of the other gifts which Clito gave me, or Archelaus induced me to accept, I have retained not one here; but the people who are bringing you this letter are also bringing them, to distribute them all there to you, my companions and friends. So how could there be anyone still so spiteful and simple-minded as to suppose that I was beguiled by greed into undertaking this expedition? Well, I suppose they'll be saying it was due to boastfulness or greed for power and influence.

5. But even when I remained in Athens I had long had enough influence with Archelaus (especially as Clito was so powerful) that I did not have to adopt a life-style different from the one I originally chose, nor to die where I didn't want to, nor, finally, to provide material for all time to those who want to slander me. And even if I were eager for some power, for what other purpose would I use this power than to serve the interests, first of my city, and then of my friends? As for boastfulness, I would much rather be influential in the eyes of my friends, and not least of my enemies. What is more, no one could accuse me of fickleness if he considers my activities or you my friends or, not less, my enemies, all of whom, from my youth up to the present, I have treated in the same way, except for one man, Sophocles. Towards him alone it is known that I have perhaps not always been consistent in my feelings.

6. I have never disliked him, I have always admired him, but I have not always felt the same degree of affection for him. Occasionally I have regarded him with suspicion, thinking him to be too ambitious; but once he was prepared to give up our quarrel I welcomed him whole-heartedly as a friend.

ὑπεδεξάμην. καὶ ἀλλήλους μέν, ἐξ ὅτου συνέβη, στέργομέν τε καὶ στέρξομεν· τοὺς δ' ἐμβάλλοντας ἡμῖν πολλάκις τὰς ὑπονοίας,ᵉ ἵνα
70 ἐκ τοῦ ἡμᾶς ἀπεχθάνεσθαι, τὸν ἕτερον θεραπεύοντες, αὐτοὶᵉ πλεῖον ἔχωσι, διαβεβλήμεθα. καὶ νῦν, ὦ βέλτιστε Κηφισοφῶν, οἶδ' ὅτι οὗτοί εἰσιν οἱ τοὺς περὶ ἡμῶν λόγους ἐμβάλλοντες εἰς τοὺς ὄχλους· ἀλλ' ὥσπερ ἀεὶ ἄπρακτοι αὐτῶν αἱ κακαὶ γλῶσσαι ἐγένοντο καὶ γέλωτα ἐξ αὐτῶν καὶ μῖσος, οὐδὲν πλέον ὠφλίσκανον, καὶ νῦν ἴσθι
75 ὅτι οὐκ ἄπρακτοι μόνον ἀλλὰ καὶ ἐπὶ κακῷ σφίσιν ἔσονται. σὺ μέντοι εὖ ποιεῖς περὶ τούτων ἡμῖν γράφων, ἐπειδήπερ οἴει ἡμῖν διαφέρειν· ἀλλ' ὥσπερ εὖ ποιεῖς γράφων, οὕτως ἀδικεῖν σε φήσαιμ' ἂν ἡμᾶς ἀντιλέγοντα ὑπὲρ αὐτῶν τοῖς οὐκ ἀξίοις.

Gösswein
   ᵉ⁻ᵉ ἵνα... αὐτοὶ *Gösswein:* εἶναι... ἄν τοι (τι) ω

From that time we have felt, and shall continue to feel, affection for each other. And I have outwitted those people who have often stirred up suspicions between us so that they can win some advantage out of our enmity by cultivating one or other of us. Even now, my good Cephisophon, I know that these are the people who are spreading the rumours about me among the public. But just as their wicked tongues have never got them anywhere, and won them nothing but derision and hatred, you can be sure that now too they will not only get nowhere but actually come to grief themselves. Still, you do well in writing to me about these things, as you think they matter to me. But though you do well in so writing, I must say that you are doing me an injury in offering a reply to people who don't deserve it.

THEMISTOCLES

9

Θεμιστοκλῆς Καλλίᾳ

Μὴ ζήλου, ὦ Καλλία, Ἀριστείδην τοῦ φθόνου. οὐδὲ γὰρ ἐκεῖνος
πολλά σε ἔφη ζηλῶσαι τοῦ πλούτου. καίτοι μακρῷ ἄμεινον ἦν νὴ
Δί’ ὃ πάντες εὔχονται σφίσιν αὐτοῖς καὶ γενεαῖς σφετέραις,
κἀκεῖνον ἀσπάζεσθαι ἢ σέ, ἃ πάντες ἐχθαίρουσιν καὶ ἐπάρατα
5 ἡγοῦνται, ἐκεῖνα μιμεῖσθαι. **2.** μηδὲν οὖν νουθέτει μηδὲ σωφρόνιζε
Ἀθηναίους ὅτι εἰκαίως χειροτονοῦσιν καὶ ἐκ τῶν ἀναξίων αἱροῦνται
προστάτας, εἰς ἐμὲ αἰνιττόμενος. **3.** ἀλλὰ πρῶτον ἐκεῖνο σκόπει,
ὅτι ἐπιπλήττεις αὐτοῖς νενικηκότας προστάτας κεχειροτονηκόσιν.
4. ἔπειτα ὅστις ὢν αὐτὸς ταῦτα ληρεῖς καὶ ὅτι οὐδὲ μετὰ πολλοὺς
10 ἄλλους Θεμιστοκλέας στρατηγὸς ὧδε ἀποδειχθῆναι δεδυνημένος.
5. οὐ γὰρ τῶν τυμβωρυχησάντων τοὺς ἐν τοῖς λάκκοις ἐν Μαραθῶνι
κατασεσηπότας Περσῶν, ἀλλὰ *ᵃτῶν καταναυμαχησάντωνᵃ* καὶ ἀπο-
κτεινάντων τοὺς ἐν Σαλαμῖνι καὶ ἐν Εὐβοίᾳ παρατατττομένους ἔδει
στρατηγῶν ⟨καὶ⟩ᵇ καθόλου τῶν ἡγεμόνων τῇ πόλει **6.** οὐδὲ πολλὰ
15 μὲν χρήματα κεκτημένων, ὁπόθεν δὲ αὐτὰ κέκτηνται εἰπεῖν οὐ
δυναμένων, ἀλλὰ μεγάλα καὶ καλὰ ἔργα διαπραξαμένων. **7.** σὺ δὲ
ἐν οἷς δυνατότατος ἦσθα αὐτὸς ἑαυτοῦ καὶ τῶν ἄλλων οὐδὲν ὤνησας
τὴν πόλιν, ἐν οἷς ⟨δὲ⟩ᶜ ἀχρηστότατος εἶ πάντων Ἀθηναίων, αὐτὴν
ἐν τούτοις περιεργάζεσθαι καὶ πολυπραγμονεῖν ἐπιχειρεῖς. **8.** καὶ
20 κατὰ πλοῦτον μὲν τοσοῦτον ὄντα, οἷον οὐκ ὀλίγαι μυριάδες Περσῶν
ἐπλούτουν, οὓς πάντας σοὶ ἐκληρονομήσω, οὐκ οἶδ’ ὅπως ἀφελόμενος
τοὺς μαχεσαμένους αὐτοῖς καὶ τὴν πόλιν σύμπασαν τὰ λάφυρα,
οὔτε μικρὸν οὔτε μέγα οὐδὲ ὤνησας οὐδέποτε τὴν πατρίδα, λόγοις
δὲ ἄρα, ἐν οἷς σὺ ἀδυνατώτατος, σωφρονίζειν αὐτὴν ἐπιχειρεῖς καὶ
25 ⟨περὶ⟩ πολεμικῶν ἔργων, ἐν οἷς ἀχρηστότατος εἶ καὶ ἀνανδρότατος,
ἐπιτιμᾷς Ἀθηναίοις οὕτω καὶ μὴ οὕτω διαγνοῦσιν. **9.** ἀλλὰ ὧδε
ἔχει, ὦ Καλλία, τοὺς λέοντας ζωοὺς μὲν ὄντας οὔτε οἱ ταῦροι
ὑπομένουσιν οὔτε ἄλλο τι τῶν παμμεγάλων καὶ ἀλκίμων θηρίων,
πεσόντων δὲ αὐτῶν καὶ κειμένων οὐδὲν θαυμαστὸν εἰ καὶ οἱ μύες ἐπ’

Doenges
ᵃ⁻ᵃ τῶν καταναυμαχησάντων *Habich*: κατὰ τῶν ναυμαχησάντων P
ᵇ ⟨καὶ⟩ *add. Doenges*   ᶜ ⟨δὲ⟩ *addidi*

THEMISTOCLES

9

THEMISTOCLES TO CALLIAS

Don't envy Aristides his malice, Callias; for he said he did not greatly envy you your wealth. And yet, by Zeus, it would be much better for him to welcome what all men want for themselves and their families than for you to imitate what all men hate and consider accursed.   **2.** So you must in no way rebuke or chastise the Athenians for voting rashly and choosing leaders from among the unworthy—hinting at me.   **3.** But first consider this, that you are reproving those who have voted for leaders who have won victories.   **4.** Then bear in mind who *you* are to talk such rubbish, and that you have not succeeded in being appointed general even after many other Themistocleses. **5.** The city did not need generals and leaders of any kind who had broken open the graves of the decayed bodies of the Persians buried at Marathon, but men who had beaten at sea and killed those arrayed against them at Salamis and Euboea. **6.** It did not need men who have a lot of money but cannot say where it came from, but men with great and noble achievements behind them.

7. In those spheres where you were more influential than you or others had ever been you did no good whatever to the city; but in those where you are the most useless of all the Athenians you are trying to be a meddlesome intriguer.   **8.** With regard to your wealth, which is equal to the wealth of many thousands of the Persians, to all of whom you have made yourself heir, I don't know how it was that after you robbed those who fought the Persians and the whole city of the booty, you never did any good great or small to your country. But it seems you are trying to chastise it in speeches in which you are completely ineffective; while in military matters, where you are most useless and cowardly, you blame the Athenians because they choose one policy rather than another.

9. It is like this, Callias. Neither bulls nor any other big, strong creatures stand up to lions when they are alive; but when they have fallen and lie dead it is not surprising if even

30 αὐτοὺς ἀναβαίνουσιν. **IO.** ὥστε καὶ σὺ νῦν μὲν ἀπόλαυε ἡμῶν ᾗ
βούλει καὶ ἐμπίπλασο, ὅτι πᾶσιν ἐσμὲν περίπατος. **II.** οὐδὲν
μέντοι τῶν ἀδοκήτων, εἰ καὶ ἡμῖν ποτε ἔτι γ᾿ οὖν ἐμπνέουσιν καὶ
τὴν ψυχὴν ἔχουσι δώσει θεὸς ὑπομνῆσαι ταύτης τῆς δημηγορίας.
δώσει δ᾿ εὖ οἶδ᾿ ὅτι δώσει. "οὐκ ἀρετᾷ κακὰ ἔργα," φασὶν οἱ ποιηταί.

mice climb over them.   **10.** So you too take advantage of me as you like and have your fill, as I am a promenade for all. **11.** But don't be surprised if, while I still have the breath of life in me, God will grant that I remember this speech of yours. He will grant it: I know he will. 'Evil deeds do not prosper', as the poets say.

HIPPOCRATES

14

Ἱπποκράτης Δαμαγήτῳ

Οἶδα παρὰ σοὶ γενόμενος ἐν Ῥόδῳ, Δαμάγητε, τὴν ναῦν ἐκείνην,
Ἅλιος ἐπιγραφὴ ἦν αὐτῇ, πάγκαλόν τινα καὶ εὔπρυμνον ἱκανῶς
⟨τε⟩ τετροπισμένην, καὶ διάβασιν εἶχε πολλήν. ἐπήνεις δὲ καὶ τὸ
ναυτικὸν αὐτῆς ὡς ὀξὺ καὶ ἀσφαλὲς καὶ εὔτεχνον ὑπουργῆσαι καὶ
5 τοῦ πλοῦ τὴν εὐδρομίην. ταύτην ἔκπεμψον ἡμῖν, ἀλλ' εἰ οἷόν τε μὴ
κώπησιν, ἀλλὰ πτεροῖσιν ἐρετμώσας αὐτήν. ἐπείγει γὰρ τὸ πρῆγμα,
φιλότης, καὶ μάλα ἐς Ἄβδηρα διαπλεῦσαι πάνυ ταχέως. βούλομαι
γὰρ νοσέουσαν ἰήσασθαι πόλιν διὰ νοσέοντα ἕνα Δημόκριτον.
ἀκούεις που τἀνδρὸς τὸ κλέος· τοῦτον ἡ πατρὶς ᾐτίηται μανίη
10 κεκακῶσθαι· ἐγὼ δὲ βούλομαι, μᾶλλον δὲ εὔχομαι μὴ ἐόντως αὐτὸν
παρακόπτειν ἀλλ' ἐκείνοισιν δόξαν εἶναι. γελᾷ, φασίν, αἰεὶ καὶ οὐ
παύεται γελῶν ἐπὶ παντὶ πρήγματι καὶ σημεῖον αὐτοῖσι μανίης
τοῦτο δοκεῖ. ὅθεν λέγε τοῖσιν ἐν Ῥόδῳ φίλοισι μετριάζειν ἀεὶ καὶ
μὴ πολλὰ γελᾶν μηδὲ πολλὰ σκυθρωπάζειν, ἀλλὰ τούτων ἀμφοῖν τὸ
15 μέτριον κτήσασθαι, ἵνα τοῖσι μὲν χαριέστατος εἶναι δόξῃς, τοῖσι δὲ
φροντιστὴς περὶ ἀρετὴν μερμηρίζων. ἔνι μέντοι τι, Δαμάγητε,
κακὸν παρ' ἕκαστον αὐτοῦ γελῶντος. εἰ γὰρ ἡ ἀμετρίη φλαῦρον, τὸ
διὰ παντὸς φλαυρότερον. καὶ εἴποιμ' ἂν αὐτῷ· Δημόκριτε, καὶ
νοσέοντος καὶ κτεινομένου καὶ τεθνεῶτος καὶ πολιορκουμένου καὶ
20 παντὸς ἐμπίπτοντος κακοῦ ἕκαστον τῶν πρησσομένων ὕλη σοι
γέλωτος ὑπόκειται. οὐ θεομαχεῖς δέ, εἰ δύο ἐόντων ἐν κόσμῳ, λύπης
καὶ χαρᾶς, σὺ θάτερον αὐτῶν ἐκβέβληκας; μακάριός τ' ἂν ἦς, ἀλλ'
ἀδύνατον, εἰ μήτε μήτηρ σοι νενόσηκε μήτε πατὴρ μήτε τὰ ὕστερον
τέκνα ἢ γυνὴ ἢ φίλος, ἀλλὰ διὰ τὸν σὸν γέλωτα, ἵνα σῴζηται,
25 εὐτυχεῖς πάντα. ἀλλὰ νοσεόντων γελᾷς, ἀποθνησκόντων χαίρεις, εἴ τί
που πύθοιο κακόν, εὐφραίνει· ὡς πονηρότατος εἶ, ὦ Δημόκριτε, καί
πόρρω γε σοφίης. ἢ νομίζεις αὐτὰ μηδὲ κακὰ εἶναι; μελαγχολᾷς οὖν,
Δημόκριτε, κινδυνεύων καὶ αὐτὸς Ἀβδηρίτης εἶναι, φρονιμωτέρη δὲ
ἡ πόλις. ἀλλὰ περὶ μὲν δὴ τούτων ἀκριβέστερον ἐκεῖσε λέξομεν,

HIPPOCRATES

14

HIPPOCRATES TO DAMAGETUS

From my stay with you in Rhodes, Damagetus, I know that ship called 'Helios', a splendid one with a good stern, serviceable keel, and plenty of deck room. You also praised her seaworthiness, saying she was nippy, safe, responsive to skilful handling, and you praised the speed of her sailing. Send her to me—but, if possible, equipping her with wings, not oars. For I have urgent business, my friend, and indeed must sail with all haste to Abdera. I want to cure a city of an illness caused by the illness of one man, Democritus. You must have heard of the man's reputation: it is he whom the city has alleged to be in a desperate plight through madness. My wish, or rather my prayer, is that he is not really deranged, but that it only seems so to them. They say he laughs all the time, and never stops laughing at everything, and that seems to them a sign of madness. So tell your friends in Rhodes to be always moderate in their behaviour, and not to laugh much or scowl much, but learn moderation in both, so that you may seem most charming to some, and to others a wise thinker pondering on virtue. And yet, Damagetus, there *is* something worrying in his laughing at everything. If excess is a bad thing, continual excess is worse. I might say to him: 'Democritus, even when people are sick, being killed, dead, besieged, or suffering any kind of evil— anything that happens to them gives you cause for laughter. Aren't you fighting against the gods, if the world offers two things, grief and joy, and you have rejected one of them? You would have been truly blessed if your mother never got ill, nor your father, nor the children you had later on, nor your wife or a friend; but this cannot be, but because of your laughter, to keep it going for ever, you are enjoying complete happiness. But it is illness you laugh at, death that rejoices you: whatever disaster you learn about cheers you up. What a worthless creature you are, Democritus, and how far you are from wisdom. Do you think these things are not evils? Then you are crazy, Democritus, and in danger of becoming a real Abderite,

30 Δαμάγητε. ἡ δὲ ναῦς καὶ τὸν χρόνον, ὃν ἐπιστέλλω σοι, χρονίζει.
ἔρρωσο.

17

Ἱπποκράτης Δαμαγήτῳ

Τοῦτ' ἐκεῖνο, Δαμάγητε, ὅπερ εἰκάζομεν, οὐ παρέκοπτεν Δημόκριτος, ἀλλὰ πάντα ὑπερεφρόνει καὶ ἡμέας ἐσωφρόνιζε καὶ δι' ἡμέων
πάντας ἀνθρώπους. ἐξέπεμψα δέ σοι, φιλότης, ὡς ἀληθέως τὴν
Ἀσκληπιάδα νῆα, ᾗ πρόσθες^a μετὰ τοῦ Ἁλίου ἐπίσημον καὶ
5 Ὑγιείην, ἐπεὶ κατὰ δαίμονα τῷ ἐόντι ἱστιοδρόμηκε καὶ ἐκείνη τῇ
ἡμέρῃ κατέπλευσεν ἐς Ἄβδηρα, ᾗπερ αὐτοῖσιν ἐπεστάλκειν
ἀφίξεσθαι. πάντας οὖν ἁλέας πρὸ τῶν πυλέων εὕρομεν ὡς εἰκὸς
ἡμέας περιμένοντας, οὐκ ἄνδρας μούνους, ἀλλὰ καὶ γυναῖκας, ἔτι δὲ
καὶ πρεσβύτας καὶ παιδία, νὴ θεούς, κατηφέας, καὶ τὰ νήπια· καὶ
10 οὗτοι μέντοι ὡς ἐπὶ μαινομένῳ τῷ Δημοκρίτῳ, ὁ δὲ μετ' ἀκριβείης
τότε ὑπερεφιλοσόφει. ἐπεὶ δέ με εἶδον, ἔδοξάν που σμικρὸν ἐφ'
ἑωυτῶν γεγονέναι καὶ χρηστὰς ἐλπίδας ἐποιοῦντο. ὁ δὲ Φιλοποίμην
ἄγειν ἐπὶ τὴν ξεινίην με ὥρμητο κἀκείνοισι ξυνεδόκει τοῦτο. ἐγὼ
δέ, Ὦ ἄνδρες, ἔφην, Ἀβδηρῖται, οὐδέν ἐστί μοι προὔργου ἢ
15 Δημόκριτον θεήσασθαι. οἱ δ' ἐπῄνουν ἀκούσαντες καὶ ἥσθησαν,
ἦγόν τέ με ξυντόμως διὰ τῆς ἀγορῆς, οἱ μὲν ἑπόμενοι, οἱ δὲ
προθέοντες ἑτέρωθεν ἕτεροι, Σῷζε, λέγοντες, βοήθει, θεράπευσον.
κἀγὼ παρῄνεον θαρρεῖν ὡς τάχα μὲν οὐδενὸς ἐόντος κακοῦ, πίσυνος
ἐτησίῃσιν ὥρῃσιν, εἰ δ' ἄρα καί τινος βραχέος, εὐδιορθώτου.
20 2. Καὶ ἅμα ταῦτα λέγων ᾔειν. οὐδὲ γὰρ πόρρω ἦν ἡ οἰκίη,
μᾶλλον δ' οὐδ' ἡ πόλις ὅλη. παρῆμεν οὖν, πλησίον γὰρ τοῦ τείχους
ἐτύγχανε, καὶ ἀνάγουσίν με ἡσυχῇ· ἔπειτα κατόπιν τοῦ πύργου
βουνὸς ἦν τις ὑψηλός, μακρῇσι καὶ λασίῃσιν αἰγείροισιν ἐπίσκιος,
ἔνθεν τε ἐθεωρεῖτο τὰ τοῦ Δημοκρίτου καταγώγια. καὶ αὐτὸς ὁ
25 Δημόκριτος καθῆστο ὑπό τινι ἀμφιλαφεῖ καὶ χθαμαλῇ πλατανίστῳ,
ἐν ἐξωμίδι παχείῃ, μοῦνος, ἀνήλιπος,^b ἐπὶ λιθίνῳ θώκῳ, ὠχριακὼς

W. D. Smith
   ^a πρόσθες Ο: πρόσθε Μ: πρόθες b
   ^b ἀνήλιπος ub (corr. b²): ἀνήληφος Μ²

and the city has more sense than you.' But we'll talk in more detail about these things over there, Damagetus: the ship is wasting the time I spend writing to you.

Farewell

17

HIPPOCRATES TO DAMAGETUS

It is as we imagined, Damagetus: Democritus was not off his head, but surpassingly wise in all things, and he gave me lessons in good sense, and through me all mankind. I have sent back your ship, my friend—a truly Asclepiadic ship, on which you must display Hygieia alongside the sign of Helios, since she really sailed by divine grace and put into Abdera on exactly the day I had told them I would arrive. We found them all gathered at the gates, obviously waiting for us, not only men but women and old men too, and children: and, by the gods, they looked depressed, even the infants. So, while these were behaving as if Democritus was mad, he was then deep in the niceties of philosophy. When they saw me they seemed to recover their senses and became more hopeful. Philopoemen began to take me off to my lodgings with their approval, but I said, 'Men of Abdera, nothing is more important to me than seeing Democritus.' They were pleased when they heard this and applauded me, and they took me quickly through the agora, some following, some hastening ahead on both sides, saying, 'Save him, help him, cure him.' I encouraged them to be cheerful, since I was confident that, as it was the season of the Etesian winds, there might be nothing the matter with him, or if there was some minor problem, it would be easily put right.

2. Saying this I went along, for his house was not far off, nor in fact was the whole city. So there we came, for it happened to be near the wall, and they took me up to it quietly. Further on, behind the tower there was a high mound, shaded by large bushy poplars, from which you could see Democritus' dwelling. And Democritus himself was sitting alone on a stone seat under a low spreading plane tree, wearing a coarse tunic, barefoot, very pale and thin, and with his beard

πάνυ καὶ λιπόσαρκος, κουριῶν τὰ γένεια. παρ' αὐτὸν δ' ἐπὶ δεξιῆς
λεπτόρρυτον ὕδωρ κατὰ πρηνοῦς τοῦ λόφου ἠρεμαίως ἐκελάρυζεν.
ἦν δέ τι τέμενος ὑπὲρ ἐκεῖνον τὸν λόφον, ὡς ἐν ὑπονοίῃ
30 κατεικάζοντι, νυμφέων ἱδρυμένον, αὐτοφυτοῖσιν ἐπηρεφὲς
ἀμπέλοισιν. ὁ δ' εἶχεν ἐν εὐκοσμίῃ πολλῇ ἐπὶ τοῖν γονάτοιν βιβλίον,
καὶ ἕτερα δέ τινα ἐξ ἀμφοῖν τοῖν μεροῖν αὐτῷ παρεβέβλητο·
σεσώρευντο δὲ καὶ ζῷα συχνὰ ἀνατετμημένα δι' ὅλων. ὁ δὲ ὁτὲ μὲν
ξυντόνως ἔγραφεν ἐγκείμενος, ὁτὲ δὲ ἠρέμει πάμπολύ τι ἐπέχων καὶ
35 ἐν ἑωυτῷ μερμηρίζων. εἶτα μετ' οὐ πολὺ τούτων ἐρδομένων
ἐξαναστὰς περιεπάτει καὶ τὰ σπλάγχνα τῶν ζῴων ἐπεσκόπει καὶ
καταθεὶς αὐτὰ μετελθὼν ἐκαθέζετο. οἱ δὲ Ἀβδηρῖται περιεστῶτές
με κατηφεῖς καὶ οὐ πόρρω τὰς ὄψεις δακρυόντων ἔχοντές φασιν,
Ὁρῇς μέντοι τὸν Δημοκρίτου βίον, ὦ Ἱππόκρατες, ὡς μέμηνεν καὶ
40 οὔτε ὅτι θέλει οἶδεν οὔτε ὅτι ἔρδει; καί τις αὐτῶν ἔτι μᾶλλον
ἐνδείξασθαι βουλόμενος τὴν μανίην αὐτοῦ, ὀξὺ ἀνεκώκυσεν εἴκελον
γυναικὶ ἐπὶ θανάτῳ τέκνου ὀδυρομένῃ· εἶτ' ἀνῴμωξεν
ὑποκρινόμενος παροδίτην ἄλλος ὀλέσαντα ὃ διεκόμιζεν. καὶ ὁ
Δημόκριτος ὑπακούων τὰ μὲν ἐμειδία, τὰ δὲ ἐξεγέλα καὶ οὐκέτι
45 οὐδὲν ἔγραφε, τὴν δὲ κεφαλὴν θαμινὰ ἐπέσειεν. ἐγὼ δέ, Ὑμεῖς μέν,
ἔφην, Ἀβδηρῖται, αὐτόθι μίμνετε· ἐγγυτέρω δ' αὐτὸς ᶜκαὶ λόγων
καὶ σώματος τἀνδρὸςᶜ γενηθεὶς ἰδών τε καὶ ἀκούσας εἴσομαι τοῦ
πάθους τὴν ἀλήθειαν.

3. Καὶ ταῦτ' εἰπὼν κατέβαινον ἡσυχῇ. ἦν δὲ ὀξὺ καὶ ἐπίφορον
50 ἐκεῖνο τὸ χωρίον· μόγις οὖν διαστηριζόμενος διῆλθον. ἐπεὶ δ'
ἐπλησίαζον, ἔτυχεν ἐπελθὼν αὐτῷ ὅτι δήποτε γράφειν ἐνθουσιωδῶς
καὶ μεθ' ὁρμῆς· εἱστήκειν οὖν περιμένων αὐτοῦ τὸν καιρὸν τῆς
ἀναπαύσιος· ὁ δὲ μετὰ σμικρὸν τῆς φορῆς λήξας τοῦ γραφείου
ἀνέβλεψέν τε ἐς ἐμὲ προσιόντα καί φησιν, Χαῖρε, ξεῖνε. κἀγώ,
55 Πολλά γε καὶ σύ, Δημόκριτε, ἀνδρῶν σοφώτατε. ὁ δὲ αἰδεσθείς,
οἶμαι, ὅτι ὀνομαστὶ μὴ προσεῖπέν με, Σὲ δέ, ἔφη, τί καλέομεν;
ἄγνοια γὰρ τοῦ σοῦ ὀνόματος ἦν ἡ τοῦ ξείνου προσηγορίη.
Ἱπποκράτης, ἔφην, ἔμοιγε τοὔνομα, ὁ ἰητρός. ὁ δὲ εἶπεν, Ἡ τῶν
Ἀσκληπιαδῶν ᵈεὐγένεια πολύ τεᵈ σοῦ τὸ κλέος τῆς ἐν ἰητρικῇ
60 σοφίης πεφοίτηκεν καὶ ἐς ἡμέας ἀφίκται· τί δὲ χρέος, ἑταῖρε, δεῦρό
σε ἤγαγε; μᾶλλον δὲ πρὸ πάντων κάθησο. ὁρῇς δὲ ὡς ἔστιν οὗτος
οὐκ ἀηδὴς φύλλων θῶκος, χλοερὸς καὶ μαλακὸς ἐγκαθίσαι,

ᶜ⁻ᶜ καὶ σώματος καὶ λόγων b: καὶ λόγου καὶ σώματος O: καὶ λόγων τἀνδρὸς καὶ
σωμάτων u
ᵈ⁻ᵈ εὐγένεια πολύ τε scripsi: εὐγένεια· πολύ γε codd.

untrimmed. Close to him on his right a small stream gurgled gently down the side of the hill. There was a shrine on that hill-top, covered with a wild grapevine, which I guessed was dedicated to the nymphs. He was holding a book very carefully on his knees, with others lying around on both sides of him. There was also a large pile of animal bodies, completely dissected. At times he wrote with concentrated attention; at times he was absolutely quiet and still, pondering to himself. Then after doing this for a short time he would get up, walk around, examine the animals' entrails, put them down again, and return to his seat. The Abderites who were standing around me downcast, and almost with tears in their eyes, said, 'You see Democritus' way of life, Hippocrates, that he's mad and doesn't know what he wants or what he is doing?' One of them, by way of illustrating his madness even more, wailed aloud like a woman lamenting her child's death. Then another one groaned in imitation of a traveller who has lost his belongings. And when Democritus heard the first he smiled; when he heard the second he laughed aloud, stopping in his writing and shaking his head repeatedly. But I said, 'You stay here, Abderites, while I get closer to his speech and body; so that having seen and heard him I can learn what is really the matter with him.'

3. With these words I moved down quietly. But the place formed a steep slope, so that I could scarcely keep my footing as I went. And as I was approaching him, he happened to be seized by a frenzied urge to write down something or other. So I stood waiting for him to pause and give me an opportunity. After a short time, stopping the movement of his pen, he looked up at my approach and said, 'Greetings, stranger.' I replied, 'Many greeting to you too, Democritus, wisest of men.' He was embarrassed, I think, because he had not addressed me by name, and said, 'And what do we call you? Addressing you as "stranger" was due to my ignorance of your name.' 'Hippocrates is my name,' I said, 'the doctor.' He said, 'The distinction of the Asclepiads, and your own great fame in the healing art, have gone abroad and come even to us. What has brought you here, my friend? But first of all do sit down. You see there is a pleasant seat of leaves here, green and soft to sit on, and more soothing than the invidious

προσηνέστερος τῶν τῆς τύχης ἐπιφθόνων θώκων. καθίσαντος δέ μου
πάλιν φησίν. Ἴδιον οὖν ἢ ἐπιδήμιον πρῆγμα διζήμενος δεῦρο ἀφῖξαι;
65　φράζε σαφῶς. καὶ γὰρ ἡμεῖς ὅτι δυναίμεθα συνεργοῖμεν ἄν. κἀγώ, Τὸ
μὲν κατ' ἀληθείην, ἔφην, αἴτιον, σέο δεῦρο χάριν ἥκω ξυντυχεῖν
σοφῷ ἀνδρί· ἔχει δὲ πρόφασιν ἡ πατρίς, ἧς πρεσβείην τελέω. ὁ δέ,
Ξεινίη τοίνυν, φησί, τὰ πρῶτα κέχρησο ἡμετέρῃ. πειρώμενος δὲ κἀγὼ
κατὰ πάντα τἀνδρὸς καίπερ ἤδη μοι δήλου μὴ παρακόπτειν ἐόντος,
70　Φιλοποίμενα οἶσθα, ἔφην, πολίτην ἐόντα ὑμέτερον; ὁ δέ, Καὶ μάλα,
εἶπεν, τὸν Δάμωνος λέγεις υἱὸν τὸν οἰκοῦντα παρὰ τὴν Ἑρμαΐδα
κρήνην; Τοῦτον, εἶπον, ᾧ καὶ τυγχάνω ἐκ πατέρων ἴδιος ξεῖνος· ἀλλὰ
σύ, Δημόκριτε, τῇ κρείσσονί με ξεινίῃ δέχου. καὶ πρῶτόν γε τί ἦν
τοῦτο ὃ γράφεις, φράζε. ὁ δ' ἐπισχὼν ὀλίγον, Περὶ μανίης, ἔφη.
75　κἀγώ, Ὦ Ζεῦ βασιλεῦ, φημί, εὐκαίρως γε ἀντιγράφεις πρὸς τὴν
πόλιν. ὁ δέ, Ποίην, φησίν, πόλιν, Ἱππόκρατες; ἐγὼ δέ, Οὐδέν, ἔφην,
ὦ Δημόκριτε, ἀλλ' οὐκ οἶδ' ὅκως προὔπεσεν. ἀλλὰ τί περὶ μανίης
γράφεις; Τί γάρ, εἶπεν, ἄλλο ἢ τίς πέλει καὶ ὅκως ἀνθρώποισιν
ἐγγίνεται καὶ τίνα τρόπον ἀπολωφέοιτο. τά τε γὰρ ζῷα, ἔφη, ταῦτα
80　ὁκόσα ὁρῇς, τούτου μέντοι γε οὕνεκα ἀνατέμνω, οὐ μισέων θεοῦ
ἔργα, χολῆς δὲ διζήμενος φύσιν καὶ θέσιν. οἶσθα γὰρ ἀνθρώπων
παρακοπῆς ὡς αἰτίη ἐπὶ τὸ πολὺ αὕτη πλεονάσασα, ἐπεὶ πᾶσι μὲν
φύσει ἐνυπάρχει, ἀλλὰ παρ' οἷσι μὲν ἐλάσσων, παρ' οἷσι δέ τι
πλείων. ἡ δ' ἀμετρίη αὐτῆς νοῦσοι τυγχάνουσιν, ὡς ὕλης ὁτὲ μὲν
85　ἀγαθῆς, ὁτὲ δὲ φαύλης ὑποκειμένης. κἀγώ, Νὴ Δία, ἔφην, ὦ
Δημόκριτε, ἀληθέως γε καὶ φρονίμως λέγεις· ὅθεν εὐδαίμονά σε
κρίνω τοσαύτης ἀπολαύοντα ἡσυχίης. ἡμῖν δὲ μετέχειν ταύτης οὐκ
ἐπιτέτραπται. ἐρεομένου δέ, Διὰ τί, ὦ Ἱππόκρατες, οὐκ
ἐπιτέτραπται; Ὅτι, ἔφην, ἢ ἀποικίη ἢ τέκνα ἢ δάνεια ἢ νοῦσοι ἢ
90　θάνατοι ἢ δμῶες ἢ γάμοι ἢ τοιαῦτά τινα τὴν εὐκαιρίην ὑποτάμνεται.

4. Ἐνταῦθα δὴ ὁ ἀνὴρ ἐς τὸ εἰωθὸς κατηνέχθη καὶ μάλα ἀθροῦν
τι ἀνεκάγχασε καὶ ἐπετώθασε καὶ τὸ λοιπὸν ἡσυχίην ἦγε. κἀγώ, Τί
μέντοι, Δημόκριτε, ἔφην, γελᾷς; πότερον τὰ ἀγαθὰ ὧν εἶπον ἢ τὰ
κακά; ὁ δὲ ἔτι μᾶλλον ἐγέλα. καὶ ἄπωθεν ὀρεῦντες οἱ Ἀβδηρῖται οἱ
95　μὲν τὰς κεφαλὰς αὑτῶν ἔπαιον, οἱ δὲ τὰ μέτωπα, οἱ δὲ τὰς τρίχας
ἔτιλλον. καὶ γάρ, ὡς ὕστερον ἔφησαν, πλεονάζοντι παρὰ τὸ εἰωθὸς
ἐχρήσατο τῷ γέλωτι. ὑποτυχὼν δ' ἐγώ, Ἀλλὰ μήν, ἔφην, σοφῶν
ἄριστε, Δημόκριτε, ποθέω γὰρ αἰτίην τοῦ περὶ σὲ πάθεος
καταλαβέσθαι, τίνος ἄξιος ἐφάνην ἐγὼ γέλωτος ἢ τὰ λεχθέντα ὅκως
100　μαθὼν παύσωμαι τῆς αἰτίης ἢ σὺ ἐλεγχθεὶς διακρούσῃ τοὺς
ἀκαίρους γέλωτας. ὁ δέ, Ἡράκλεις, ἔφη, εἰ γὰρ δυνήσῃ με ἐλέγξαι,
θεραπείην θεραπεύσεις οἵην οὐδένα πώποτε, Ἱππόκρατες....

thrones given by good fortune.' When I had sat down he resumed: 'Have you come on private or public business? Tell me clearly, for I would do all I could to help.' I replied, 'The real reason for my coming is on account of you, to meet a wise man; but my excuse is supplied by your country, for whom I am performing an embassy.' He said, 'First enjoy my hospitality.' Then, making a detailed test of the man, although it was already clear to me that he was not deranged, I said, 'Do you know Philopoemen, your fellow-citizen?' 'Yes, indeed,' he replied, 'You mean the son of Damon, who lives by Hermes' fountain?' 'That's the man,' I said; 'I am his personal guest-friend through our families. But you, Democritus, must accept me in a stronger bond of hospitality. And first will you tell me what is that you are writing?' He paused for a moment and then said, 'A work on madness.' 'O King Zeus,' I said, 'you are writing a most opportune reply to the city.' He said, 'What do you mean by the city, Hippocrates?' 'Nothing, Democritus,' I replied, 'that slipped out somehow. But what are you writing about madness?' 'Exactly what it is, how it comes on people, and the way to relieve it. All the animals you see here', he went on, 'I am dissecting for that reason, not because I dislike the works of God, but seeking the nature and location of the bile. You know that excess of this is usually the cause of dementia in people, since it is naturally present in everyone, but less in some and a bit more in others. Diseases occur through a disproportion of it, as it is a substance whose presence is sometimes beneficial, sometimes harmful.' Then I said, 'By Zeus, Democritus, you speak truly and wisely; and so I judge you a happy man to enjoy such leisure. It is not my lot to share it.' When he asked, 'why is it not, Hippocrates?', I replied, 'Because my leisure is cut down by travelling, children, debts, illnesses, deaths, servants, marriages, and so on.'

4. At that the man reverted to his usual state, with a sudden burst of laughter, mockery, and then was silent. 'But what are you laughing at, Democritus?', I said, 'the good things I spoke of or the bad?' He just laughed even more; and, watching from a distance, some of the Abderites struck their heads, and some their foreheads, and some pulled their hair, because, as they said later, his laughter was even more excessive than usual. But I took him up, saying, 'Truly, Democritus,

...9. Ἐγὼ μὲν οὐδαμῶς δοκέω γελῆν· ἐξευρεῖν δὲ κατ' αὐτῶν
ἤθελόν τι λυπηρόν. ἀλλ' οὐδὲ ἰητρικὴν ὑπὲρ τούτων ἐχρῆν εἶναι
105 μητιωμένην παιήονα φάρμακα. ὁ σὸς πρόγονος Ἀσκληπιὸς
νουθεσίῃ σοι γενέσθω· σῴζων ἀνθρώπους κεραυνοῖσιν ηὐχαρίστη-
ται. οὐχ ὁρῆς, ὅτι κἀγὼ τῆς κακίης μοῖρά εἰμι; μανίης διζήμενος
αἰτίην ζῷα κατακτείνω^e καὶ ἀνατάμνω, ἐχρῆν δὲ ἐξ ἀνθρώπων τὴν
αἰτίην ἐρευνῆσαι. οὐχ ὁρῆς, ὅτι καὶ ὁ κόσμος μισανθρωπίης
110 πεπλήρωται; ἄπειρα κατ' αὐτῶν πάθεα ξυνήθροικε. ὅλος ἄνθρωπος
ἐκ γενετῆς νοῦσός ἐστι· τρεφόμενος ἄχρηστος, ἱκέτης βοηθείης·
αὐξανόμενος ἀτάσθαλος, ἄφρων διὰ χειρὸς παιδαγωγίης· θρασὺς
ἀκμάζων, παρακμάζων οἰκτρός, τοὺς ἰδίους πόνους ἀλογιστίῃ
γεωργήσας· ἐκ μητρῴων γὰρ λύθρων ἐξέθορε τοιοῦτος. διὰ τοῦτο οἱ
115 μὲν θυμικοὶ καὶ ὀργῆς ἀμέτρου γέμοντες, οἱ δ' ἐν φθορῇσι καὶ
μοιχείῃσι διὰ παντός, οἱ δ' ἐν μέθῃσι, οἱ δ' ἐν ἐπιθυμίῃσι τῶν
ἀλλοτρίων, οἱ δ' ἐν ἀπωλείῃσι τῶν σφετέρων. ὄφελον δύναμις
ὑπῆρχεν τὰς ἁπάντων οἰκήσεις ἀνακαλύψαντα μηθὲν ἀφεῖναι τῶν
ἐντὸς παρακάλυμμα, εἶθ' οὕτως ὁρᾶν τὰ πρησσόμενα ἔνδον. εἴδομεν
120 ἂν οὓς μὲν ἐσθίοντας, οὓς δὲ ἐμέοντας, ἑτέρους δὲ αἰκίῃσι
στρεβλέοντας, τοὺς δὲ φάρμακα κυκέοντας, τοὺς δὲ ξυννοέοντας
ἐπιβουλίην, τοὺς δὲ ψηφίζοντας, ἄλλους χαίροντας, τοὺς δὲ
κλαίοντας, τοὺς δὲ ἐπὶ κατηγορίην φίλων ξυγγράφοντας, τοὺς δὲ διὰ
φιλοδοξίην ἔκφρονας. καί γε τινὲς βαθύτεραι πρήξιες τῶν κατὰ

---

^e κατακτείνω *bO;* κατατίνω *u*

wisest of men, I want to grasp the cause of your condition,
why I, or what I said, seemed to prompt your laughter, so that
when I know I can check my fault, or when you are proved
wrong you can curtail your ill-timed laughter.' 'By Hercules,'
he replied, 'if you can prove me wrong you will achieve such a
cure as you never yet managed for anyone, Hippocrates. ...

[Hippocrates and Democritus have a long discussion, in which
Democritus explains that the sole cause of his laughter is humanity, subject
to empty desires and fruitless activities, never learning from bitter experi-
ences, and paying the inevitable penalty for their mindless schemes.]

...9. 'I don't in the least aim to laugh: I wanted to find
something to distress them. But there is no place for medical
skill to devise drugs to heal them. Let your ancestor Asclepius
be a warning to you: while saving men he was rewarded by a
thunderbolt. Do you not see that I too am a part of the evil?
As I seek the cause of madness I kill animals and dissect
them, whereas I should be looking for the cause in men. Do
you not see that even the cosmos is full of hatred for humanity? It has collected innumerable afflictions for them. Man is
one complete illness from birth: while being nurtured he is
useless and a suppliant for help; as he grows up he is pre-
sumptuous and a fool in his tutor's hands; in his prime he is
reckless; when past it he is pitiable, with a crop of troubles
brought on himself by his own witlessness. Such he is from
when he sprang from the blood of his mother's womb. That is
why some men are hot-tempered and full of uncontrolled passion; some spend their whole time in corrupt and adulterous
activities, some in drink; some in coveting other people's
property; some in squandering their own. If I only had the
power to uncover everybody's house, leaving nothing to veil
what is within, so as to see the activities inside. We would see
some people eating; some vomiting; others torturing men
with outrageous treatment; some concocting poisons; some
devising plots; some voting; some rejoicing; some weeping;
some composing accusations against their friends; some driven out of their minds by love of fame. What is more, there are
some deeper activities among those hidden in the soul. And all
these people, both young and old, are begging, refusing, too
poor, too rich, oppressed by famine, sinking under their

125 ψυχὴν κευθομένων. καὶ τούτων ὁκόσοι μὲν νέοι, ὁκόσοι δὲ πρεσβῦ-
ται, αἰτεῦντες, ἀρνεόμενοι, πενόμενοι, περιουσιάζοντες, λιμῷ
θλιβόμενοι, οἱ δὲ ἀσωτίῃ βεβαρημένοι, ῥυπῶντες, δέσμιοι, οἱ δὲ
τρυφῇσι γαυριῶντες, τρέφοντες, ἄλλοι σφάττοντες, ἄλλοι θάπτοντες,
ὑπερορέοντες ἃ ἔχουσι, πρὸς τὰς ὑπερορίους κτήσιας ὡρμημένοι, οἱ
130 μὲν ἀναίσχυντοι, οἱ δὲ φειδωλοί, οἱ δὲ ἄπληστοι, οἱ μὲν φονεῦντες,
οἱ δὲ τυπτόμενοι, οἱ δὲ ὑπερηφανεῦντες, οἱ δὲ ἐπτερωμένοι κενο-
δοξίῃ· καὶ οἱ μὲν ἵπποισι παρεστῶτες, οἱ δὲ ἀνδράσι, οἱ δὲ κυσίν, οἱ
δὲ λίθοισιν ἢ ξύλοισιν, οἱ δὲ χαλκῷ, οἱ δὲ γραφῇσι· καὶ οἱ μὲν ἐν
πρεσβείῃσιν, οἱ δ’ ἐν στρατηγίῃσιν, οἱ δὲ ἱερωσύνῃσι, οἱ δὲ στεφα-
135 νηφορίῃσιν· οἱ δὲ ἔνοπλοι, οἱ δὲ ἀποκτεινόμενοι. φέρονται δὲ τούτων
ἕκαστοι οἱ μὲν ἐπὶ ναυμαχίην, οἱ δὲ ἐπὶ στρατείην, οἱ δὲ ἐπ’
ἀγροικίην, ἕτεροι δὲ ἐπὶ φορτίδας ναῦς, οἱ δὲ ἐς ἀγορήν, ἕτεροι δ’
ἐπ’ ἐκκλησίην, οἱ δ’ ἐπὶ θέητρον, οἱ δὲ ἐς φυγήν, ἄλλοι δὲ
ἀλλαχόσε. καὶ οἱ μὲν ἐς φιληδονίην καὶ ἡδυπαθείην καὶ ἀκρασίην, οἱ
140 δὲ ἐς ἀργίην καὶ ῥαθυμίην. τὰς ἀναξίους οὖν καὶ δυστήνους σπουδὰς
ὁρεῦντες καὶ τοσαύτας, πῶς μὴ χλευάσωμεν τὸν τοιῆσδε ἀκρασίης
ἔχοντα βίον αὐτῶν; κάρτα γὰρ ἔλπομαι μηδὲ τὴν σὴν ἰητρικὴν
ἀνδάνειν αὐτοῖσιν. δυσαρεστέονται γὰρ ὑπ’ ἀκρασίης ἅπασι καὶ
μανίην τὴν σοφίην νομίζουσι. ἦπου γὰρ ὑπονοέω λωβᾶσθαί σου τὰ
145 πολλὰ τῆς ἐπιστήμης ἢ διὰ φθόνον ἢ δι’ ἀχαριστίην. οἵ τε γὰρ
νοσέοντες ἅμα τῷ σῴζεσθαι τὴν αἰτίην θεοῖσιν ἢ τύχῃ προσνέμουσι,
πολλοὶ δὲ τῇ φύσει προσάψαντες ἐχθαίρουσι τὸν εὐεργετήσαντα,
σμικροῦ δεῖν προσαγανακτεῦντες εἰ νομίζονται χρεωφειλέται. οἵ τε
πολλοὶ τὸ τῆς ἀτεχνίης ἐφ’ ἑωυτοῖσιν ἔχοντες ἄιδριες ἐόντες
150 καθαιροῦσι τὸ κρέσσον· ἐν ἀναισθήτοισι γάρ εἰσιν αἱ ψῆφοι. οὔτε δ’
οἱ πάσχοντες συνόμιλοι εἶναι θέλουσι οὔτε οἱ ὁμοτεχνεῦντες μαρ-
τυρεῖν. φθόνος γὰρ ἐνίσταται. οὐκ ἀπείρῳ σοὶ τῶν τοιούτων
λεσχηνέω ταῦτα, σαφέως δὲ εἰδὼς ταῦτα ἐν ἀναξιοπαθείῃσί σε
πολλάκις γεννηθέντα καὶ οὐ δι’ οὐσίην ἢ βασκανίην
155 φιλοτωθάσσοντα. ἀτρεκείης γὰρ οὐδεμία οὔτε γνῶσις οὔτε μαρτυρίη.

10. Ἐπεμειδία λέγων ταῦτα καί μοι, Δαμάγητε, θεοειδής τις
κατεφαίνετο καὶ τὴν προτέρην αὐτοῦ μορφὴν ἐξελελήσμην καί φημι,
Ὦ Δημόκριτε μεγαλόδοξε, μεγάλας γε πάντων σῶν ξεινίων δωρεὰς
ἐς Κῶ ἀποίσομαι· πολλοῦ γάρ με τῆς σοφίης θαυμασμοῦ
160 πεπλήρωκας. ἀπονοστέω δέ σου κῆρυξ ἀληθείην ἀνθρωπίνης φύσεως
ἐξιχνεύσαντος καὶ νοήσαντος, θεραπείην δὲ λαβὼν παρὰ σεῦ τῆς
ἐμῆς διανοίης ἀπαλλάσσομαι τῆς ὥρης τοῦτο ἀπαιτούσης καὶ τῆς
τοῦ σώματος τημελείης. αὔριον δὲ καὶ κατὰ τὸ ἑξῆς ἐν ταὐτῷ
γενησόμεθα. ἀνιστάμην ταῦτα εἰπὼν καὶ ὃς ἦν ἕτοιμος ἀκολουθεῖν.
165 προσελθόντι δέ τινι οὐκ οἶδ’ ὅθεν ἐπεδίδου τὰ βιβλία. κἀγὼ

wastefulness, living in filth or in chains, glorying in their luxury, some nurturing children, others slaughtering or burying, some despising their own possessions while eager to get those of their neighbours, shameless, miserly, insatiable, some murdering, others being beaten up, some full of arrogance, others exalted by vainglory. Then there are those who are beside themselves over horses, or men, or dogs, or precious stones, or woodwork, or bronze, or paintings. Then there are those in embassies, or in military commands, or in priesthoods, or wearing crowns, or under arms, or being killed. All of these are borne along to sea battles, or military campaigns, or farming, or merchant ships, or the market place, or the assembly, or the theatre, or into exile, or elsewhere. Some indulge in love of pleasure, or luxurious living, or wantonness, or idleness, or indifference. When we look at these worthless, wretched pursuits, and so many of them, how can we avoid mocking at their lives that cling to such wantonness? I truly believe that not even your healing art is welcome to them. Through their wantonness they are displeased with everything and they regard wisdom as madness. Indeed, I suspect they insult much of your skill from either envy or ingratitude. For as soon as they recover from an illness they ascribe the cause to the gods or to fortune, and many assign it to nature. They hate anyone who does them a service, and they get almost more annoyed if they are regarded as owing a debt. And most of them, lacking skills themselves, in their ignorance destroy anything superior to them, for the votes go to the unintelligent. Those who are affected by it do not wish to be associated with it, nor do fellow practitioners wish to acknowledge it: for jealousy stands in their way. I am not chattering about all this to you as if you don't know of such things: I am well aware that these things have often got you into situations where you didn't deserve your treatment, and that you don't enjoy mocking people for their possessions or through spite. For we have neither knowledge nor evidence of exact truth.'

10. He smiled as he said this, and to me he had a divine look, Damagetus. I forgot his former appearance and said, 'O glorious Democritus, I shall take back to Cos the great gifts of all your kindly hospitality. You have filled me with a great wonder at your wisdom. I go away to proclaim that you have

ξυντονώτερον ἤπειξα καὶ πρὸς τοὺς ἐόντως Ἀβδηρίτας ἐπὶ τῆ
σκοπιῆ ἀναμένοντάς με· Ἄνδρες, ἔφην, τῆς πρὸς ἐμὲ πρεσβείης
χάρις ὑμῖν πολλή. Δημόκριτον γὰρ εἶδον, ἄνδρα σοφώτατον,
σωφρονίζειν ἀνθρώπους μοῦνον δυνατώτατον. ταῦτ' ἔχω σοι περὶ
170   Δημοκρίτεω, Δαμάγητε, φράζειν γηθόσυνα πάνυ. ἔρρωσο.

tracked down and understood the truth about human nature, and taking from you the means to heal my understanding I'll make my departure, as the hour and my bodily needs require it. But we shall meet tomorrow and thereafter.' With these words I got up, and he was ready to accompany me: he gave his books to a man who came up from somewhere. I hastened back eagerly to the real Abderites, who were waiting for me at their watching-point. 'Men,' I said, 'I am very grateful to you that you sent for me. For I have seen Democritus, wisest of men, who is alone best qualified to teach mankind good sense.'

That is my news for you about Democritus, Damagetus— and what joyful news!

Farewell

CHION

3

Μάτριδι

Πολλὴν χάριν οἶδα τοῖς ἐπισχοῦσιν ἡμᾶς ἀνέμοις καὶ τὴν ἐν
Βυζαντίῳ διατριβὴν βιασαμένοις, καίτοι τὸ πρῶτον ἠχθόμην αὐτοῖς
ἐπειγόμενος. ἀλλὰ γὰρ ἀξία πρόφασις καὶ χρονιωτέρας μονῆς ἐφάνη
Ξενοφῶν ὁ Σωκράτους γνώριμος. οὗτος γὰρ ὁ Ξενοφῶν εἷς τῶν ἐπ'
5 Ἀρταξέρξην στρατευσαμένων Ἑλλήνων, Κύρῳ δὲ συμμάχων ἐστί.
καὶ τὸ μὲν πρῶτον μετά τινος τῶν στρατηγῶν ἦν οὐδὲν πολυπρα-
γμονῶν ὅ τι μὴ στρατιώτην ἐχρῆν, καίπερ εἷς ὢν τῶν Κύρῳ τιμίων·
ὡς δὲ Κῦρός τε ἀπέθανεν ἐν τῇ πρώτῃ μάχῃ καὶ οἱ στρατηγοὶ τῶν
Ἑλλήνων παρασπονδηθέντες ἀπετμήθησαν τὰς κεφαλάς, ᾑρέθη
10 στρατηγός ἀνδρείας τε ἕνεκα καὶ τῆς ἄλλης σοφίας, δοκῶν ἄριστα
ἂν διαπράξασθαι τὴν σωτηρίαν τοῖς Ἕλλησι. καὶ οὐκ ἔψευσεν
αὐτοὺς τῆς ἐλπίδος, ἀλλὰ διὰ μέσης πολεμίας γῆς ὀλίγην στρατιὰν
ἄγων περιεσώσατο, ἑκάστης ἡμέρας τοῖς βασιλέως στρατηγοῖς
παραστρατοπεδευόμενος.
15 **2.** Θαυμαστὰ μὲν οὖν καὶ ταῦτα, πολὺ δὲ τούτων θαυμασιώτερόν
τε καὶ μεῖζον ὅπερ αὐτὸς ἐγὼ νῦν ἐθεασάμην. πεπονημένοι γὰρ οἱ
Ἕλληνες πολυχρονίῳ καὶ χαλεπῇ στρατείᾳ καὶ μηδὲν ἄλλο
εὑρημένοι τῶν κινδύνων ἆθλον πλὴν τῆς σωτηρίας, δεξαμένων
αὐτοὺς κατὰ φόβον Βυζαντίων, ἔγνωσαν διαρπάσαι τὴν πόλιν, καὶ
20 πολὺς τάραχος αἰφνιδίως κατέσχε τοὺς Βυζαντίους. ἐπεὶ δ'
ὡπλίζοντό τε οἱ ξένοι καὶ ὁ σαλπιγκτὴς ἐσήμηνεν, ἐγὼ μὲν ἀσπίδα
καὶ λόγχην ἁρπάσας ἔδραμον ἐπὶ τὸ τεῖχος, οὗ καὶ τῶν ἐφήβων
τινὰς συνεστηκότας ἑώρων. ἦν δ' ἡ φυλακὴ τῶν τειχῶν οὐδὲν
ὠφέλιμος πολεμίων κατεχόντων τὴν πόλιν, ἀλλ' ὅμως ῥᾷον
25 ἐνομίζομεν ἀμυνεῖσθαι πλεονεκτοῦντες τῷ τόπῳ ἢ ἀπολεῖσθαί γε
βραδύτερον. **3.** κἂν τούτῳ ταραττομένων τῶν Ἑλλήνων ἑωρῶμεν
κομήτην ἄνδρα, καλὸν πάνυ καὶ πρᾶον ἰδέσθαι, διεξιόντα δι' αὐτῶν
καὶ παύοντα τῆς ὁρμῆς ἕκαστον· οὗτος δ' ἦν ὁ Ξενοφῶν. ὡς δ' ἐκ
τῶν ἐναντίων παρεκάλουν αὐτὸν οἱ στρατιῶται ἕνα ὄντα πολλοῖς
30 πείθεσθαι καὶ ἀναπαῦσαί ποτε αὐτοὺς τῆς ταλαιπώρου καὶ χαλεπῆς
ἄλης, "ἀνάγετε οὖν ἐπὶ πόδα, ἔφη, καὶ βουλεύσασθε· οὐ γὰρ δέος
μὴ διαφύγῃ βουλευομένους τὸ πρᾶγμα ἐφ' ἡμῖν κείμενον." ὡς δὲ
τοῦτό γε αὐτὸ ἀπειθεῖν ᾐδέσθησαν, εἰς μέσον καταστὰς ὁ Ξενοφῶν
θαυμαστοὺς λόγους διέθετο, ὡς τὸ τέλος αὐτῶν ἐδήλωσεν· οὐ γὰρ ἡμῖν

CHION

3

TO MATRIS

I am very grateful to the winds for delaying me and forcing me to stay awhile at Byzantium, though at first being in a hurry I was angry with them. In fact it was worth staying even longer there for the opportunity it gave of seeing Xenophon, the pupil of Socrates. This Xenophon is one of the Greeks who served as an ally of Cyrus in the expedition against Artaxerxes. At first he simply served under one of the generals, doing nothing of special note beyond a soldier's duty, though personally esteemed by Cyrus. But after Cyrus was killed in the first battle and the Greek generals were beheaded in violation of the truce, he was chosen as general: his bravery as well as his intelligence seemed to make him the most likely to secure deliverance for the Greeks. Nor did he disappoint their hopes, but he brought his little band safely through the heart of enemy territory, though every day he had to encamp close to the king's commanders. **2.** This was indeed a remarkable achievement, but much more remarkable and impressive was what I myself now witnessed. The Greeks were worn out by their long and difficult campaign, and had won nothing except survival from their dangers; so when the Byzantines received them with fear, they decided to plunder the city, at which a great panic suddenly seized the Byzantines. When the mercenaries were armed and their trumpeter sounded the call, I seized a shield and spear and ran to the wall, where I saw some youths assembled. But there was no point in guarding the wall as the enemy was in possession of the city. Still, we thought that with more room for manoeuvre we would more easily defend ourselves, or at least put off our destruction. **3.** In the mean time, while the Greeks were still in disorder, we saw a long-haired man, remarkably handsome and mild of aspect, moving about among them and calming their impulsiveness. This was Xenophon. When the soldiers on their side called on him as he stood alone to yield to the majority and let them cease at last from their cruel and

35 γε σαφῶς ἐξηκούοντο. τοὺς γοῦν πρὸ μικροῦ διαρπάζειν ἐγνωκότας
τὴν πόλιν μετρίους κατὰ τὴν ἀγορὰν ἑωρῶμεν ὠνουμένους τὰ
ἐπιτήδεια, ὡς τῶν ἄλλων Βυζαντίων ἕκαστον, καὶ μηδὲν ἔτι ἐκείνου
τοῦ ἀδίκου καὶ ἁρπακτοῦ Ἄρεος πνέοντας. 4. αὕτη δ᾽ ἡ ὄψις
ἐπίδειξις ἦν τῆς Ξενοφῶντος ψυχῆς, ὅπως καὶ φρονεῖν καὶ λέγειν
40 ἐδύνατο. οὐ μὴν ἔγωγε ἡσυχίᾳ τὸν ἄνδρα παρελθεῖν ὑπέμεινα, καὶ
ταῦτα ὁμοίως Βυζαντίοις εὖ πεπονθὼς ὑπ᾽ αὐτοῦ (ἐπεὶ διὰ τοὺς
ἀνέμους καὶ αὐτὸς εἷς ἦν τῶν διαρπασθησομένων), ἀλλ᾽ ἐγνώρισα
αὐτῷ ἐμαυτόν. ὃ δὲ καὶ τῆς σῆς πρὸς Σωκράτην φιλίας
ἀνεμιμνήσκετο κἀμὲ φιλοσοφεῖν παρίστατο, καὶ τἆλλα οὐ στρατι-
45 ωτικῶς μὰ Δί᾽ ἀλλὰ καὶ πάνυ φιλανθρώπως διελέγετο. νῦν δ᾽ εἰς
Θρᾴκην ἄγει τὸ στράτευμα· Σεύθης γὰρ ὁ τῶν Θρᾳκῶν βασιλεὺς
πρός τινας ὁμόρους πολεμῶν μετεπέμψατο, ἐντελῆ μισθὸν αὐτοῖς
ὑποσχόμενος, οἳ δ᾽ ὑπήκουσαν. οὐ γὰρ ἄποροι διαλυθῆναι βούλον-
ται, ἀλλὰ καὶ κτήσασθαί τι ἐκ τῶν πόνων, ἕως γ᾽ ἔτι στράτευμά
50 εἰσιν.
　　5. Ἴσθι δὴ πολύ με νῦν προθυμότερον εἰς Ἀθήνας πλευσεῖσθαι
φιλοσοφήσοντα· μέμνησαι γὰρ δήπου ὅτι προτρέπων με συνεχῶς
ἐπὶ φιλοσοφίαν καὶ θαυμαστὰ διεξιὼν περὶ τῶν καθ᾽ ὁτιοῦν
σπουδασάντων περὶ αὐτὴν μέρος τἆλλα μὲν εἶχες πειθόμενον, ἐκεῖνο
55 δὲ καὶ πάνυ φοβούμενον. ἐδόκει γάρ μοι τὰ μὲν λοιπὰ ὄντως
σπουδαιοτέρους ποιεῖν ὅσων ἐφάψαιτο (καὶ γὰρ τὸ σῶφρον καὶ τὸ
δίκαιον οὐκ ἄλλοθεν ἀρύεσθαι τοὺς ἀνθρώπους ἢ φιλοσοφίας ᾤμην),
τὸ δὲ πρακτικὸν καὶ σφόδρα λύειν τῆς ψυχῆς καὶ μαλθάσσειν ἐπὶ τὸ
ἥσυχον. ἀπραγμοσύνη γὰρ ἦν καὶ ἠρεμία τὰ θαυμαστά, ὥς μοι
60 ἔλεγες, ἐγκώμια φιλοσόφων. 6. δεινὸν οὖν μοι κατεφαίνετο, εἰ
φιλοσοφήσας τἆλλα μὲν ἀμείνων ἔσομαι, θαρραλέος δ᾽ οὐκέτι οὔτε
στρατιώτης εἶναι δυνήσομαι οὔτ᾽ ἀριστεύς, εἰ δέοι, ἀλλὰ μεθήσω
ταῦτα πάντα ὥσπερ ἐπιλήσμονί τινι ἐπῳδῇ παντὸς ἔργου
λαμπροτέρου κηληθεὶς τῇ φιλοσοφίᾳ. ἠγνόουν δ᾽ ἄρα, ὅτι καὶ πρὸς
65 ἀνδρείαν εἰσὶν ἀμείνους οἱ φιλοσοφήσαντες, καὶ μόλις γ᾽ αὐτὸ παρὰ
Ξενοφῶντος ἔμαθον, οὐκ ἐπειδὴ διελέχθη μοι περὶ αὐτοῦ, ἀλλ᾽ ἐπεὶ
τοιοῦτος ὢν ἐφάνη ὁποῖός ἐστι. μάλιστα γὰρ δὴ μετασχὼν τῶν
Σωκράτους λόγων ἀρκεῖ καὶ στρατεύματα καὶ πόλεις σῴζειν, καὶ
οὐδὲν αὐτὸν ἐποίησε φιλοσοφία αὐτῷ τε καὶ τοῖς φίλοις
70 ἀχρειότερον. 7. ἡσυχία μὲν οὖν ποιητικωτέρα τάχα εὐδαιμονίας·
ἤδη μέντοι καὶ πράξει καλῶς ἕκαστα ὁ καλῶς ἠρεμεῖν δυνάμενος,
ἐπεὶ καὶ μείζων ἂν εἴη τοῦ πολεμοῦντος ὁ πλεονεξίαν καὶ ἐπιθυμίαν
καὶ τἆλλα πάθη χειρούμενος, ὧν καὶ οἱ νικῶντες τοὺς πολεμίους
ἡττῶνται. κἀγὼ οὖν ἐλπίζω φιλοσοφήσας τά τε ἄλλα κρείττων

grievous wanderings, he replied 'Retire in good order and take counsel. There is no risk that we shall lose control of the situation for which we are responsible while we are deliberating.' They were ashamed to disobey this order, and so Xenophon came forward into their midst and made an admirable speech, as the outcome of it indicated: for I could not hear it clearly. At any rate, the men who shortly before had been intent on plundering the city we saw calmly buying provisions in the market square, just like any of the Byzantines, and no longer breathing fire and sword.

4. This sight was a revelation of Xenophon's personality—his mental and oratorical powers. I did not wait quietly until he had gone, especially since, like the Byzantines, I had been well served by him, for because of the winds I too would have been a victim of the plundering. I made myself known to him, and he remembered your friendship with Socrates, urged me to study philosophy, and in general spoke not at all in a military way but like an extremely civilized man. He is now taking his army to Thrace; for Seuthes, the Thracian king, is at war with some of his neighbours and has sent for him. He has promised Xenophon's men full pay, and they have agreed to go. They do not want to disband unpaid, but to get something to show for their toils while they still form an army.

5. I must tell you that I am now much more keen to sail to Athens and study philosophy. No doubt you remember that you used to urge me constantly to take up philosophy, giving me marvellous descriptions of those who had devoted themselves to its various branches. You won me over in most respects, but on one point I was very anxious. It seemed to me that in other areas it dealt with philosophy did in fact make men better (indeed I thought that philosophy was man's only source of prudence and justice); but that it greatly weakened the practical instincts of the mind and softened them into inactivity. For philosophers, as you told me, have written marvellous eulogies of non-intervention and tranquillity. 6. There seemed to me to be a danger that, even if in other ways philosophy taught me to be a better man, I would not manage to become brave or soldierly or heroic if I needed to be, but would forego all that, as if charmed by the enchantment of philosophy into forgetting every noble deed. I did not know

75 ἔσεσθαι καὶ οὐχ ἧττον ἀνδρεῖος, ἀλλ' ἧττον θρασύς. ταῦτα μὲν οὖν
*ᵃ*οὐ τοῦ ἱκανοῦ*ᵃ* μόνον, ἀλλὰ *ᵇ*καὶ πάνυ πολλῷ πέρα.*ᵇ* γίνωσκε δέ με
ἤδη πρὸς τῷ πλεῖν ὄντα· καὶ γὰρ δὴ γέγονε καὶ τὰ τῶν ἀνέμων
αἰσιώτερα.

Düring
ᵃ⁻ᵃ οὐ τοῦτο ἱκανοῦ B
ᵇ⁻ᵇ καὶ πάνυ πολλῷ πέρα Düring: καὶ τοῦ πάνυ πολλοῦ πέρα codd.: καὶ τοῦ
πάνυ πέρα Ald.

13

Μάτριδι

Ὄντως Κλέαρχος, ὥς μοι ἔγραφες, οὐχ οὕτως Σιληνὸν δέδοικε
κατειληφότα αὐτοῦ τὸ φρούριον ὡς ἡμᾶς φιλοσοφοῦντας. ἐπ'
ἐκεῖνον μέν γε οὐκ ἀπέστειλε τέως τοὺς πολιορκήσοντας, ὡς
πυνθάνομαι, ἐπ' ἐμὲ δ' ἧκε Κότυς Θρᾷξ, δορυφόρος αὐτοῦ
5 γενόμενος (ἔγνων γὰρ μετὰ ταῦτα), κυὶ μικρὸν ὕστερον ἢ γραφῆναί
σοι τὴν περὶ τῆς νόσου παρ' ἡμῶν ἐπιστολὴν ἐπεχείρησεν
(ἀνειλήφειν δ' ἐμαυτὸν ἱκανῶς ἤδη), καί μοι περὶ ἕκτην ὥραν μόνῳ
περιπατοῦντι ἐν τῷ Ὠιδείῳ καὶ περί τινος σκέμματος φροντίζοντι
αἰφνιδίως προσῆξεν. 2. ἐγὼ δ' εὐθέως μὲν ὑπενόησα ὅπερ ἦν· ὡς
10 δὲ ξιφίδιόν τι ὁρῶ κακῶς μεταλαμβάνοντα, βοήσας τ' αὐτὸν
ἐξέπληξα καὶ προσδραμὼν τὴν δεξιὰν αὐτοῦ μετειληφότος ἤδη τὸ
ἐγχειρίδιον καταλαμβάνω, καὶ τὸ λοιπὸν δὴ λακτίζων καὶ περια-
γνύων τὸν βραχίονα ἐξέβαλον αὐτοῦ τὸ ξίφος, καὶ ἐτρώθην μὲν
κατενεχθέντος αὐτοῦ ἐπὶ τὸν πόδα, οὐ χαλεπῶς δ' ὅμως. ἐκ τούτου
15 δὴ ἰλιγγιῶντα ἔδησα τῷ ἰδίῳ ζώματι, ἀποστρέψας εἰς τοὐπίσω τὼ
χεῖρε καὶ πρὸς τοὺς στρατηγοὺς ἄγω. κἀκεῖνος μὲν ἔτισε δίκην, ἐγὼ
δ' οὐδὲν δειλότερος εἰς τὸν πλοῦν γέγονα, ἀλλὰ τῶν ἐτησίων
παυσαμένων ὅπως ἂν ἔχω πλεύσομαι· ἄτοπον γὰρ τυραννουμένης
τῆς πατρίδος ἡμᾶς δημοκρατεῖσθαι.

that in bravery too philosophers are superior, and I've just learnt that from Xenophon—not from his talking to me about it but when he exemplified his qualities in his actions. For he spent a great deal of time talking to Socrates, and he is also capable of saving armies and cities. In no way has philosophy made him less serviceable to himself and his friends.

7. Perhaps a quiet life will sooner lead to happiness. Yet a man who can honourably live quietly will also be acting honourably, since he who subdues greed, desire, and the other passions is superior to the warrior: for even those who conquer their enemies are defeated by their own passions. So I too hope through philosophy to become a better man, especially in being not less brave but less reckless.

Well, this is more than enough from me—in fact far too much. Be assured that I am now about to sail, as the winds have become more favourable.

13

To Matris

You were clearly correct in writing to tell me that Clearchus is not so afraid of Silenus, who captured his citadel, as of me, a mere student of philosophy. At any rate, to my knowledge he has not yet despatched men to attack him, but Cotys the Thracian (one of his bodyguard, as I found out afterwards) has come after me. Shortly after I wrote you the letter about my illness he assaulted me. I had made a pretty good recovery and was taking a walk alone about midday in the Odeum, pondering some question or other, when he suddenly attacked me.

2. I realized straightaway what was up, and as soon as I saw him getting out his dagger in a hostile way, I startled him by shouting loudly. Then I rushed at him, grabbed his right hand which now held the dagger, followed this with a kick, and twisting his arm around made him drop the blade. As he fell backwards I was wounded, but not badly. Then as he lay dazed I tied his hands behind his back with his own belt, and took him to the magistrates. So he paid the penalty, while I am nothing daunted regarding my voyage, but whatever my state of health I'll set sail as soon as the north-west winds

20   **3.** Καὶ τὰ μὲν ἐμά, ὡς ἂν ἔχῃ, ἀσφαλῶς ἔχει· ἀγαθὸς γὰρ καὶ
ζῶν καὶ ἀποθνήσκων ἔσομαι· ὅπως δέ τι καὶ ὑπὲρ τῆς πατρίδος
πολιτευώμεθα, πεῖθε τὸν Κλέαρχον, ὅτι φιλοσοφήσαντες ἡσυχίας
γλιχόμεθα καὶ τελέως ἀπολίτευτοι τὰς ψυχάς ἐσμεν· ταῦτα δὲ
καὶ διὰ Νύμφιδος πεῖθε αὐτόν, ὃς ἡμῖν μὲν φίλος, ἐκείνῳ δὲ καὶ
25 συγγενής ἐστιν· οὕτως γὰρ ἂν πορρωτάτω πάσης ὑποψίας
ἀπάγοιτο. ἀπροκαλύπτως δέ σοι γράφομεν, ἐπεὶ καὶ πιστοῖς
ἐπιτιθέμεθα ἀνδράσι τὰς ἐπιστολὰς καὶ Κλέαρχος, ὡς ἐδήλους
καλῶς ποιῶν, περὶ γοῦν ταῦτα οὐ πολυπραγμονεῖ.

14

Μάτριδι

Εἰς Βυζάντιον θρασυτέρῳ μέν, ταχεῖ δ᾽ οὖν πλῷ διασωθεὶς ἔγνων
αὐτός τε ἐπιμεῖναι χρόνον, ὃν ἄν μοι καλῶς ἔχειν   δοκῇ, καὶ πρὸς
ὑμᾶς ἐκπέμψαι Κρωβύλον τὸν θεράποντα, ἵνα τὴν κάθοδον πράττωμεν
ὠφελίμως τῇ πατρίδι. τὸ μὲν γὰρ ἡμέτερον ἀσφαλὲς οὐκ ἐπὶ
5   Κλεάρχῳ ἐστίν. βούλομαι δ᾽ ἐπεὶ προήχθην ἅπαξ, καὶ καθόλου σοι
τὴν ἐμὴν γνώμην δηλῶσαι. ἐμοὶ γὰρ δοκεῖ τῇ μὲν πατρίδι ὁ μέγιστος
εἶναι κίνδυνος μετ᾽ ἀτυχίας ἤδη παρούσης. νῦν τε γάρ, ὡς πυνθάνομαι,
σφαγάς τ᾽ ἀνδρῶν καὶ φυγὰς ὑπομένει, στερομένη μὲν τῶν ἀρίστων
πολιτῶν, τοῖς δ᾽ ἀσεβεστάτοις δουλεύουσα, καὶ εἰσαῦθις οὐχ ὁ τυχὼν
10 αὐτῇ κίνδυνος, μήποτ᾽ ἐκ τῆς περὶ τοῦτον εὐτυχίας οἷς μὲν πόθος τοῦ
τυραννεῖν, οἷς δὲ συνήθεια δουλείας γένηται, καὶ τὸ λοιπὸν εἰς
μοναρχίαν ἀκατάλυτον περιστῇ τὰ πράγματα. **2.** μικραὶ γὰρ δὴ
ῥοπαὶ καὶ τῶν πολυχρονίων καὶ σχεδὸν εἰπεῖν ἀπαύστων ἄρχουσι
κακῶν καὶ ἔγγιστα ὅμοιόν τι ποιοῦσι τοῖς νοσήμασι τῶν σωμάτων.
15 ὥσπερ γὰρ ἐκεῖνα περὶ μὲν τὰς ἀρχὰς ῥᾷον ἀπολύεται τῶν ἀνθρώπων,
ἐνισχύσαντα δὲ δυσίατα ἢ καὶ τελέως ἀνίατα γίνεται, οὕτω καὶ τὰ ἐν
ταῖς πολιτείαις νοσήματα· μέχρι μὲν μνήμη τε ἐλευθερίας ἰσχύει καὶ
ἐπέρχεται [a]τὸν δουλούμενον,[a] παράταξις λίαν ὀχυρὰ γίνεται [b]πρὸς
βουλομένου τοῦ πλήθους·[b] ἐπειδὰν δ᾽ ἅπαξ ὑπερισχύσῃ τὸ κακὸν καὶ

Düring
[a-a] τὸν δουλούμενον *Düring*: τὸ δουλόμενον aBc: τὸ δουλούμενον β *rell.*: τὸ
βουλόμενον ε: τοῖς δουλουμένοις *Ald*
[b-b] πρὸς βουλομένου τοῦ πλήθους *Düring*: πρὸς βουλόμενον τὸ πλῆθος *codd.*

cease. It is quite wrong for me to live here in a democratic state when a tyrant rules my native city.

3. As for me, one thing at least is certain: living or dying I shall remain virtuous. But in order that I can also do a good public service for my city, get Clearchus to believe that I am wrapped up in the tranquillity of philosophical studies and that public life is totally alien to my nature. Nymphis can help you persuade him—he is a friend of mine and a relative of Clearchus. In this way he can be made completely unsuspicious. I am writing to you quite openly as I entrust my letters to loyal bearers, and, as you were careful to tell me, Clearchus is not inquisitive about our communications.

14

To Matris

After a risky but quick crossing I arrived safely at Byzantium, and decided to remain here myself as long as it seemed right, and to send my servant Crobylus to you to see how my return could benefit my city. For Clearchus is not the only threat to our safety, and now I have come this far I want to explain to you how I see things in general.

It seems to me that the city is in the greatest danger from our current misfortune. From what I can gather, it is enduring butchery and banishments, deprived of its finest citizens and a slave to the most ungodly of men. And for the future there is no small danger that this man's success will give some men the urge to be tyrants and cause others to become used to slavery, and eventually the situation will end in a perpetual monarchy. **2.** For small movements lead to long-lasting, almost, you might say, unstoppable troubles, and produce very similar effects to those of diseases on the body. Just as the latter more easily relax their hold on people at their early stages, but when they have strengthened their grip they are hard to cure or indeed quite incurable, so it is with diseases in the state. While the memory of freedom persists and stays in the mind of the enslaved, the people keep a very strong will to resist. But once the evil becomes too strong, and men no

20 μηκέτι ᾖ τοῖς ἀνθρώποις λόγος, ὅπως αὐτὸ ἀπαλλάξωσιν ἑαυτῶν, ἀλλ'
ὅπως ἂν ῥᾷστα ἐν αὐτῷ διάγοιεν τότε ὁ παντελὴς ὄλεθρος γίνεται.
3. Ἡ μὲν οὖν πατρὶς ἐν τοιούτοις κακοῖς καὶ κινδύνοις ἐστίν,
ἐγὼ δ', εἰ μὲν αὐτὸ ἐφ' ἑαυτοῦ βούλοιο τοὐμὸν σκέπτεσθαι, καὶ
πάνυ ἀσφαλής εἰμι. δουλείαν γὰρ ταύτην ἔγωγε νομίζω, ἢ μετὰ τῶν
25 σωμάτων καὶ τὰς ψυχὰς ὑφ' ἑαυτὴν ἔχει. ἡ δὲ τῆς μὲν ψυχῆς οὐδ'
ὁτιοῦν ἁπτομένη, τὸ δὲ σῶμα μόνον ἔχουσα οὐδὲ δουλεία τυγχάνειν
ἔμοιγε δοκεῖ. τεκμήριον δέ· εἴ τι δουλείας κακόν, τοῦτο ἐπὶ ψυχὴν
καταβαίνει, ἐπεὶ ἄλλως οὐδὲ κακὸν λέγοιτ' ἄν· φόβος γὰρ τοῦ παθεῖν
τι καὶ ἐκ τοῦ παθεῖν λύπη τὰ δεινότατα τοῖς μὴ ἐλευθέροις. τί οὖν;
30 ἄν τις μὴ φοβῆται μέλλον κακὸν μηδ' ἐπὶ τῷ γινομένῳ ἄχθηται,
δουλεύσει; καὶ πῶς, ὅ γε μὴ ἔχων τὰ δουλείας κακά; 4. ἴσθι οὖν
τοιοῦτόν με ὑπὸ φιλοσοφίας γενόμενον, ὁποῖον κἂν δήσῃ Κλέαρχος,
κἂν ὁτιοῦν δράσῃ τῶν χαλεπῶν, οὐδέποτε ποιήσει δοῦλον· οὐδέποτε
γάρ μου τὴν ψυχὴν χειρώσεται, ἐν ᾗ τὸ δοῦλον ἢ τὸ ἐλεύθερον, ἐπεὶ
35 σῶμά γε ἀεὶ συντυχίας ἧττον, κἂν ὑπ' ἀνδρὶ μὴ τάττηται δεσπότῃ.
ἢν δέ μ' ἀποκτείνῃ, τότε καὶ τὴν τελείαν ἐλευθερίαν χαριεῖταί μοι.
ἢν γὰρ οὐδὲ τὸ περιέχον σῶμα ᾠκείωσε τῇ ἑαυτοῦ δουλείᾳ, ταύτῃ
τίνα οἰκονομίαν ἐλλείψειν δοκεῖς κεχωρισμένῃ τοῦ σώματος; οὐ
μόνον δ' ἐγώ, ὃ ἂν πάσχω, ἐλεύθερος, ἀλλὰ καὶ Κλέαρχος, ὃ ἂν
40 διαθῇ με, δοῦλος γενήσεται· φοβούμενος γὰρ διαθήσει, δέος δ'
οὐδὲν ἔχει ψυχῆς ἐλευθερία.
5. Τὰ μὲν οὖν ἐμὰ ἐφ' ἑαυτῶν σκοπεῖν, ὡς ὁρᾷς, ἀσφαλέστερα εἰς
τὸ παθεῖν ἢ Κλεάρχῳ εἰς τὸ δρᾶσαι, καὶ τό γ' ἐμὸν οὐκ ἐπιμελείας
ἀλλ' ὀλιγωρίας δεῖται. τὸ γὰρ ἀρχὴν φροντίζειν περὶ αὐτῶν ἀνδρός
45 ἐστιν οὐ πάντῃ ἐλευθέρου. τὰ δὲ τῆς πατρίδος συνημμένα μοι οὐκ
ἐπιτρέπει τὴν αὐτόνομον ταύτην ἐλευθερίαν, ἀλλὰ καὶ πολιτεύεσθαι
ἀναγκάζει καὶ κίνδυνον ἔχειν, κίνδυνον δ' οὐχὶ μὴ αὐτός τι πάθω,
ἀλλὰ μὴ πάσχουσάν τι τὴν πατρίδα οὐκ ὠφελήσω. διὰ τοῦτό μοι
ἀνάγκη καίπερ μὴ φοβουμένῳ θάνατον προνοεῖν, ὅπως μὴ πρότερον
50 ἀποθάνω ἢ ὑπὲρ τῆς πατρίδος ἀποθανεῖν δυνήσομαι. πολιτεύου δὴ
πρὸς τὸν τύραννον ἃ καὶ πρότερόν σοι ἔγραφον, πείθων αὐτὸν ὅτι
ἡσυχίας ἐρασταί ἐσμεν, καὶ γράφε ἡμῖν, ἐὰν καὶ ἄλλο τί σοι δοκῇ
πρὸς τὴν αὐτόθι πολιτείαν ἀνήκειν, ἐπεὶ ἀνάγκη μοι εἰς τὴν τῆς
πατρίδος ἐλευθερίαν ὑφαιρεῖν τι τῆς ἐμαυτοῦ, φροντίζοντι περὶ
55 τούτων καὶ βουλευομένῳ.

longer consider how to rid themselves of it but how to live with it most comfortably, then follows their total ruin.

3. Such, then, are the evils and dangers that afflict our city; whereas if you care to look at my own particular position I am pretty safe. For I consider to be slavery only that which possesses souls as well as bodies; that which subdues the body alone and has no grip at all on the soul does not strike me as slavery. The proof is that if slavery is some kind of evil this affects the soul, otherwise it cannot be called an evil. For the fear of suffering and the pain resultant from suffering are only really horrifying to those who are not free. So, will anyone be a slave who is not afraid of a future evil or oppressed by a present one? How can a man be a slave who does not suffer the evils of slavery?

4. You can be sure therefore that philosophy has made me the sort of person Clearchus will never enslave, even if he puts me in chains or whatever suffering he inflicts on me. For he will never subdue my soul, which is what decides whether I am free or a slave; since the body is always subject to fortune even if not under a human master. And if he kills me, then he will be presenting me with the ultimate freedom. For if the body has not reconciled the soul to its own slavery while still containing it, do you suppose the soul will lack a function when divorced from the body? So not only am I free whatever I suffer, but whatever he does to me Clearchus will in fact be the slave: he will be acting out of fear, whereas freedom of the soul knows no fear.

5. You can see, then, that regarding my own position I am at less risk in suffering than Clearchus is in acting. My fate is not something to be troubled about, but a matter of total unconcern; for even to think about it is the sign of a man not completely free. But my links with my native city do not allow me such total independence, but compel me to public action which involves danger—a danger not of suffering personally but of being unable to assist my suffering city. Because of this, though not afraid of death I am bound to take precautions not to be killed until I can die for my city. So in your dealings with the tyrant, as I've written before, persuade him that I am devoted to the tranquil life; and write to me if you think of anything else relevant to the political situation there. For the sake of my city's freedom I have to give up some of my own, reflecting on these things and making my plans.

16

Κλεάρχῳ

Ἐν Ἀθήναις μοι φιλοσοφίας χάριν διατρίβοντι τῶν τε κοιῶν τινες
φίλων καὶ ὁ πατὴρ ἔγραψεν ὡς δἰ ὑποψίας εἴην πρός σε καὶ τὰς
αἰτίας ἐκέλευον ἀπολύσασθαι· τοῦτο γὰρ δίκαιον εἶναι καὶ αὐτῷ μοι
ἄμεινον. ἐγὼ δὲ ὅτι μὲν ὀρθῶς παρήνουν ταῦτα σαφῶς ᾔδειν, ἠγνόουν
5   δὲ ἀφ' ὧν διεβλήθην, καὶ τοῦτό μοι πρὸς τὴν ἀπολογίαν ἦν ἄπορον·
οὐδὲ γὰρ αὐτὸς παρῆν ὅτε περιεβάλου τὴν ἀρχήν, οὔτε ἀπὼν
ἐδυνάμην ἐναντιοῦσθαι, οὐδ' ὅλως ἢ λόγος ἢ ἔργον τι τῶν ἐμῶν
ἐπιμιξίαν τινὰ ἔσχε πρὸς τὰ αὐτόθι πράγματα. τίνες οὖν αἱ
διαπόντιοι πρὸς μόναρχον ἐναντιώσεις ἀνθρώπου μετ' ὀλίγων
10   οἰκετῶν ἀποδημοῦντος οὐκ ἐγὼ ηὕρισκον, καὶ διὰ τοῦτό γε ἠπόρουν
ἀπολογίας, ὅτι οὐδὲν ἑώρων τὸ κατηγορούμενον. 2. οὐκ ἠπόρουν δὲ
πάλιν τῷ μηδὲν ἐννοεῖσθαι τοιοῦτον, ὁποῖον ἴσως ὑποπτεύομαι,
ἀλλὰ καὶ πάνυ ἔχων πείθειν σε, ὅτι ἡ ἐμὴ ψυχὴ οὐδενὶ εὐέμβατός
ἐστι τῶν τοιούτων βουλευμάτων. οἶμαι μὲν οὖν εἰ καὶ μὴ
15   πεφιλοσοφήκειν, ἱκανὸν ἂν γενέσθαι τεκμήριον τοῦ μὴ ἀπεχθῶς ἔχειν
πρός σε τὸ μηδὲ ἠδικῆσθαί τι ὑπὸ σοῦ. οὐδὲ γὰρ οἱ ἀφιλοσόφητοι μὴ
παντάπασί γε μανέντες καθ' ἡδονήν τινα τὰς ἀπεχθείας ἐπαναιροῦν-
ται, οὐδ' ἔρωτάς τινας ὥσπερ παιδικῶν ἐπιτηδευμάτων οὕτω καὶ
μίσους λαμβάνουσι (πολλοῦ δεῖ) ἀλλὰ καὶ πάνυ ἐπίστανται ὅτι οὐδὲν
20   ἀνθρώποις ἀπεχθείας ἀνιαρώτερον· ὅταν δὲ ὑπ' ἀνηκέστου τινὸς
διαιρεθῶσιν ἀπ' ἀλλήλων τὰς ψυχάς, τότε ἀπεχθάνονται καὶ οὐδὲ
τότε ἑκόντες. 3. ἡμῖν δὲ μέχρι τῆς νῦν ἡμέρας οὐδὲν οὔτε μέγα
οὔτε μικρὸν ὑπῆρκται πρὸς ἀλλήλους ἀπεχθείας ἔργον, ἀλλὰ σοὶ μὲν
οὐδὲν πλέον ὑπονοίας καὶ λόγου, ἐγὼ δὲ καθαρεύω τὴν ψυχὴν καὶ
25   ἀπὸ τούτων. τί οὖν βουλόμενος ἐξαίφνης στασιάζω πρός σε, καὶ
ταῦτα μηδέπω καὶ τήμερον ἑορακὼς ἀρχομένην ὑπὸ σοῦ τὴν
πατρίδα; ἢ νὴ Δία φυσῶσί με αἱ πολλαὶ τριήρεις καὶ οἱ ἱππεῖς, ἵνα εἰ
μηδὲν ἄλλο ὑποπτεύοις τό γε δύνασθαί με ἐχθρὸν εἶναι; ἀλλ'
ἀπεδήμησα μὲν σὺν ὀκτὼ θεράπουσι καὶ φίλοις δύο, Ἡρακλείδῃ καὶ
30   Ἀγάθωνι, ἀναλύω δὲ δύο τῶν οἰκετῶν ἀποβαλών. ταῦτα δὲ οὐκ οἶδ'
ὅπως πείθουσί σε ἱκανὴν εἶναι παρασκευὴν ἐπὶ σέ· ἐκεῖνο δ' οὐ
σκοπεῖς ὅτι εἰ συνῄδειν ἐμαυτῷ δικαίως ὑποπτευομένῳ, οὐκ ἄν ποτε
ἑκὼν ἐμαυτὸν ἐνεχείριζον τῷ ὑποπτεύοντι. 4. ἢ οὕτω τις ἐραστής
ἀπεχθειῶν εἰμι, ὥστε μηδὲ τὴν πρὸς ἐμαυτὸν φυλάττειν φιλίαν, ἀλλ'
35   ἑκοντὶ ἐγχειρίζειν τὸ σῶμα τοῖς δικαίως αὐτὸ τιμωρησομένοις; ἀλλὰ
ταῦτα μὲν καὶ τοῖς μὴ φιλοσοφήσασιν ἱκανή. μᾶλλον δὲ πέρα τοῦ
ἱκανοῦ ἀπολογία.

16

TO CLEARCHUS

While I was staying in Athens studying philosophy my father and some of our joint friends wrote to say that you were suspicious of me, and told me to clear myself of the charges as this was the right thing to do and in my own interest. I know this is good advice, but I am ignorant of the grounds of the accusations and this makes it difficult to defend myself. For I wasn't around when you seized power, being absent I couldn't oppose you, and not a single word or deed of mine had any connection with events in Heraclea. I cannot see what hostility there can be that crosses the seas between a despot and someone who has gone abroad with a few servants. Moreover, I am in a difficulty how to work up my defence because I have not seen the accusation.

2. However, I am in no difficulty about the fact that I have not plotted anything I may be accused of: on the contrary, I have strong arguments to show you that my mind is not receptive to such plots. Even if I had not studied philosophy I think the fact that I have never been injured by you would be sufficient proof that I am no enemy to you. For not even unphilosophical people, unless they are quite mad, take pleasure in making enemies. They do not acquire a passion for hatred in the way they do for childish pursuits: far from it, as they are well aware that nothing is more painful to men than hatred. It is only when men's minds become divided on some intractable issue that they hate each other, and even then reluctantly.

3. Until this very day there has been no single act of hostility between us, great or small; and yet you offer nothing but suspicion and a charge, while my mind does not even harbour such things. What motive could I have in suddenly starting a faction against you, especially when to this day I have not yet seen my city under your rule? Heavens! Is my pride so swollen by the thought of quantities of triremes and a cavalry force that you suspect me at least of being a potential foe? But I went away with eight servants and two friends, Heraclides and Agathon, and I return having lost two of the servants. I can't see how anyone can convince you that this is a sufficient

Ἐγὼ δὲ οὐδ' ἄλλως ἀφυὴς γενόμενος πρὸς τὰ ἐκ φιλοσοφίας
ἀγαθὰ συνέλαβον τῇ φύσει ὡς μάλιστα ἐνῆν, καὶ νεανίας γενόμενος
40 οὐκ ἀρχὰς οὐδὲ φιλοτιμίας εἱλόμην, ἀλλ' εὐθέως θεατὴς ἤρων
γενέσθαι τῆς φύσεως τῶν λόγων. καὶ οὗτός με ὁ ἔρως ἤγαγεν εἰς
Ἀθήνας καὶ Πλάτωνι ἐποίησε φίλον, καὶ μέχρι γε νῦν οὔπω αὐτοῦ
πέπλησμαι. 5. φύσεως μὲν οὖν οὕτως ἔσχον πρὸς ἡσυχίαν, ὡς
ἔτι παντελῶς νέος ὢν καταφρονῆσαι πάντων ὅσα ἄρχειν
45 ταρακτικωτέρου βίου δύναται, ἐλθὼν δ' εἰς Ἀθήνας οὔτ'
ἐκυνηγέτουν, οὐδὲ ναύτης εἰς Ἑλλήσποντον ἐπὶ Λακεδαιμονίους σὺν
Ἀθηναίοις ἔπλεον, οὐδὲ ταῦτα ἐπαιδευόμην, ἀφ' ὧν τυράννοις καὶ
βασιλεῦσιν ἐχθρὸς ἔσομαι, ἀλλ' ἀνδρὶ ἡσυχίας ἐραστῇ διελεγόμην,
τὸν ἔγγιστα θεῷ λόγον παιδευόμενος. καί μοι πρῶτόν τι ὑπ' αὐτοῦ
50 παρηγγέλθη ἡσυχίαν ποθεῖν· ταύτην γὰρ τοῦ κατὰ φιλοσοφίαν λόγου
φῶς εἶναι, τὴν δὲ πολιτείαν καὶ πολυπραγμοσύνην ὥσπερ ζόφον
τινὰ ἐπικαλύπτειν καὶ ἀνεύρετον ποιεῖν τοῖς ἐρευνῶσιν. 6. ὡς δ'
οὔτε πεφυκέναι κακὸς ἐδόκουν πρὸς αὐτὴν οὔτε πείθεσθαι ῥᾳδίως
περὶ αὐτῆς, τηνικαῦτα ἤδη θεὸν πάντων ἐπόπτην καὶ κόσμου
55 κατασκευὴν ἐμάνθανον καὶ φύσεως ἀρχὰς ἑώρων καὶ δικαιοσύνην
τιμᾶν ἐδιδασκόμην καὶ ὅσα τοιαῦτ' ἄλλα παιδεύει φιλοσοφία. καὶ
οὐδὲν οὐχ ὅπως τοῦ εἰδέναι ταῦτα ἀλλ' οὐδὲ τοῦ ζητεῖν τιμιώτερον.
τί γὰρ κάλλιον ἢ ἄνθρωπον ὄντα θνητῆς φύσεως καὶ θεοῦ
κεκραμένον μοίρᾳ μόνοις εὐκαιρεῖν τοῖς ἀθανάτοις ἑαυτοῦ καὶ ταῦτα
60 πρὸς τὸ συγγενὲς ἄγειν; συγγενῆ δὲ τῷ θείῳ τὰ θεῖα λέγω.
7. Ταῦτα ηὐχόμην τε καὶ ἐσπούδαζον μαθεῖν, πολιτείας δὲ (ἀνέξῃ
γὰρ μετὰ παρρησίας μου λέγοντος) οὐδὲ μεμνῆσθαι ἠξίουν,
ἔμαθον δ' ἄλλα τε πολλὰ καὶ ταῦτα, οἷς νῦν χρήσομαι πρός σε, τὸν
μὲν μὴ ἀδικοῦντα τιμᾶν, τὸν δὲ ἀδικοῦντα ἄριστον μὲν εὐεργεσίαις
65 ἀμύνεσθαι[a], εἰ δὲ μή γε, ἡσυχίᾳ· καὶ φίλον μὲν τιμιώτατον ἡγεῖσθαι,
ἐχθρὸν δὲ μηδένα ἑαυτῷ κατασκευάζειν, ἀλλὰ καὶ τὸν ὄντα φίλον
ποιεῖσθαι, καὶ μηδὲν τηλικοῦτον νομίζειν κακόν, ὅσον ἂν ταράξειε
τὴν ψυχὴν καὶ οἰκείων ἔργων τρέψειε[b] πρὸς ἕτερα. ἆρά γε ἐπιβούλῳ
μοι νομίζεις χρῆσθαι ταῦτα εἰδότι; μηδαμῶς, ἀλλὰ σοὶ μὲν
70 ἀποκείσθω πολέμων ἔργα καὶ πολιτειῶν, ἡμῖν δὲ τῆς σῆς τοσοῦτον
ἀποτετμήσθω τυραννίδος, ὅσον ἀταράχῳ ἀνδρὶ δοκεῖ ἐνησυχάσαι.
πείθομαι δ' ὅτι, ἢν καὶ διαλέγεσθαί με ἀφῇς τοῖς φίλοις, ἠρεμαίους
ἂν αὐτοὺς ποιήσαιμι καὶ ἀπολιτεύτους ὧν σὺ βούλει, διεξιὼν τὰ ἀεὶ

Düring
[a] ἀμύνεσθαι βc: ἀμείβεσθαι αε Ald.   [b] ἀποτρέψειε Ald.

force to bring against you. And you don't reflect that, if I had been aware of being justifiably under suspicion, I would not voluntarily have entrusted myself to the man who suspected me.   **4.** Or am I so keen on hostilities that I do not cherish friendship, but willingly give up my body to those who will rightly punish it? But all this is enough, and more than enough, of a defence even for those not expert in philosophical arguments.

I myself was in any case naturally equipped to benefit from studying philosophy, and I assisted nature as best I could. In my youth I did not crave civic offices or distinctions, but early on I longed to study the natural sciences. This longing took me to Athens and into Plato's circle, and I have still not had my fill of him.   **5.** Indeed I was so naturally inclined to quietude that even as a very young man I scorned everything that would lead to an agitated life. So when I came to Athens I didn't go hunting, nor serve as a sailor with the Athenians to the Hellespont against the Spartans, nor was I indoctrinated to hate tyrants and kings. Instead I conversed with a man who loves tranquillity and I was trained in a thoroughly divine doctrine. The first lesson he taught me was: yearn for tranquillity. For that (he said) lights the way to philosophical enquiry, while public life and being a busybody cover it in darkness and make it hard to find for those who seek it.

6. Since I seemed by nature not unfitted for philosophy, though not readily convinced of its value, that was the time I began to learn about God, who oversees all things, and the structure of the world. I learnt to contemplate the first principles of nature, to honour justice, and all the other lessons of philosophy. And nothing is more worthy not only to know but also to search out. For what is nobler than for a man, whose mortal nature also has a share in the divine, to devote his time solely to the immortal elements of his being, and to bring them close to what they are akin to? By that I mean that his godlike elements are akin to the divine.   **7.** This was what I longed for and tried my best to learn; as for politics—you must excuse my bluntness—I did not even think it worth my attention. But I did learn a lot, including these principles I shall now apply to you: to honour a man who does not act unjustly; ideally to repay one who acts unjustly with kindness,

ἡμῖν μελετώμενα ἡσυχίας[c] ἐγκώμια, ἐπεὶ καὶ τελέως ἂν εἴην μὴ
75 ταῦτα φρονῶν ἀχάριστος.

8. Φέρε γάρ, εἴ μοι ταραττομένῳ τι ὧν σὺ ὑποπτεύεις ἡ πραεῖα
ἐπισταίη θεὸς Ἡσυχία καὶ ταῦτα λέγοι, "Ἀχάριστος εἶ καὶ
πονηρός, ὦ Χίων, καὶ οὔτε τῶν καλῶν ἐκείνων μαθημάτων οὔθ᾽
ὅλως σεαυτοῦ μνήμην ἔχεις. ἐμοὶ χρώμενος δικαιοσύνην ἤσκησας
80 καὶ σωφροσύνην ἐκτήσω καὶ θεὸν ἔμαθες, καὶ τὴν σεαυτοῦ πρὸς
αὐτὸν συγγένειαν ἀνενεώσω καὶ τῶν ταπεινοτέρων τούτων, θαυμασ-
τῶν δὲ τοῖς ἄλλοις κατεφρόνησας, φιλοτιμίας καὶ πλούτου καὶ ὅσα
τούτοις ὅμοια. εἶτα νῦν, ὅτε ἀποδιδόναι σε δεῖ τὴν χάριν μείζονι
ἤδη νόμῳ καὶ κρείττονι ψυχῇ συνόντα μοι καὶ διαλεγόμενον,
85 ἀπολείψεις με οὐδὲ μεμνημένος, ὅτι οὐ τὰ ἄλλα μόνον ἐκ
φιλοσοφίας ἔμαθες, ἀλλὰ καὶ τὸ ζητεῖν δεξιῶς ἃ μήπω οἶδας. καὶ
πῶς ἂν σύ γε ζητήσειας ἢ εὕροις ἐμοῦ στερόμενος;" 9. ταῦτ᾽ εἰ
λέγοι, τί ἂν ἀποκριναίμην πρὸς αὐτὴν δίκαιον; ἐγὼ μὲν γὰρ οὐδὲν
ὁρῶ.

90 Ἀλλὰ μὴν εὖ ἴσθι ὡς ἐγὼ ταῦτα πρὸς ἐμαυτὸν ἀεὶ λέγω (λέγει
γὰρ ἕκαστος πρὸς ἑαυτὸν ἃ φρονεῖ) καὶ οὐκ ἄν ποτε ἀπολειφθείην.
ὥστ᾽ οὐδέν σοι δέος ἐξ ἡμῶν εὔλογον· οὐδὲ γὰρ οὐδ᾽ ἅψεται τῶν
σῶν πραγμάτων ἡ ἐμὴ ἡσυχία.

---

[c] ἡσυχίας βc: φιλοσοφίας αε Ald.

but if that doesn't work, with resignation. Again, to consider a friend your most valuable possession; to make no man your enemy, but if you have one to turn him into a friend; to regard no evil as important enough to agitate your mind and distract you from your proper pursuits towards other ones. Do you really think that with these principles I should be regarded by you as a conspirator? Certainly not. Let the activities of war and politics be your province, and allow me just enough of your sovereignty as befits a man of tranquil nature to lead a quiet life. If you will let me talk to my friends I believe I can calm them down, and make them desist from the public activities you wish them to give up, by offering them the panegyric on tranquillity which I am always rehearsing to myself. If I had any other idea I should be utterly ungrateful to you.

8. Come then: suppose I were disturbed in some such way as you suspect, and the gentle goddess Tranquillity stood beside me and said, 'Chion, you are ungrateful and wicked, and you have forgotten those fine lessons and indeed yourself. With my help you practised justice, acquired temperance, learnt to understand God, and renewed your kinship with him. You despised ambition, wealth, and the like—those baser things that others admire. And now, when you should be giving your thanks by remaining my pupil and associate under a higher law and with a superior spirit, you are going to abandon me, not even remembering that among the lessons philosophy taught you is to seek with skill what you do not yet know. And how can you seek or find that without my help?' If she were to say that, what could I honestly reply? **9.** I can see nothing.

Let me assure you that I am always putting these thoughts to myself—everyone says what he thinks to himself—and I shall never fall short of them. You have no good reason to fear me, for never will my tranquillity meddle with your affairs.

COMMENTARY

AELIAN 5

Baiton bitterly regrets the loss of his bees.

Bee-keeping was of course an important part of ancient food-economy, and there are many references to it in both technical works and literature. Aristotle is an important scientific source (*GA* 3. 10, and *HA* 5. 21–3, 9. 40), and Aelian himself has many allusions to bees in his work on animals (e.g. *NA* 1. 9–11, 5. 10–13). For a detailed modern discussion see Davies and Kathirithamby, *Greek Insects* (London, 1986), 47–79. We should remember too that one of the peaks of Latin literature, Virgil's fourth *Georgic*, is devoted to bees, with its famous double inserts of the stories of Aristaeus and of Orpheus and Eurydice. We meet another enthusiastic bee-keeper in Alciphron 2. 20, and [Quint.] *Decl. Maiores* 13 records a dispute between a poor bee-keeper and a rich neighbour who has poisoned his bees.

Note that Baiton regards his bees collectively as female (and μέλισσα, like the Latin *apis*, is feminine), though, apart from the 'king' bee, which we now know to be a 'queen', we learn from Aristotle (*HA* 5. 21) that the drones were known to be male and the others female.

4 πανδαισίᾳ: a feast offering every type of food—the wealth of flowers in the meadow.

6 ὠδῖνος: ὠδίς is literally the product of birth-pangs, a child, but it has extended meanings and is used of honey also by Nonnus, *D.* 5. 228.

7 Ἀρισταῖον: Aristaeus, son of Apollo and the water-nymph Cyrene, was a mythical hero and cult figure associated with various aspects of country life. Virgil seems to have invented the story (*G.* 4. 315 ff.) that credited Aristaeus with discovering how to generate a new swarm of bees from the carcase of a bull.

9 περὶ αὐτά: it is difficult to make sense of this phrase and it may be corrupt: perhaps we should read περίλυπα, 'grief-stricken'. The flowers have lost the bees that used to visit them.

14 ἀνιχνεῦσαι: interestingly Aristotle (*HA* 624ᵃ28) uses the same verb of wandering bees 'tracking down' their king by his scent.

15 καὶ τοῦτο: difficult to punctuate, but it seems to refer back to and to emphasize the previous words τίς... ὑπεδέξατο. This use of οὗτος, used resumptively but without special emphasis, is noted as a mannerism of Aelian by Schmid, *Der Atticismus*, iii. 65.

15–16 ἔχει...μηδὲν προσηκούσας: in fact a new colony of swarming bees, if sufficiently far from the original hive, could legally become the property of someone else: see Mynors on Virg. *G.* 4. 61, quoting Gaius in the *Digest* 41. 1. 5. 4.

AELIAN 13

Callipides appeals to his neighbour to stop his outrageous behaviour.

This and the following letter are the first of two pairs (Letters 13–16) of exchanges between the same writers, in which Callipides utterly fails to make any impression on his crusty neighbour.

A bad neighbour is a pest, as Hesiod put it (*Op.* 346 πῆμα κακὸς γείτων), and Cnemon is the type of the bad-tempered boor familiar to us from Mime and Greek and Roman Comedy. In particular, he recalls the δύσκολος in Menander's play of that name, who looks after his wild pears and throws a clod at an intruder (*Dysk.* 101, 110–11). The archetypal misanthrope was Timon of Athens, immortalized in Lucian's dialogue (25) and Shakespeare's play—and he also turns up in Alciphron 2. 32 (another letter from a farmer).

2 τοῖς τῆς γῆς: the text is uncertain, but with this reading these words go together ('to country matters') after τὸ ἄγειν σχολὴν (= σχολάζειν).

4 βάλλεις...βώλοις: like Menander's δύσκολος, and as we are told Timon does in Alciphron 2. 32.

6 ἁλμυρὸν γειτόνημα: the phrase proverbially refers to the sea, which is said to be an undersirable neighbour: see Alcman, fr. 116; Plato, *Lg.* 705a; Leutsch–Schneidewin, ii. 271–2.

AELIAN 14

Cnemon rudely rejects his neighbour's advice.

For Cnemon as the type of the μισάνθρωπος see introduction to Letter 13.

2 κεκέρδαγκα: irregular perfect of κερδαίνω.

4 Σκυθῶν: the Scythians were traditionally (λεγομένη) regarded as a rough, harsh people. We should also recall the Scythians' riddling reply to Darius, reported by Herodotus (4. 131).

7 Περσέα: the mythical hero with winged shoes, who cut off the head of the Gorgon Medusa and thereafter used it to turn his enemies to stone.

9 εὖ μάλα: the words strongly emphasize ἐκείνου ('well-known').

12 τί... μαθών: (also below) lit. 'having learnt what?', 'with what idea?': commonly used in an ironical or exasperated tone when faced with something inexplicable.

14–15 ἀργὸν εἴασα... χῆρόν ἐστι καρπῶν: Cnemon is afraid that passers-by would raid his produce: also he avoids being near the road in case he meets someone. (For this crusty attitude cf. Libanius, *Decl.* 27. 5.) In the same spirit of distrust he goes on to imply that Callipides need not hope to gain any advantage by claiming to be a friend or kinsman.

AELIAN 19

Mormias is thoroughly disgusted at being deceived over his son's choice of a wife.

The situation seems to be that Mormias has been duped by his son about the nature of the new wife he is bringing home, who turns out to be an ex-music-girl whom his son has bought out of slavery.

1 χρυσοῦς: occasionally used in an ironically derogatory sense, like English 'fine' and 'precious': cf. Lucian, *Laps.* 1.

2 οὐδὲν δέον: the 'accusative absolute' construction ('there being no need'), used like the genitive absolute, but mainly confined to the neuter singular of participles of impersonal verbs.

2 ἔνδον καὶ... ἔξω θεοὺς: the gods of the household (like Hestia and Zeus Herkeios) and more public gods, in this case perhaps those associated with the countryside (like Demeter).

6 φάτταν ἀντὶ περιστερᾶς: a proverbial expression for getting the worse of two alternatives: so too Plato, *Tht.* 199b5.

11 ἐς κόρακας: lit. '(go and be food) for the crows': a very common imprecation, much like the English 'go to the devil'. ἀποκηρύσσειν is literally 'to sell by public auction', and then more generally 'to banish', 'renounce'.

12–13 ταφρεύῃ καὶ βωλοκοπῇ: these jobs typify the essential, if humdrum, routine of running a farm, and the son cannot expect to avoid them.

AELIAN 20

The countryside is beautiful—and countrymen are not stupid.

We find praise of the country in comparison with the city from Virgil (*G.* 2. 458–74) to Libanius (8. 353 ff. Foerster)—who is particularly relevant to our letter as he includes praise of rural σωφροσύνη, and criticizes urban σοφία for just producing clever speakers.

This is the last letter in Aelian's collection, and it is in a sense a delayed programmatic statement, winding up the series with a paean on the countryside which has been the setting of the preceding letters. It ends appropriately with a sort of authorial σφραγίς, or seal, where the Roman Aelian masquerades as an Athenian farmer, the pose he has adopted throughout the letters.

4 θεοὶ ... ἡ γῆ ...: this reflects the immemorial myths of sky mating with earth, or rain from heaven impregnating the ground, whereby mother earth produces and nurtures all growing things. For the importance of the earth as mother in ancient scientific and biological thinking see e.g. Lucretius 5. 793 ff. (with my notes thereto).

4 αὕτη: translated 'also', like *eadem*: a Latinism would be natural to Aelian (see Schmid, *Der Atticismus*, iii. 66).

5 δικαιοσύνη καὶ σωφροσύνη: the rustic farmer shows that he knows the importance of these key terms in Greek ethical thinking. (See also below, Chion 16.77 n.) He goes on to claim that country wisdom is of the strong silent type, and not garnished with sophistic tricks of rhetoric. (Cf. Libanius loc. cit. above.)

10 χορηγίαν: originally the resources required to pay for a public chorus, and then more generally 'supplies', 'means'.

11 οὔτε Λίβυες οὔτε Λυδοί: these may be named simply as types of remote and unsophisticated rustics, but there could be an allusion to the proverbial saying Λυδοὶ πονηροί, δεύτεροι δ' Αἰγύπτιοι, τρίτοι δὲ πάντων Κᾶρες ἐξωλέστατοι (Leutsch–Schneidewin i. 274, ii. 514).

ALCIPHRON 1.1

A fine catch of fish after a prolonged storm.

This is a vivid little vignette of fishing life, set at Phalerum on the Attic coast. A violent storm drives a group of fishermen to shelter on the beach; afterwards they make a huge catch of fish (apparently driven near the shore by the storm), and dispose of most of it to fish-mongers waiting for them on their return.

1 τὸ τήμερον εἶναι: an equivalent to the simple τήμερον, as at Plato, *Crat.* 396e.

2 ὡς γὰρ...: the long ὡς construction continues down to ἐρρήγνυτο, followed by the main clause ἀεργία ... ἦν.

4 ἀφρὸς ἐξηνθήκει: a vivid metaphor, picturing the foam as white flowers on the sea's surface: cf. Eur. *IT* 300 ὡς αἱματηρὸν πέλαγος ἐξανθεῖν ἁλός.

10 ἀλκυονίς: adjective from ἀλκυών. The halcyon was a semi-mythical bird, usually identified with the kingfisher, and 'halcyon days' were supposedly a few days of calm around the winter solstice when the bird could nest on the sea: Arist. *HA* 542^{b}4 ff. The problems concerning the bird's identity and the legend about it are notorious: for discussions see D'Arcy Thompson, *A Glossary of Greek Birds*, 46–51; Dunbar on Aristoph. *Av.* 250–1, 1591–5.

15 χαλάσαντες: sc. τὰ δίκτυα.

16 εὐοψίας: a rare word, also used of a good catch of fish at Alc. 1. 13. The genitive is exclamatory, often with an interjection like φεῦ here: cf. Philostratus 12.

18 ἀσίλλας: yokes or poles balanced over the shoulders: a very rare word, but a likely conjecture of Hemsterhuys for meaningless manuscript readings.

19 ὑπὲρ αὐτῶν: in payment 'for them', i.e. the fish: ὑπέρ is used in later Greek in the sense of payment 'on account of' (LSJ s.v. A II 4).

20 ἄστυδε: i.e. to Athens. Phalerum remained a port of Athens even after Peiraeus became the main one.

ALCIPHRON 1.4

A plea from a husband to his discontented wife to choose between his fisherman's life and the risky delights of the city.

We have here a variation on the familiar contrast between the simplicities of country life and the sophistications of the city. (For a similar complaint from a farmer husband see below, 2. 8.) It is a recurrent element in pastoral, e.g. the first Eclogue of Virgil and the seventh of Calpurnius Siculus, and it appears perhaps most famously and attractively in the fable of the town mouse and the country mouse in Horace, *Sat.* 2. 6. 79. ff. The city might produce simply a culture shock for the visiting rustic, as in Calpurnius, or it could be positively dangerous for a woman (see below 14 n.).

7 τὰ νήματα τοῦ λίνου: used for mending her husband's nets—an appropriate occupation for a fisherman's wife.

8 Ὠσχοφόρια ... Λήναια: these were both Athenian festivals of Dionysus, the names being derived respectively from ὠσχός, a vine-shoot covered with grapes, and λήνη, a maenad, or ληνός, a wine-vat. The chief rite in the autumn Oschophoria was a procession, led by two young men of noble birth dressed as women and carrying ὠσχοί, from the temple of Dionysus to that of Athena Skiras at Phalerum. The Lenaea was a winter festival, the main interest of which was the dramatic performances there, mainly of comedy.

11 μνεῖσθαι ... γάμῳ: for this metaphorical use of the verb see Plato, *Symp.* 209e τὰ ἐρωτικὰ ... μυηθείης.

14 ἀπατηλῶν θεαμάτων: in literature, as no doubt in life, attendance at theatrical and other shows was regarded as potentially dangerous for unescorted women. Undesirable liaisons and even rapes at such assemblies feature in New Comedy, e.g. Menander's *Epitrepontes*. The theme is also brilliantly exploited by Ovid in his *Ars Amatoria* 1. 89 ff. (the theatre is an obvious place for a man to go to pick up a girl); and Tacitus comments on the licentious behaviour, imported from Greece, at theatres in Neronian Rome (*Ann.* 14. 20).

ALCIPHRON 1. 11

This is the first of a pair of connected letters. Here a fisherman's daughter tells her mother that she cannot take the man her father intends for her husband, as she is totally smitten with another man she saw at a festival in Athens. In the reply (Alc. 1. 12) her mother tells her bluntly that she must abandon these mad thoughts or her father will throw her to the sharks.

The scene again is set on the Attic coast, near Athens: notice ἄστυδε and the reference to Peiraeus.

2 Μηθυμναίῳ: Methymna was after Mytilene the most important city in Lesbos. (It does not seem significant that allusions to Lesbos frame the letter.)

3 ἀστικὸν: the word suggests sophistication and urbane charm, with an implied contrast to the nautical suitor favoured by Glaucippe's father.

4 τὸν ὠσχοφόρον: for the Oschophoria see above, on 1. 4. The young man was conspicuous as playing a leading role in the festival.

6 βρύων: βρύον is used of various kinds of moss, seaweed, and lichen, but a fisherman's daughter would think naturally of seaweed for a comparison. It is usually identified as the type called oyster-green or sea-lettuce.

6 μειδιᾷ ... χαριέστερον: for the imagery cf. Meleager, *Anth. Pal.* 5. 156 ἁ φίλερως χαροποῖς Ἀσκληπιὰς οἷα γαλήνης/ὄμμασι συμπείθει πάντας ἐρωτοπλοεῖν. But there may be irony here, as the smiling of a quiet sea was an image of treachery: see Nisbet–Hubbard on Hor. *C.* 1. 5. 13.

8–9 τὸ ... πρόσωπον: the phrase does not fit strictly into the syntax of the sentence. The girl simply highlights her beloved's features, which she then describes in a loosely attached sentence.

9 τὰς Χάριτας: for the Graces see note on Philostratus 51.

9–10 ἐνορχεῖσθαι ...᾿ Ὀρχομενὸν: an obvious pun, which we find also in a fragment of the 3rd-cent. BC epic poet Euphorion: Ὀρχομενὸν Χαρίτεσσιν ἀφαρέσιν ὀρχηθέντα (fr. 87). The old Boeotian city Orchomenus had a temple to the Graces (Strabo 9. 2. 40).

10 τῆς Ἀργαφίας κρήνης: there is very little evidence for this Boeotian spring, and there may be a confusion in spelling with another one there, Gargaphia. See the entry in the *Etymologicum Magnum*, which also records a verse that seems to lie behind our text: νιψάμεναι κρήναις ἔδραμον Ἀργαφίης.

11 τὰ ῥόδα: for roses and Aphrodite see below, note on Philostratus 20.

11 τὼ χείλη ... διήνθισται ... ἐπιθέμενος: literally 'as to his lips he is adorned with flowers, having put them (the roses) on the tips (of his lips)'—τὼ χείλη being accusative of respect.

13 Σαπφὼ: the story that Sappho leapt to her death from the Leucadian promontory for love of Phaon was probably a Hellenistic invention. For references to it see Menander fr. 258 Körte, [Ovid] *Ep. Sapph.* 171 ff. Leucas or Leucadia is an island in the Ionian Sea, off the coast of Acarnania.

ALCIPHRON 1. 15

Some rich Athenian youths and their girl friends hire a fishing-boat for a party, and to see how the other half lives by joining in the fishing. Their luxurious life-style is an eye-opener for the fisherman, but he takes his money and is content.

15 φερομένων: the sentence rambles. Understand ἡμῶν with φερομένων, which is followed by a long parenthesis listing the passengers, οὐ μόνος … ἐπεκρότει, and then the main clauses ἐγένετο … καὶ ἦν. Within the parenthesis understand παρῆν or the like with Πάμφιλος.

16 γυναίων: from γύναιον, a by-form of γυνή.

17 Κρουμάτιον …: the musicians all have significant names. Kroumation, 'Musical Note' (κροῦμα—properly the note produced by striking (κρούειν) a stringed instrument, but applied also to wind instruments). Erato, 'Lovely' (ἐρατός), also the name of a Muse. Euepis, 'Melodious' (εὐεπής).

21 ὀλίγοι, Γλαυκίας: both subjects of ἦν … βασκαίνων, which agrees in number with the nearer Γλαυκίας. In this kind of periphrastic construction (εἰμί with present participle) the participle is virtually an adjective (Weir Smyth, §§ 1857, 1961).

22 Τελχῖνος: the Telchines were a semi-divine race, mainly associated with Rhodes. They were known chiefly as metal-workers, who were skilled in magic and also malicious sorcerers: hence Callimachus calls his spiteful literary detractors Telchines (*Aetia* prol. fr. 1).

24 διέχει: διαχεῖν ('scatter', 'disperse') is metaphorical here: 'relax', 'cheer'.

24 ἀγαπῶ: the verb has here its more diluted sense 'tolerate', 'be content with'.

ALCIPHRON 2. 2

Iophon tells his neighbour how he was woken by a cock's crowing from a marvellously happy dream. But the dream would have been deceptive anyway.

It is difficult to see the point of the name Iophon: 'Venomous' (from ἰός) or 'Violet-man' (from ἴον). Neither this nor Eraston seems to be a typical farmer's name. (Sophocles had a son called Iophon, but that seems irrelevant.)

Alciphron's resemblance to Lucian is nowhere more obvious than in this letter, which has striking similarities to Lucian's *Gallus*, esp. sects. 1 and 12. (On the general relationship between the two writers see Introduction, xvi.)

1 ἐπιτριβείη: literally 'may he be crushed *or* rubbed out'): a fairly common expletive, as in Lucian, *Gallus* 1, Aristoph. *Av.* 1530, *Th.* 557. The farmer makes up in energy of diction what he lacks in variety—κακὸς κακῶς ... κάκιστος.

8 Γρυλλίωνα ... Παταικίωνα: both these characters appear elsewhere. Gryllion ('Piglet') is a parasite referred to in Athenaeus (6. 244 F); and Pataecion a notorious robber: Aeschines, *Ctes.* 189, Plut. *De audiendis poetis* 21 F.

9–10 ὁ δῆμος ... στρατηγόν: Iophon dreams that the general assembly of Athenian citizens (*ekklesia*), meeting in the theatre of Dionysus, were electing him general, i.e. one of the annually elected *strategoi* (political as well as military leaders). The voting was done by a show of hands (χειροτονία).

12 ἐνθύμιον ποιησάμενος: this periphrasis (= ἐνθυμεῖσθαι) often suggests having a worrying or anxious thought: see the citations in LSJ s.v. ἐνθύμιος.

12–13 τοὺς φυλλοχόους ...: this strange idea is discussed in Plut. *Quaest. Conv.* 8. 10. 734D ff.: the reason given by those who support the theory is that the type of food and drink we consume in autumn makes our dreams untrustworthy.

ALCIPHRON 2. 8

A farmer complains that his wife is no longer interested in her family or in country life, but has fallen under the spell of the city and the sophisticated women there.

This letter reminds us of the fisherman's similar complaint in 1. 4 above. There are links too with Comedy and the Novel. In Aristophanes' *Clouds* 41 ff. Strepsiades laments the problems he had as a rustic married to a city girl; and in Longus (4. 27) Daphnis, like the wife here, is accused of forsaking the nymphs.

2 ὅλη... ἄστεος: cf. below, 2. 9 ὅλαι τοῦ μέλους, and Plut. *Arat*. 48. 3 ὅλος ἦν ἐκείνου: the genitive is unusual with ὅλος, but is clearly a type of the common genitive expressing fulness: Chronium is entirely taken up with the city.

2–3 Πανὶ... Νύμφαις: the farmer's point is that his wife is spurning the simple country deities in favour of other more sophisticated ones, with sexual and erotic associations. The three groups of nymphs are characterized as those who look after flocks (Epimelides), tree nymphs (Dryads), and river nymphs (Naiads). Colias is a cult title for Aphrodite, after Cape Colias on the Bay of Phalerum, where she had a shrine (Pausanias 1. 1. 5). The Genetyllides were birth goddesses who are regularly associated with Aphrodite Colias: Paus. loc. cit.; [Lucian] *Am*. 42; Aristoph. *Nu*. 52 (see Dover's note on the variations between singular and plural in these cult-names); *Lys*. 2. The farmer's despairing remark that he cannot even remember the names of his wife's new deities recalls the similar complaint in [Lucian] *Am*. 42.

7 ἀπώλισθέ: (Hemsterhuys' conjecture for ἀπολεῖσθαί): aorist of ἀπολισθάνειν.

9 ἀστικαῖς: (Ruhnken for ἀττικαῖς): if right this is used just as in 1. 11 (see note there).

10–11 φύκει, παιδέρωτι: both were kinds of rouge or face paint used by Greek women (cf. Alc. 4. 6). Along with the white lead (ψιμύθιον) they would procure the desired proportions of a 'pink and white' complexion. For further details on φῦκος see Gow on Theoc. 15. 16. There is a similar warning to a wife against using ψιμύθιον in Xen. *Oec*. 10. 2 ff.

ALCIPHRON 2. 9

A goatherd charms his goats by his pipe-playing, and thus fancies himself to be a second Orpheus.

The imagined names of the correspondents conjure up the world of early Greek poetry and music. Pratinas of Phlius (6th/5th cent.) was a celebrated lyric and dramatic poet and a distinguished musician. Epigonus of Sicyon (6th cent.) was another talented musician, who was credited with inventing a type of harp named after him (Athen. 4. 183D).

1 σταθερᾶς: in this and similar phrases the word has been explained as meaning either the point at which the sun seems to stand still, or

the time when physical activity generally pauses because of the heat. (See Rowe on Plato, *Phaedr.* 242a).

1 φιλήνεμόν: this very rare adjective is also applied to the pine in Plut. *Quaest. Conv.* 5. 3. 676a (the pine is φιλήνεμος ὥσπερ ἡ θάλασσα). Perhaps something in the way the tree sways in the wind suggested the fancy that the pine loved it.

4 σύριγγα: the syrinx was the pan pipe, the traditional shepherd's pipe: a set of pipes (usually seven) fastened together, and played by blowing across their ends. It is not clear what the player is doing with his tongue—perhaps moistening the ends of the pipes before blowing onto them. μετὰ τῶν χειλέων must mean that his lips funnelled the breath as they moved along the row of pipes.

8 ὅλαι τοῦ μέλους: for the construction see above, note on 2. 8.

9–10 τὸν Ἠδωνὸν ... Καλλιόπης: the goatherd displays his little bit of erudition: this is Orpheus, whose music could charm all nature. He came from Thrace—the Edonians were a Thracian people—and the Muse Calliope was his mother.

ALCIPHRON 2. 15

An invitation to a birthday party—and bring the dog too.

The first of a pair of letters: in the reply (2. 16) Pithacnion accepts on behalf of his wife and children.

1 γενέσια: used in later Greek for γενέθλια. Birthdays seem not to have been greatly observed in Classical Greece; more extensive celebrations came in during the Hellenistic and Roman periods: see *OCD*[3] s.v. 'Birthday'.

1 πανδαισίαν: see Aelian 5 and note.

3 συνέργαστρον: the word does not seem to occur elsewhere, and Reiske suggested σύργαστρον (which is found in the reply 2. 16 and in 3. 27), literally 'belly-trailer', and apparently applied to a day-labourer.

7–8 κορδακίζειν: the κόρδαξ was an indecent dance, associated with Comedy and characteristic of drunken behaviour: Theophr. *Char.* 6. 3: Athen. 14. 631D.

9 κατ᾽ εὐχὰς: 'according to one's wishes', and so 'perfect, ideal': the phrase is commoner in the singular, κατ᾽ εὐχήν.

ALCIPHRON 2. 17

The writer describes a mind-boggling sleight-of-hand act he saw when he visited a theatre.

The conjurer here was a professional ψηφοπαίκτης, and the cups-and-balls trick seems to have been universal, in the East as well as the West: see *Encyclopaedia Britannica* s.v. 'Conjuring'.

1 καταγαγόντα: without further explanation this presumably means putting the donkey in its stall; but this detail seems unrelated to the main episode of the letter, and Schepers' supplement ἄστυδε gives a plausible link with the writer's visit to the theatre.

5 ἀχανὴς: we have the choice of two opposing meanings of ἀχανὴς: 'not opening the mouth', i.e. dumb with astonishment and strengthening ἄναυδος; or 'wide-mouthed', i.e. gawping but mute.

5 σοι: translated 'let me tell you': the so-called ethic dative, used 'to secure the interest of the person spoken to', Weir Smyth § 1486.

12–13 τὴν ... τὴν ... τὴν ...: surprising, as the words refer to the neuter λιθίδια: we can either emend with Hirschig to τὸ ... τὸ ... τὸ ... or assume that Alciphron has jumped mentally from λιθίδια to λιθάδας (from feminine λιθάς).

15 Εὐρυβάτην: Eurybates or Eurybatos was a proverbial rogue, sometimes associated with the Cercopes, a race of mischievous gnomes from Oechalia in Euboea. For the confusing tradition about him see *RE* 6. 1319 s.v. 'Eurybatos' (2).

ALCIPHRON 2. 36

The writer bought a slave in high hopes of having made a good purchase, and the man turns out to be a dead loss. What to do?

Assessing a good slave for purchase was clearly a tricky business, as in buying farm animals at market. There is another complaint about an over-sleeping servant in Alc. 2. 18.

The addressee's name must be intended to recall the Pasion who was the richest Athenian banker of his time (he died in 370 BC): the *OCD* entry gives details about him.

2 Νουμήνιον: he is named after the first day of the month, νουμηνία (new moon). This was a regular market day (cf. Aristoph. *Equ.*

43–4, *Vesp.* 169–71), but there were clearly activities like inspection and bargaining on the previous day (ἔνῃ καὶ νέᾳ) as well.

4 ἐπὶ τῆς ἐσχατιᾶς: literally 'on the edge *or* border', used in Attic geography of an estate which is either up-country or by the coast, depending on the speaker's viewpoint. Here we are starting in Athens, and so moving inland. Also in Alc. 2. 32 καταλαβὼν γὰρ τὴν ἐσχατιάν.

5 λαμπρὰ ζημία: similarly in 2. 18 the somnolent labourer is a ζημία καθαρά ('pure loss').

7 Ἐπιμενίδην: an early teacher and cosmogonist of very uncertain date (*c.*600 or *c.*500 BC), to whom miraculous anecdotes were attached. He was the proverbial Rip Van Winkle of antiquity, because he was alleged to have fallen asleep for fifty-seven years (Diog. Laert. 1. 109). For a similar allusion see Lucian, *Timon* 6 ὑπὲρ τὸν Ἐπιμενίδην γὰρ κεκοίμησαι.

7–8 τὴν Ἡρακλέους τριέσπερον: according to the well-known story, Hercules was conceived during a miraculously prolonged night when Zeus slept with Alcmene. The legend is the theme of Plautus' *Amphitruo*, and it is widely referred to.

ALCIPHRON 2. 38

The writer complains bitterly that his son has become a drop-out through association with the Cynics, and he has no more use for farm-life or even his parents.

With their sturdy anti-social independence the Cynics had always been regarded with a mixture of wariness and disfavour, though their moral austerity was frequently praised. There was a revival of the movement during the 1st cent. AD, which led to large numbers of rather more disreputable Cynic beggar philosophers wandering around both Rome and the Greek East. There were of course civilized and intelligent men in the imperial period who were still sympathetic to Cynic views, like the distinguished orator Dio Chrysostom. But Dio himself gives a cuttingly critical account (32. 9) of the Cynic beggar philosophers; and other writers, notably Lucian, are full of jeers at them, sometimes contrasting true Cynics with these depraved specimens of the sect. Lucian never tires of hitting them hard: see e.g. *Vit. Auct.* 10–11, *Fug.* 16, *Pisc.* 44–5, *Symp.* 12 ff. Alciphron's description here is the routine picture of the untidy, dirty figure in a tattered cloak, carrying pouch and stick—an offence to civilized society.

1 ἀποδόσθαι: the infinitive of purpose is uncommon in prose after πέμπειν and its compounds: see Weir Smyth § 2009, citing Thuc. 6. 50.

2 τὴν αὐτὴν: sc. ἡμέραν.

5 κύνας: the nickname ὁ κύων ('dog') was applied first to the founder of the sect himself, Diogenes of Sinope.

6 ἔστιν ἰδεῖν θέαμα...: the syntax is loose, with ἀνασείων and the subsequent participles and adjectives attached in free apposition to θέαμα and no further main verb in the sentence.

11 φύσει λέγων γεγονέναι...: the theory here outlined is remarkably similar in phraseology to one of the letters attributed to Diogenes: γονεῦσι χάριτας οὐχ ἑκτέον οὔτε τοῦ γενέσθαι, ἐπεὶ φύσει γέγονε τὰ ὄντα, οὔτε τῆς ποιότητος· ἡ γὰρ τῶν στοιχείων σύγκρασις αἰτία ταύτης (*Ep.*21)]. Of course these late spurious letters are no sure guide to Diogenes' own theories, but Alciphron may be following a general Cynic tradition.

14 τὴν αἰδῶ... ἀπέξυσται: a striking phrase which probably derives from Diogenes' own advice in Lucian, *Vit. Auct.* 10 τὸ ἐρυθριᾶν ἀπόξυσον τοῦ προσώπου παντελῶς. Very similar is *Alc.* 1. 12: ἀπέξεσας τὴν αἰδῶ τοῦ προσώπου.

15 ὦ γεωργία: the abstract Farming must be addressed as representing the deluded young farmer. (Hercher's ὦ γεωργέ gives the address to the son himself. Or was the son's name Γεωργίας?)

15 φροντιστήριον: a clear allusion to Socrates' 'thinking-shop of wise souls' in Aristoph. *Nu.* 94—but here the wise souls have become cheats and deceivers.

16 Σόλωνι, Δράκοντι: Solon (early 6th cent.) and Draco (late 7th cent.) were the two most famous Athenian lawgivers. Little is known with certainty about Draco, but since Solon repealed all his laws except those concerning homicide, Alciphron is obviously suspect in coupling them in this way.

18 ἀνδραποδίζοντας ἀπὸ τοῦ φρονεῖν: a condensed expression, meaning that they snatch young men out of their senses and make slaves of them.

ALCIPHRON 3. 2

The writer relays an invitation for dinner to a courtesan and nearly gets scalded with boiling water for his pains.

The writer's name here reflects the parasite's character: he is the man who is in a hurry to get to the dinner-hour.

In this anecdote the *hetaira* shares the spotlight with the parasite, and both types, of course, had designs on the well-to-do. Other courtesans from the Cerameicus appear in Alc. 3. 12 and below, 3. 28, and the area had the reputation for dissolute living (2. 22).

1 ὁ Ἐτεοβουτάδης: the Eteoboutadai were an aristocratic family: they had the distinction that the priestess of Athena Polias was always chosen from among them (Aeschin. 2. 147).

4 Ἀηδόνιον: 'Little Nightingale' (ἀηδών): her musical talents would add to her attractions as a guest.

6 Λεωκορίου: the Leocorium was a sanctuary in the Cerameicus area of Athens. The name was derived from the daughters of a mythical Attic king Leos, who were sacrificed to ensure the preservation of the city (Aelian, *VH* 12. 28).

7 Μενδησίου: in spite of the form of the adjective (which should mean from Mendes in the Nile delta), this must refer to Mendaean wine (properly Μενδαῖος), from the town of Mende in Chalcidice, which was highly rated (Athen. 1. 29D–E).

9 ἐδέησα: here (and below ἐδέησε) the verb is used without a genitive like ὀλίγου or μικροῦ, which is more frequently found in this idiom.

13 τοῦ ὕδατος: 'some of the water': a type of the partitive genitive.

15 ἡδονῶν: the writer means, so much for my hopes of pleasurable company at dinner.

ALCIPHRON 3. 11

A thieving parasite has a narrow escape, and plans a new life-style with his ill-gotten gains.

1 κερδῷε, ἀλεξίκακε: both are common titles of gods, κερδῷος being specially applicable to Hermes, the god of gain and lucky finds. Here the two gods are given thanks, one for help with the theft and the other for help in avoiding the dogs.

3 δρόμῳ δοὺς φέρεσθαι: in this and similar constructions δίδωμι is intransitive, 'give oneself up to': LSJ s.v. V.

5-6 *Μολοττοὶ καὶ Κνώσιοι:* two famous breeds of dog in antiquity. Both were hunting-dogs, and the Molossians were also used as watchdogs and sheepdogs. They are widely referred to: for Molossians see Arist. *HA* 608ᵃ26; Grattius, *Cyn.* 181; Nemesianus, *Cyn* . 107; for Cretan dogs see Oppian, *Cyn.* 1. 373, *Hal.* 4. 273; Xen. *Cyn* . 10. 1. The two breeds are linked also at Sen. *Phae.* 32–3.

6 *Ἄρτεμιν:* a reference to the story of Actaeon, who was torn apart by his own dogs as a punishment for seeing Artemis bathing (Ovid, *Met.* 3. 138 ff.).

13 *τὰ πρυμνήσια:* the stern-cables of a boat, which were loosened (*λύειν*) for departure.

18-19 *κύων ... ἐπιλήσεται:* a proverbial saying found also in Lucian, *Ind.* 25. It seems to mean that a dog if flayed would chew even its own skin: Leutsch–Schneidewin, ii. 643.

ALCIPHRON 3. 17

Another thieving parasite has a nasty fright, but manages to get away with his stolen feast.

Greed is of course the governing characteristic of the parasite in life and in literature, and this letter is in line with writers of New Comedy and satirists in portraying the type who will lie, toady, and even steal to satisfy an insatiable appetite.

The name of the addressee, *Χωνοκράτης,* must pick up a story in Athenaeus (10. 436E) about a heavy drinker, who was nicknamed *Χώνη* ('Funnel') from his habit of putting a funnel in his mouth through which to drink the wine poured into it.

1 *Καρίωνος:* presumably the cook in the household in which the writer is a hanger-on. Carion occurs as a name for a cook in New Comedy, e.g. Menander's *Epitrepontes.*

3-4 *ἀφύας Μεγαρικὰς:* ἀφύας, here translated 'anchovies', is the name for various kinds of small-fry: see D'Arcy Thompson, *A Glossary of Greek Fishes* (Oxford, 1895), 21 ff. Plutarch gives us the alleged origin of the Megarian variety: Poseidon sent them to the Megarians as a favour to the philosopher Stilpo (*De profectibus in virtute* 83C–D).

5-6 *τὴν Ποικίλην:* sc. *Στοάν:* the public hall at Athens which gave its name to the Stoic school because Zeno had taught there. Alciphron has another uncomplimentary reference to 'barefoot, cadaverous' Stoic philosophers at 1. 3.

8 τηλίας: the word is used of a gaming-table in general, and more particularly of a stage on which cock-fighting took place.

10 Ἀποτροπαίοις: sc. θεοῖς. The epithet, meaning much the same as ἀλεξίκακος (above, 3. 11), is often applied to Apollo, but also as here to gods unspecified.

11 νέφος: used just like the English 'cloud' of something gloomy or ominous.

11–12 χόνδρους ... λιβανώτου ... εὖ μάλα εὐρωτιῶντας: the identical phrase appears in Alc. 2. 33 (a poor man's contribution to a sacrifice) and in Lucian, *Jup. Trag.* 15 (a stingy man's offering). Frankincense was produced by burning small lumps or grains of the gum of the λίβανος tree; but as the Lucian passage explains, mouldy grains would be quenched at once without providing any smoke to smell. So our parasite is not offering much to his averting deities. Scavenging from the remains of sacrificial offerings was a common activity of the mean and the hungry.

15 χάρισμα: the word usually has the meaning of divine grace or favour, but a general sense of 'gift', 'favour' is occasionally found in late Greek: see Arndt–Gingrich s.v. Alciphron may of course be using the word humorously in its usual sense: the innkeeper is divinely favoured with a pot and a plate.

16 ἐπιεικής, δεξιὸς: decent to the innkeeper, and clever in his successful theft.

ALCIPHRON 3. 23

A truly horrific dream: can the experts say what it means?

Dreams and their interpretation were taken very seriously in the Greek and Roman world from the earliest times: they were part of the general practice of divination which played an important part in people's lives, and there were professional interpreters to be consulted on the meaning of dreams. Aristotle discussed the theory of dream interpretation in his short treatise *De Divinatione per Somnia*; and from the Hellenistic period onward we find practical handbooks of interpretation, like the surviving treatise *Onirocritica* of Artemidorus (late 2nd cent. AD). Whether or not this dream was really experienced, the reaction described must have been a common one—I must find out what it portends.

The answer from Artemidorus (2. 20: pp. 135–6 Pack) would be that it is a good thing for a poor man to be carried by an eagle.

A journey to heaven (2. 68: p. 192) may indicate acceptance in a rich household, or a trip to Italy—or death (4. 72: pp. 293–4). Vultures (p. 136) are bad omens for most people. Perhaps the point here is that the parasite is to have some great hopes suddenly dashed.

The letter shows an interesting literary lineage. In [Theoc.] *Id.* 21 one fisherman consults another about a frustrating dream he has had about catching a fine fish; while the eagle/vulture which carries the parasite up to heaven recalls Lucian's *Icaromenippus*, where Menippus flies up to heaven with wings of eagle and vulture (*Icar.* 10). For another recitation of a dream see also Herodas 8, with Headlam's note (p. lii) on dreams in Greek literature.

1 τὸ ʼΙακχεῖον: Iacchus was a minor god, sometimes said to be the son of Dionysus and sometimes identified with him. He was also linked with Demeter, and this temple is probably the temple of Demeter in Athens described by Pausanias (1. 2. 4). If there is any significance in the interpreters posting their professional cards here, it might be that they thereby acquired some aura of divine inspiration for their consultations.

7 ἐδόκουν...: the verb governs the whole construction, with its string of infinitives, down to ηὐτρεπισμένον; though from μέλλοντα onwards the dreamer appears in the accusative, a fairly natural transition.

8 περίψηκτος: 'well-groomed' (from ψήχειν): the word seems not to recur, and Schepers followed Bergler in reading περίψυκτος, ('dear', 'beloved'); but that too is extremely rare.

9 Γανυμήδης: a young Trojan, remarkable for his beauty, who was carried off by an eagle to Olympus to become Zeus' cup-bearer and lover: Homer, *Il.* 20. 231 ff.; Virgil, *Aen.*5. 252 ff.

11–12 γαμψώνυχα, ἀγκυλοχείλην: elevated language for his exciting story: both words are epithets of large birds of prey in Homer (*Il.* 16. 428, *Od.* 19. 538, 22. 302).

15 Ὧραι: minor goddesses of the seasons. They were stationed at the gate of Olympus to control entry by moving aside the clouds that formed it: Homer, *Il.* 5. 749–51.

ALCIPHRON 3. 28

The writer exploits a young man's infatuation, and sees his way to getting an attractive wife for himself.

The unflattering picture we have here of the philosopher with double standards—a severe teacher by day and a frequenter of brothels by night—is something of a *topos*: cf. the randy philosopher in 4. 7 below, and Lucian, *Dial. Mort.* 20. 11 (quoted below).

1–2 εἰς φιλοσόφου φοιτᾶν: φοιτᾶν is regularly used of attending a teacher for instruction: LSJ s.v. 5. With φιλοσόφου understand οἶκον, as frequently in this type of phrase.

3 Ποικίλης: see above, 3. 17 and note: another hit at the Stoics.

4 σκινδαλμοὺς: literally 'splinters', 'slivers': used of hair-splitting, logic-chopping argumentation. See Aristoph. *Nu.* 130 (the despairing Strepsiades) λόγων ἀκριβῶν σκινδαλάμους μαθήσομαι; Lucian, *Hes.* 5.

9–10 νύκτωρ... εἰλούμενον: Lucian has a very similar jibe against a philosopher grieving because he cannot νύκτωρ ἐξιὼν ἅπαντας λανθάνων τῷ ἱματίῳ τὴν κεφαλὴν κατειλήσας περίεισιν ἐν κύκλῳ τὰ χαμαιτυπεῖα (*Dial. Mort.* 20. 11).

11 Ἀκαλανθίδος: i.e. Siskin or Goldfinch: another songbird from the Cerameicus, like Aëdonion in Alc. 3. 2.

16 Ἀφροδίτη πάνδημε: in Plato, *Symp.* 180e ff. Ἀφροδίτη Πάνδημος is distinguished from Ἀφροδίτη Οὐράνια as representing physical, sexual love of the body rather than of the soul. We hear from Xenophon (*Symp.* 8. 9) that there were separate altars and sacrifices to each. Our writer is quite clear which Aphrodite is looking after his interests.

18 θεραπεύομαι: the boy realizes that success with Acalanthis depends on bribing Turdosynagus.

21 λυσάμενον: Acalanthis is clearly not a common slave, but she might be under contract to a pimp from whom Turdosynagus has to buy her out. For the same use of λύειν see Aristoph. *Vesp.* 1353.

21–2 τοῦ ζῆν... τοῦ ζῆν: there is a play on two different meanings of the verb, 'make a living' and 'exist'.

ALCIPHRON 4. 7

Thaïs reproaches her lover for preferring to attend lectures on philosophy to enjoying her company.

The letter playfully exploits *topoi* we find elsewhere in similar contexts. The general theme recalls Lucian, *DMeretr.* 10, in which a courtesan complains that her young man's philosophy tutor has forbidden him to visit her any more. Similar too is Aristaenetus 2. 3 (below), where Glycera complains that her rhetorician husband spends his time practising his speeches instead of making love to his wife. In our letter Thaïs also claims that her lover's teacher is no better than he should be (we have had the *topos* of philosophers visiting brothels in disguise in 3. 28 above: see introductory note there); and that anyway courtesans are a better influence on young men than are sophists. This argument too has echoes. In Athenaeus (13. 584A) the influence of courtesans over men is compared to that of philosophers: whereas philosophers teach them sophistic tricks courtesans teach them erotic ones (ἐρωτικὰ σοφίσματα compared with ἐριστικὰ).

2 τὰς ὀφρῦς... ἐπῆρας: a visible expression of pride: cf. a very similar phrase in Lucian, *Am.* 54, and others cited in LSJ s.v. ὀφρῦς I.

3 τὴν Ἀκαδημίαν: Euthydemus is thus a budding Platonist. His name may be intended to recall the sophist who appears in Plato's dialogue of that name, where he cuts a very unflattering figure.

3–4 τὴν δὲ ἡμετέραν... παρέρχῃ: walking past her house is clear evidence that he has rejected his mistress: Myrtale makes the same complaint in Aristaenetus 2. 16.

7 ἐντυχεῖν: the verb is found with this sense in later Greek prose: e.g. 4. 8 below; Plut. *Sol.* 20.

14 διαφέρειν ἑταίρας σοφιστήν: for the argument see introductory note. Thaïs' defence of courtesans includes references to one of the charges against Socrates ('We don't say there are no gods'), and to Democritean physics ('the nature of the atoms'). She goes on to compare two famous pupils of a courtesan and a philosopher respectively: Pericles, who was allegedly much influenced by his mistress Aspasia, and Critias, the associate of Socrates who was afterwards one of the Thirty Tyrants at Athens in 404–3 BC. Critias also appears in a similarly unfavourable comparison in Plutarch (*De Alex. Magni fort.* 328B–C), where the pupils of Plato and Socrates, like Critias, are matched unflatteringly with those of Alexander the Great.

30–1 ἀπὸ Λυκείου: the well-known gymnasium at Athens, made famous as the place where Aristotle taught and which thus gave its name to his philosophical school.

32–3 τέλος τῆς ἡδονῆς... σοφή: Thaïs suitably labels herself an Epicurean in following their ideal of pleasure—though it is un-Epicurean to suggest that the gods have any interest in our life-span.

34 ἔρρωσο: perfect imperative middle of ῥώννυμι: the conventional signing off in Greek letters, with exactly the sense of the Latin *vale* (lit. 'be strong').

ALCIPHRON 4. 8

This is the first of a connected pair of letters. Here a rejected lover complains bitterly of his mistress's treatment of him. In the reply (below, 4. 9) he gets short shrift, and is told he has no chance with her unless he improves his offerings.

Both letters illustrate the long-lasting influence of erotic poetry and certain familiar themes from it. Simalion is the traditional *exclusus amator* of elegy: observe his self-pity, his prediction that the lady's current favourites will in turn soon fall from grace and suffer as he now suffers, his warning to Petale that she risks divine displeasure for her treatment of him, and his threat to kill himself.

2 διαλεγομένων: the verb has here its sense of 'have sexual intercourse' (LSJ s. v. B 5). Cf. next note.

6 ἐντυγχανόντων: for the sense 'lovers' see above, note on 4. 7.

7 Εὐφρονίῳ: Fobes (Loeb edn.) suggests a link with a wine expert of this name mentioned by Pliny (*NH* 14. 19. 24), but it may simply be a suitable type-name for a host, 'Cheerful'.

11–12 μικρὰ ... παραψυχὴ: normally a flower thrown to a lover is a sign of favour, but this was an act of bad temper, and any comfort quickly withered (μαραινόμενον) as the flowers would wither— rather a laboured pun.

18 ἀνιασομένοις: the prediction follows a traditional theme of lyric and elegy, e.g. Horace, *C.* 1. 5. 5–6 (Pyrrha's current lover) 'heu quotiens fidem | mutatosque deos flebit'.

21 μιμήσωμαί...: i.e. I'll kill myself.

ALCIPHRON 4. 9

Petale's reply to the last letter. Your protestations are unconvincing and there is no future for us together unless you can be more generous.

Petale is, like Simalion, a figure with a long literary history: the mercenary courtesan, who is not incapable of affection, but who has to ensure that her business interests do not come second to her emotions. Contrast the style and ἦθος, delineation of character, in Glycera's warm response to Menander (below, 4. 19).

3–4 διοίκησις ... ἐντεῦθεν: understand a verb meaning 'depend on', such as ἀρτᾶται or ἀνάκειται.

4 Μυρρινοῦντι: Myrrhinus was one of the coastal demes of Attica: the implication is that it was a choice area in which to own property.

5 ἐν τοῖς ἀργυρείοις: the famous silver mines in the hilly area of Laurium in southern Attica.

9 ταραντινίδια: these were filmy, diaphanous cloaks, originally from Tarentum, and conventionally regarded as a courtesan's garment: Philostratus 22, Aristaenetus 1. 25, Lucian, *DMeretr* 7. 2, Gomme–Sandbach on Menander, *Epitr.* 489. Petale's girl friends are her fellow-courtesans, who are better dressed than she is.

12 τὸ καλόν: a Hellenistic adverbial usage: cf. Herodas 1. 54 πλουτέων τὸ καλόν, 'well and truly rich' (with Headlam's note).

15–16 ὑμῖν;—μὴ χρυσία...: most editors assume a lacuna here, with the general sense '⟨Stay away⟩ unless you bring...'. Meiser's ἔρρε is the simplest of the suggested supplements: '⟨Off with you⟩ unless ...'. But we might seriously consider Hercher, who dispensed with the lacuna and read κομιουμένοις;: 'Can't you bring goblets even if you can't get hold of ... ?'

17 Χάριτες: for the Graces see below, note on Philostratus 51. In this standard phrase they look with kindly eyes on their favourites: cf. Alc. 3. 8, Aristaenetus 1. 11.

ALCIPHRON 4. 18

Menander writes to tell Glycera of a flattering invitation from Ptolemy to go to Egypt. However, he has resolved to decline it as he could not bear to be without her.

This is the first of a pair of letters: in the reply (4. 19) Glycera urges him to think again, and offers to go with him to Egypt.

(Alciphron 4. 2 also purports to be by Menander's Glycera, telling a girl friend about his plans to go to Corinth.)

Two questions arise at once in relation to this letter: the reality of Glycera and the reality of Ptolemy's invitation. The invitation seems

to be confirmed by Pliny the Elder, who tells us: 'magnum et
Menandro in comico socco testimonium regum Aegypti et
Macedoniae contigit classe et per legatos petito' (*NH* 7. 111).
Glycera is more elusive. The name occurs in Menander's plays (e.g.
Perikeiromene), one or other of which Glycera seems to allude to in
4. 19. 20 (τὸ δρᾶμα ἐν ᾧ με γέγραφας); and there is a surviving frag-
ment which Alciphron adapts in the first sentence of this letter:

> Γλυκέρα, τί κλάεις; ὀμνύω σοι τὸν Δία
> τὸν Ὀλύμπιον καὶ τὴν Ἀθηνᾶν, φιλτάτη,
> ὀμωμοκὼς καὶ πρότερον ἤδη πολλάκις.   (fr. 87 Körte)

So we might suppose that a real Glycera has been immortalized in
Menander's comedies; or alternatively that the repeated presence of a
Glycera in the plays may have led to the story that Menander had
a mistress of that name. See A. Körte in *Hermes* 54 (1919), 87ff., and
a response by M. A. Schepers in *Mnemosyne* 54 (1926), 258ff.

The two letters 4. 18 and 4. 19 were discussed by F. Wilhelm
(*RhM* 71 (1916), 137ff.), who argued that Alciphron took them from
an earlier collection of love letters, because of evidence he detected
that they influenced Ovid's *Amores* 2. 16. In any case, we have here a
letter, whether or not invented, attached to the greatest figure in
Greek New Comedy.

On the two letters see also Bungarten, *Menanders und Glykeras
Brief bei Alkiphron*.

1 τὰς Ἐλευσινίας θεάς: Demeter and Persephone, in whose honour
the mysteries were celebrated. The following words derive in part
from some surviving lines of Menander: see introductory note.

14 τὰ Ἁλῷα: a festival held in December in honour of Demeter and
Dionysus. The connection with ἅλως, 'threshing-floor', is disputed,
as it was the wrong time of year for a harvest-home, and it is likely
to have been in origin a fertility festival. There was an orgy of ban-
queting and a generally indecent atmosphere, and, interestingly,
allusions to it in literature associate it with courtesans. See
L. Deubner, *Attische Feste* (Berlin, 1932), 60ff.; H. W. Parke,
Festivals of the Athenians, (London, 1977) 98ff.

15 Πτολεμαίου: Ptolemy Soter, the first of the line, who reigned
305–282 BC. He was himself a historian and a patron of learning,
and he was originally responsible for the founding of the great
library at Alexandria. So an invitation to Menander would be in
line with a policy of attracting Greek culture to Egypt.

18 Φιλήμονα: a distinguished contemporary New Comedy poet, perhaps second only to Menander. This is our only evidence of his invitation to Egypt, and it is not known whether he accepted it. Menander seems to be suggesting that Ptolemy's contrasting styles in his invitation letters reflected his own assessment of the two poets' styles.

22 σύ μοι... γνώμη...: Menander has, as he says, made up his mind, but he wants Glycera to sit in judgment between him and Ptolemy and endorse his decision. The Areopagus was the most venerable ancient court of Athens, still retaining some powers in the Hellenistic period. The Heliaea was the court presided over by the *thesmothetai*, the six junior archons.

25 ἵνα δή: δή seems a necessary correction by Meineke of the MSS μή (retained by Schepers). μή might mean 'so I don't cause you double boredom' by transcribing the king's letter into mine (instead of enclosing it separately), but that seems very strained.

28 τοὺς δώδεκα θεούς: the full Olympic pantheon: Zeus, Hera, Apollo, Aphrodite, Ares, Athena, Poseidon, Artemis, Demeter, Hermes, Hephaistos, Dionysos.

32 ἐρημίαν πολυάνθρωπον: an emphatic oxymoron. It was a popular rhetorical device, and a comparable Latin example is Seneca's 'inquietam inertiam' (*Tranq.* 12).

36 τὰς θηρικλείους: sc. κύλικας: Thericles was a famous 5th-cent. Corinthian potter, whose work was so good that 'thericlean' became a generic term for fine pottery (Athen. 11. 470E ff.; see also Bentley's vigorous comments in *Dissertation upon the Epistles of Phalaris*, i. 169 ff. (ed. Dyce, 1836)).

38 τῶν... Χοῶν...: from here to the end of the section Menander lists some characteristic features of Athenian life—political, cultural, religious—which are unique to Athens and which he could not bear to give up. The Χόες and the Χύτροι below were both features of the Anthesteria, the springtime festival of flowers. On the day called Χόες ('Jugs') the new wine was blessed, with everyone present carrying his own jug. On another day called Χύτροι pots filled with fruit were brought as offerings to the dead. The Lenaea was the winter festival, notable for the production of comedies (see above, note on 1. 4). The Lyceum was the famous gymnasium (see above, note on 4. 7), contrasting with Plato's Academy as physical with mental exercise.

Editors point to Browning's debt to this part of the letter for some lines in *Balaustion's Adventure* 32 ff.:

> Ours the fasts and feasts,
> Choës and Chutroi; ours the sacred grove,
> Agora, Dikasteria, Poikile,
> Pnux, Keramikos; Salamis in sight,
> Psuttalia, Marathon itself, not far!
> Ours the great Dionusiac theatre ...

39 Ἀμαλλολογίας: 'gathering of sheaves': *faute de mieux* this is Wilamowitz's conjecture for MSS readings which are hard to make sense of (ἀμαλογίας, ὁμολογίας, ἀνολογίας: see Schepers's apparatus for many other conjectures). In the context it must refer to something public and typically Athenian, and χθιζῆς seems to tie it to the Haloa, which was believed by Pausanias (and perhaps Alciphron) to be a harvest festival. (See Deubner and Parke cited above: and Bungarten, 55–6, for a discussion of the problem.)

45–6 θεσμοθέτας ... κεκισσωμένους: ἱεροὶ κῶμοι here are assemblies in honour of gods, e.g. the Dionysia. The ivy-garlanded lawgivers must refer loosely to the fact that the *archon eponymos* was in charge of the City Dionysia, and the *archon basileus* looked after the Lenaea, though strictly these archons were not called *thesmothetai*.

46 περισχοίνισμα: a large area in the northern part of the agora, which was roped off at ostracisms and other occasions when stricter control of the assembly was necessary.

48 τὰς σεμνὰς θεάς: the Erinyes or Furies, known also under their euphemistic title of Eumenides. Traditionally they had a cave and sanctuary on the NE slope of the Areopagus.

48–9 Σαλαμῖνα ... Μαραθῶνα: all four places were redolent of triumphant patriotic feelings relating to the Persian invasions of Greece. At Marathon in 490 the Persians were famously defeated; and in 480, in the area including Salamis, the straits between Salamis and the Attic coast, and the little island of Psyttalia, Xerxes' fleet was completely routed.

52 λαβεῖν: infinitive of purpose, but uncommon after a verb meaning to come or go: Weir Smyth § 2009.

55 σποδός: a *topos* of love poetry: see e.g. Tib. I. 9. 11–12 'at deus illa | in cinerem et liquidas munera vertat aquas' (with K. F. Smith's note on this commonplace).

58 ψόφοις: ψόφος has here its meaning of an empty sound, and hence a specious or pretentious title, something like the colloquial English 'big noise'.

60 ἅπαξ: Benner's rejection of this (Loeb edn.) is unwarranted: Menander means that usually one kiss is enough to bring Glycera round.

68 καταβαπτισθήσετα: 'utterly swamped' keeps what must be an intended pun in the Greek.

70 ἀποτεθηρίωται: referring especially to the notorious crocodiles.

73 ἐπ' ἐσχάρας: as part of the celebration of the City Dionysia the image of Dionysus was escorted ceremonially from his altar near the Academy to the Theatre (*IG* 2² 1006. 12). Menander wants to join in the ritual singing there.

ALCIPHRON 4. 19

Glycera's reply: don't be hasty in your decision; let us take counsel on this, and of course I will come with you anyway.

On the question whether there was a real Glycera see introduction to 4. 18. Throughout the letter Glycera stresses the close bond between Menander and herself: e.g. the episode of her girl friend whom Menander was hesitant to praise, and her own practical help in the staging of his plays. She comes across as a strong character, whose views and feelings deserve to be taken seriously.

2 Καλλιγένειαν: a cult title for Demeter ('Bearer of fair offspring'), linked with the name of the third day of the Thesmophoria, τὰ Καλλιγένεια: cf. Aristoph. *Thesm.* 297, Deubner, *Attische Feste*, 55. As the last letter tells us, Glycera is currently attending the goddess's Haloa.

6 ἀττικισμόν: here means correct Attic standards of speech; below it suggests Attic wit, which in Latin literature at least was proverbial: Cic. *Fam.* 9. 15. 2 'non Attici, sed salsiores quam illi Atticorum Romani ... sales'; Mart. 3. 20. 9.

18 τὰς θεάς: Demeter and Persephone.

18–19 βοῦς ... φθέγξαιτο: the portent of the talking ox that speaks the truth seems to be confined to Roman literature and contexts. Pliny remarks 'est frequens in prodigiis priscorum bovem locutum' (*NH* 8. 183); and Livy records the phenomenon several times: 3. 10. 6, 24. 10. 10, 35. 21. 4 (all passages giving lists of prodigies). There is a Greek allusion in Cassius Dio (48. 21. 2), but he too is writing a Roman history. So perhaps Alciphron has slipped up in bringing the speaking ox into his classical Greek context.

32 τὴν ... κεφαλὴν: the text follows Hercher's deletion of τῶν δραμάτων as a gloss, with which κεφαλὴν would have to mean 'source', 'origin'.

36 Πρωτέως ἀκρωτήρια: the sea god Proteus frequented the island of Pharos in the bay of Alexandria (Homer, *Od.* 4. 384 ff.). Here stood the celebrated lighthouse also mentioned, which was reckoned one of the seven wonders of the world.

38 φιλαργύρων...: this is a fair summary of the main character types who appear in Greek New Comedy, some of whom may well have been given their initial impetus on the stage by Menander.

42 αἰτούμενον: Professor D. A. Russell's suggestion for MSS αὐτοῦ, which seems pointless, and we need an adjective or participle. -μενον may have dropped out by haplography with the following Μένανδρον.

43 οὐ μὴν ἀλλ' εἴγε...: Glycera now deals with the possibility that Menander might actually want to go, but be hindered by his feelings for her.

45 τῶν ἠχούντων ἀγαλμάτων: this refers to the statue at Thebes of Memnon, a legendary king of Ethiopia. He was the son of Eos, the Dawn, and the statue was supposed to echo musically when first struck by the rays of the sun at dawn: it was a great tourist attraction. (See Paus. 1. 43. 2, Lucian, *Tox.* 27, Tac. *Ann.* 2. 61, Courtney on Juv. 15. 5.) But the reference is an anachronism for the 4th cent. BC, as the phenomenon only began after an earthquake in 27 BC (and stopped when the statue was repaired by Septimius Severus in 199/200).

46 λαβυρίνθου: the 'Labyrinth' was the name the Greeks gave to the great mortuary temple of the Pharaoh Amenemhat III at Hawara in the Fayyum. Dating from *c.*1800 BC, it was an enormous structure, said to have been carved from a single rock, and it greatly impressed Herodotus when he visited it (2. 148).

50 Διὶ οὐρίῳ: literally 'with Zeus sending a fair breeze', as at Aesch. *Supp.* 594: a variation on δεξιοῖς πνεύμασι.

54 ἐκκλωμένης κώπης: the breaking of an oar might be the effect of a bad storm, which would also cause seasickness.

55 Ἀριάδνη: in this sentence the text may be astray or Glycera may be distorting the myth to fit her own case. Ariadne guided Theseus in Crete, and was subsequently abandoned by him in Naxos, where Dionysus found her. Glycera is saying that she will guide Menander to Egypt (not to the Cretan labyrinth), and Menander to her is not

Theseus, nor even Dionysus, but Dionysus' representative being a famous poet. This is all rather contrived, but it allows Glycera also to contrast the faithful Menander with the faithless Theseus. (See Schepers's apparatus for suggestions for textual surgery here.)

73 λύσεις ... γνώμην: λύειν is odd if the sense is 'make up your mind' or 'act on your decision', and perhaps we should read Meineke's θήσει.

74 διδάσκεις: the lover or mistress as a teacher is a conventional notion (e.g. Prop. 1. 10. 19 'Cynthia me docuit semper ... '): the lesson may be in physical technique, but here περὶ τούτων seems to mean more general issues in the relationship. See also below σὺ γάρ με ἐδίδαξας ...

76 Ἀττικοὺς σφῆκας: a clear reference to Aristophanes' comedy *Wasps*, in which the chorus of jurors behave waspishly and are dressed to look like wasps. So here too Glycera's critics will be acting waspishly as they pass judgment on her. The charge of depriving Athens of her wealth refers back to the corn which could be expected to come from Egypt in return for Menander.

80 Θεοφράστου, Ἐπικούρου: Menander was said to be a pupil of the philosopher Theophrastus (Diog. Laert. 5. 36). He was also an exact contemporary and fellow-student of Epicurus, and there is a surviving epigram attributed to him and addressed to Epicurus and his brother, in which he salutes Epicurus for saving his country from slavery (*Anth. Pal.* 7. 72).

84 πάτριος ... θεός: Apollo was claimed thus by the Athenians: see Plato, *Euthd.* 302d Ἀπόλλων πατρῷος διὰ τὴν τοῦ Ἴωνος γένεσιν; Arist. *Ath.* 55. 3.

87 γαστρομαντεύεσθαι: this was a form of inspired prophecy which was delivered by means of ventriloquism, usually by a woman called ἐγγαστρίμαντις or ἐγγαστρίμυθος. The other activities of Glycera's practitioner are not clear because of the very uncertain sense of σπαρτῶν διατάσει. It may (as Benner and Fobes suggest) be a reference to the ἴυγξ. This was a spoked wheel or a disc used in incantations, onto which a cord was threaded, and the wheel was made to revolve by increasing or relaxing the tension on the cord: see Gow on Theoc. 2. 17. θεῶν δείξει is also obscure: perhaps it means 'calling up' the gods for consultation. We also have here a list of ingredients for ritual and sacrifice. στύραξ was a kind of aromatic gum; σελήνη was a moon-shaped wheat cake; the ἄγνος was the chaste tree, *Vitex agnus castus*: Pliny has a full account of its various medicinal properties (*NH* 24. 59 ff.).

96–8 καὶ εἰ μελετᾶν ... ψυχῆς: textual difficulties here make it hard to be sure of the sense, but Glycera seems to be taking another tack, and saying that if Menander were to consider going and try to banish his old Greek associations from his mind, he would not be able to, any more than she could.

105 τὸν αὑτοῦ Διόνυσον: if αὑτοῦ is right Ptolemy's 'Dionysus' is his taste in plays, which is not for 'popular' ones that appeal to the masses.

106 Θαΐδα ...: of these plays by Menander substantial amounts survive of *Epitrepontes* (773 lines), *Misoumenos* (466 lines), and *Sikyonios* (423 lines), and all three are printed in Sandbach's OCT text. Surviving passages from the other three are much more meagre, and they can be found in Körte's Teubner: *Thaïs* (fr. 185–91), *Thrasyleon* (fr. 203–7), *Rhapizomene* (fr. 358–70). From *Thaïs* comes the famous 'evil communications' line φθείρουσιν ἤθη χρήσθ᾽ ὁμιλίαι κακαί (187).

113–14 τὸ δρᾶμα ... γέγραφας: e.g. *Perikeiromene* or *Misogynes*: see introduction to 4. 18.

115–16 ὅσον ἰσχύει ... φέρειν ... ἀφεὶς: the construction is elliptical: understand ὥστε.

122 Θεοφορουμένης: the surviving fragments of this play can be found conveniently in Sandbach's OCT text.

PHILOSTRATUS 12

Our eyes are the means by which we enjoy the ecstasy and suffer the pain of love.

The eyes are widely referred to in the imagery of Greek and Latin elegy and other erotic poetry, though commonly it is the starry brilliance or the fiery power of the beloved's eyes which is described: e.g. Ovid, *Am.* 2. 16. 44, Tib. 4. 2. 5–6 (see K. F. Smith's note here). Or it is the eyes which make the capture: Philostratus 56 ἑάλω κάλλους ὄμμασι; Prop. 1. 1. 1. (Shackleton Bailey gives parallels in his *Propertiana*, 268).

1 πόθεν: i.e. from what vantage point or attacking position.

6 κατὰ μικρόν: this seems at first sight to contradict ταχέως below, but we can picture Love making a sly ('invidiously') but swift onslaught.

7 γυμνός: probably literal in sense, but it might mean 'unarmed' (except for his bow). Eros' conventional attributes are bow-and-arrows and a torch (e.g. Tib. 2. 1. 81–2).

11 δᾳδοῦχοι: because they carry Love's fires into the soul, but with reference also to the torch-bearers in the Eleusinian mysteries.

16 μακαρίων ... τυφλῶν: an instance of the use of the genitive in exclamations, usually regarded as a type of the causal genitive: Weir Smyth §407; cf. above, Alciphron 1. 1.

PHILOSTRATUS 18

The address should more logically be 'To a boy wearing tight shoes': the point of the letter is to persuade him to go barefoot, both to save himself discomfort and to give pleasure to the earth and to his lovers.

This little bit of whimsy is linked with other love literature by motifs like kissing the beloved's footprints; and it is also given a sort of mock seriousness by the heavyweight *exempla*, including Cynic philosophers and Homeric heroes.

6 φθονεῖς: i.e. do you grudge the earth the pleasure of feeling your bare feet, a point picked up at the end of the letter.

8 Φιλοκτήτην: Philoctetes led one of the Greek contingents that went to fight against Troy, but on his way there he was bitten in the foot by a snake which caused him an agonizing and festering wound. His story is the theme of Sophocles' play of that name.

9 τὸν ἐκ Σινώπης φιλόσοφον: Diogenes: he and Crates were Cynic philosophers (both 4th cent. BC), whose creed encouraged its followers to live their lives with the barest physical essentials. Ajax and Achilles are the types of the tough epic warrior. The episode of Jason losing his shoe is told by Ap. Rhod. (1. 8–11: cf. Pindar, *Pyth.* 4. 75, 95–6). The comment below that he was lucky to be deprived of his shoe, καλῶς σεσυλημένος, must mean that otherwise he would have been stuck in the river and drowned. In fact having one foot bare was ultimately unlucky for him, as Pelias, seeing him thus and warned by an oracle, promptly sent him on the perilous hunt for the Golden Fleece.

10–11 ἐξ ἡμισείας: sc. μοίρας: literally 'with a half share', 'half and half': one shoe on and one off.

12–13 ἐς ἀντίληψιν ... γενομένης: an elaborate phrase meaning that the mud offered a 'resisting grip' to his foot.

15 ἤτω: a later form of the imperative ἔστω from εἰμί, not literary but found in the Septuagint, NT, and inscriptions: only here in Philostratus (Schmid, *Der Atticismus*, iv. 35).

16–17 τὸ ἴχνος προσκυνήσομεν ...: the letter ends with two *topoi* of erotic literature: kissing the loved one's footprints (also at Alciphron 3. 31), and plants springing up from where the feet have walked (Theoc. 8. 46–7; Persius 2. 38).

PHILOSTRATUS 20

To a woman sleeping with a garland of roses on her breast: are they a new sort of lover for her?

For a famous picture of another girl lying among roses see Horace's Pyrrha ode (1. 5).

1 τῷ Διί: a reference to the famous scene of the seduction of Zeus in *Iliad* 14. 153ff., when Hera assists Poseidon to rally the Achaeans by diverting Zeus' attention from the fighting below. To aid her own allurements she borrows Aphrodite's charmed girdle (κεστός), and she and Zeus sleep together on a bed of flowers—the three mentioned here are duly quoted from *Il.* 14. 348. Two of the flowers are not certainly identifiable. The 'lotus' might also be tre-foil; the 'hyacinth', notoriously difficult to identify, could be a scilla or iris: see Janko on *Il.* 14. 347–8.

2 ῥόδα δὲ οὐ παρῆν: a more practical reason is offered by Schol. bT on *Il.* 14. 347: οὐκ εἶπε δὲ ῥόδον διὰ τὸ ἀκανθῶδες.

3 Ἀφροδίτης κτήματα: roses are universally associated with Aphrodite and legends about her: e.g. they sprang from the blood of her beloved Adonis as he died (Bion 1. 66).

5 οἱ δὲ ἐδέοντο ...: i.e. Hera and Poseidon (see above).

8 ποιητῶν ἐξουσία: *licentia poetica*: exactly our 'poetic licence'. For the phrase see Strabo 1. 2. 17, and the discussion in W. Kroll, *Studien* (Stuttgart, 1924), 52 ff.

9 ἀγροίκως: the girl is ill-mannered in choosing to sleep with flowers instead of a lover; but she is also behaving unnaturally in not stay-ing awake to enjoy the fragrance of the roses.

9–10 σωφρονήσασα ἐν οὐ σώφροσιν: the girl's 'chastity' is contrasted with the roses' supposed randy and unchaste nature (derived from their association with Aphrodite). So too in *Ep.* 46 Philostratus refers to roses as ἐρωτικὰ καὶ πανοῦργα.

10–11 ἢ τὸν Δία: Huet's νὴ τὸν Δία is attractive, as there were no roses for Zeus on Ida and therefore he seems out of place here;

but Philostratus may be deliberately suggesting the girl could be Hera's rival.

PHILOSTRATUS 25

This letter and the previous Letter 24 form a pair that ring the changes on a familiar theme, the ravaging physical effects of extreme anger: a good example of how persistent were rhetorical *topoi* in Greek and Latin literature. For other uses of this one see Aristaenetus 1. 17 εἰ γὰρ φοβερὰ γένοιο ἧττον ἔσῃ καλή, and Seneca's vigorous words in *Ira* 2. 35. 3: 'non est ullius adfectus facies turbatior. pulcherrima ora foedavit, torvos vultus ex tranquillissimis reddit...'.

6 βοῶπιν: a routine epithet of Hera in the *Iliad*: literally 'ox-eyed', with perhaps the implied meaning of having large, placid eyes. This would make sense here, where placidity would naturally be incompatible with wrath. (See Kirk on *Il.* 1. 551.)

6 ἅλα δῖαν: here δῖος has the derived sense 'bright' from 'heavenly'.

7 ἡ δὲ Ἀθηνᾶ...: Aristotle reports the same story about Athena (*Pol.* 8. 1341^{b}3ff.), though he suggests that a more likely reason was that playing the pipes contributes nothing to the education of the mind, in which Athena had a vested interest.

8 Ἐρινῦς Εὐμενίδας: the Erinyes were fierce avenging spirits, whose conversion to become the 'Kindly Ones' (Eumenides) is a major theme in Aeschylus' play of that name.

14 τὸ κάτοπτρον λαβοῦσα...: Ovid gives the same advice in a similarly warning passage in *Ars Amatoria* 3. 501 ff.: 'pertinet ad faciem rabidos compescere mores... vos quoque si media speculum spectetis in ira, | cognoscat faciem vix satis ulla suam.'

15 εὖγ' ὅτι ἐπεστράφης: the writer imagines that at this point in reading the letter the woman does as she is told and goes to her mirror. (The reading ἀπεστράφης of some MSS would mean that she 'turned away' because she did not like what she saw in the mirror.)

16 μετενόησας: μετανοεῖν often has the sense 'repent' in later Greek, and it seems appropriate here (LSJ s.v. 3).

PHILOSTRATUS 32

This letter is one of a sequence of three addressed to a γυνὴ καπηλίς, the hostess of an inn (the order in one of the families of MSS being

60, 33, 32). In all three there is much interplay between the hostess's personal charms and her activities as a dispenser of wine. The theme is traditional: see also the little poem *Copa* which is included in the *Appendix Vergiliana.*

Our letter has an added interest (along with Philostratus 2, 33, and 46) in being an important source of one of Ben Jonson's most famous poems, *To Celia*, perhaps through the Latin translation of Antonio Bonfini (1606). (See C. H. Herford and P. Simpson, *Ben Jonson* (Oxford 1925), i. 251, ii. 386; A. D. Fitton, *Modern Language Review*, 54 (1959), 554–7.)

1 διαυγέστερα: διαυγής is used of eyes also by Aristaenetus 1. 1.

5 ὕδωρ: for the drinkers to mix with their wine: cf. Anacreon 396 φέρ' ὕδωρ, φέρ' οἶνον, ὦ παῖ.

6–7 πόσους ... καλεῖς: the hostess is like a temptress Siren, diverting all male passers-by.

9 τὸ μὲν οὐ προσάγω ... πίνων: Jonson, *To Celia* 3–4: 'Or leave a kiss but in the cup | And I'll not look for wine.'

PHILOSTRATUS 51

A delicate little love letter, the main interest of which is the continuing influence and popularity of Sappho's poetry.

1 τοῦ ῥόδου: Sappho's surviving poems and fragments are full of flower imagery: Philostratus refers in particular to fr. 53 LP: βροδοπάχεες ἄγναι Χάριτες δεῦτε Δίος κόραι, 'Come hither, pure rosy-armed Graces, daughters of Zeus'.

1 στεφανοῖ: the flower, which often forms a crown or wreath, is itself wreathed by Sappho's poetry.

2–3 τῶν Χαρίτων: the Charites or Graces were minor goddesses, usually three in number, who dispensed beauty and charm. They were regularly associated with Aphrodite, and they made roses grow (*Anacreontea* 44. 2).

6–7 μετόπωρον τοῦ κάλλους: perhaps a recollection of a saying of Euripides about a boy, reported by Aelian, *VH* 13. 4: οὐ γὰρ μόνον τὸ ἔαρ τῶν καλῶν κάλλιστον, ἀλλὰ καὶ τὸ μετόπωρον. Plutarch too has a version of it (*Alc.* 1. 3).

PHILOSTRATUS 71

A letter of recommendation in which the writer appeals to a friend for his interest and support on behalf of a poet. The letter reminds us that poets at this period continued to depend for their living on either private or civic patronage ('houses and cities'), according to the nature and importance of their work, and they could be expected to reciprocate in their poems by complimentary allusions to their benefactors. (Philostratus 67 is another letter of recommendation, for a τραγῳδός.)

1 οἱ τῶν μελιττῶν ἐσμοί: the linking here of poets with bees recalls a famous passage in Plato's *Ion* (534b), where Socrates talks of lyric poets culling their songs, like bees, from fountains flowing with honey. Horace too used the poet/bee analogy: 'quae circumvolitas agilis thyma?' (*Ep.* 1. 3. 21).

3 αἱ μὲν κηρίοις: the translation follows Kayser's conjecture αἱ for MSS οἱ, contrasting bees reciprocating with real honey and poets with a metaphorical banquet. ὀψοποιίᾳ λαμπρᾷ suggests the higher genres (epic, tragedy). τραγήματα (properly the last course of a meal, dessert) are more trivial productions: οἱ ἐρωτικοί would be the elegists. (Cf. Dion. Hal. *Rhet.* 10, p. 373 U–R: epilogues are τραγήματα τῶν λόγων.)

5 οὗτος: this suggests that Celsus himself is delivering the letter of introduction.

6 τέττιγες: the song of the cicada seems to have been much enjoyed in antiquity, as a fair range of authors testifies: Homer, *Il.* 3. 151–2, Hesiod, *Op.* 582–4, Aelian *NA* 1. 20, *Anth. Pal.* App. III 225 (Cougny). For the belief that cicadas fed on dew see Aristotle *HA* 5. 30, Aelian loc. cit., and for further details see Davies and Kathirithamby, *Greek Insects* (London, 1986), 123–4.

PHILOSTRATUS 73

The letter is written to Julia Domna, the Syrian wife of the Emperor Septimius Severus (reigned 193–211). From all accounts she was a notable Blue Stocking, who collected around her a group of philosophers and scholars, including Philostratus himself. Certainly she herself was intelligent and learned enough to discuss the Greek classics, as we see from this letter, and her court was clearly a famous centre of literary activity.

It must be admitted that this letter on the face of it is not a fiction, but a literary manifesto, arguing for acceptance of both Plato and the sophists. It could be a reply to one from Julia which made some point about the influence of the sophists and Plato's dislike of them. But whether genuine or not the letter at least is interesting as showing how the form could be used to make a literary point.

Philostratus uses the letter to discuss the influence on some well-known writers of the literary forms and rhetorical tricks of the sophists, in particular Gorgias. His main points are perfectly valid—the oratorical teaching and practices of the sophists were widely pervasive—but the tone of the letter is fairly lighthearted, as when we are told of Plato's refusal to be outdone in 'Gorgianizing', and in the jocular reference to Plutarch at the end. Of course Philostratus shows here his own abiding interest in the subject, which we see most extensively in his work on the *Lives of the Sophists*, in which there are obvious links with our letter.

The chief sophist discussed, Gorgias of Leontini, was indeed the most important and influential of them all: Philostratus calls him the father of the sophists' art, *VS* 1. 9. His arrival in Athens in 427 BC was a turning-point in the history of rhetoric. His main influence was in style: he founded the practice of epideictic (display) oratory, and he popularized those 'figures' of balance, antithesis, and parallelism which were seen as the hallmarks of his own style, and are characteristic of the work of his most famous pupil Isocrates.

There has been much discussion of this letter: see e.g. G. W. Bowersock, *Greek Sophists in the Roman Empire* (Oxford, 1969), 101–9 (also on Julia's circle); R. J. Penella in *Hermes* 107 (1979), 161–8; G. Anderson, *Philostratus*, 4 f., 276 f., and in *CP* 72 (1977), 43–5.

1 Πλάτων: Plato's use of sophistic figures of style is discussed by E. Norden in his great book *Antike Kunstprosa* (Leipzig, 1909), 106 ff. Essentially, Plato was a master stylist himself, who used Gorgianic and other rhetorical tricks whenever and for whatever purposes he wanted, e.g. parody in Agathon's speech in the *Symposium* 194 ff.; while Socrates' report of Aspasia's funeral oration (*Menexenus* 236 ff.) is a prolonged exercise in the Gorgianic style.

3 διεφοίτων... πόλεις: the sophists were predominantly itinerant teachers, giving paid instruction in the cities they visited.

4 Θαμύρου: Thamyras was, like Orpheus, a Thracian singer, who was blinded by the Muses because he compared his skill with theirs.

8 τὰς ἰδέας: the word is used in its technical rhetorical sense of a literary style: *VS* 2. 30; LSJ s.v. I 4 b.

9 γοργιάζειν: Philostratus may have invented the verb: he uses it again at *VS* 1. 16.

9–10 Ἱππίου καὶ Πρωταγόρου: both celebrated 5th-cent. sophists, who appear in Plato's dialogues. Hippias claimed encyclopaedic knowledge and wrote a huge number of works. Protagoras did important pioneering work in grammar, and in philosophy he was best known for his claim to teach virtue, and for his maxim 'Man is the measure of all things'.

11 ὁ τοῦ Γρύλλου: Xenophon, who had heard Prodicus lecture. Prodicus was a contemporary and friend of Socrates, and was particularly interested in synonyms and subtle distinctions in the use of words. Philostratus alludes to Xenophon's use of his famous myth 'The Choice of Heracles' (*Mem.* 2. 1. 21 ff.).

14–15 οἱ κατὰ Θετταλίαν Ἕλληνες: we hear of Gorgias' influence in Thessaly from Plato, *Meno* 70a–b; Isocrates 15. 155. Philostratus mentions it again at *VS* 1. 16.

16 Ὀλυμπίασι διελέχθη: for what we know of Gorgias' *Olympian Oration* see *VS* 1. 9 and Diels–Kranz, ii. 287.

18 Ἀσπασία: the mistress of Pericles. For her alleged influence over him see above, Alciphron 4. 7 and not there, and for her own Gorgianic style see note above on Plato.

19 θῆξαι: 'whet' metaphorically both in Greek and in English—but Philostratus might have known that Aristotle condemned the usage as frigid (*Rhet.* 1406ᵃ10).

19 Κριτίας, Θουκυδίδης: Critias was a pupil of Socrates and subsequently one of the Thirty Tyrants at Athens. He wrote tragedies and elegies, of which very little survives. For the influence of Gorgias on Thucydides see Norden, op. cit. 96–101.

21 Αἰσχίνης: Aeschines 'the Socratic' (not to be confused with the famous orator), so called from his great loyalty and devotion to his master Socrates, and as the author of a number of Socratic dialogues. Diogenes Laertius (2. 63) also tells us that Aeschines was an imitator of Gorgias. The point about the Thargelia passage quoted is (*a*) the careful gradation in the number of syllables in the four successive cola: 8, 8, 9, 10 (Norden, op. cit. 103); (*b*) the striking repetition of the same word at the ends of the cola (illustrating the rhetorical figure called *epiphora* or *antistrophe*).

26 ἀποστάσεις, προσβολαί: 'detachings, '?verbal attacks': there is some uncertainty about the exact meaning of these terms (which also occur together at *VS* 1.9 as characteristic of Gorgias). They both seem to be some form of asyndeton, which produce an effect of lively emphasis and transition by causing a break between successive clauses. See Hermogenes 267. 11 Rabe; Apsines 3. 28 Spengel–Hammer; and the useful discussion in the Glossary in W. C. Wright's Loeb edition of Philostratus and Eunapius, *Lives of the Sophists*. What Philostratus means by saying that the figures were much used by epic poets defeated even Norden (op. cit. 380 n. 1).

28 θαρσαλεώτερον τοῦ ʽΕλληνικοῦ: the translation assumes the use of comparative for superlative which is common in later Greek; but it might mean 'more audacious than the Greek manner', i.e. 'un-Hellenically bold'.

29 Πλούταρχον: this request to Julia Domna is of course tongue-in-cheek and anachronistic, as Plutarch was long since dead; but perhaps she was writing something about him to which Philostratus refers. (See the discussions referred to in the introductory note.) Plutarch's dislike of the sophists was well known, e.g. *De Recta Ratione Audiendi* 41C: see also Norden, op. cit. 380, quoting from a now lost work of Plutarch strongly attacking Gorgias (= fr. 186 Sandbach).

31–2 εἰπεῖν ἔχων οὐκ ἔχω: this looks like mock coyness, and a suitably sophistic paradox to end with. If we have to supply a word κακοήθης would do as well as any.

ARISTAENETUS 1. 13

A crafty doctor persuades a doting father to give up his mistress to his own son, who is sick with love for her.

This anecdote clearly derives from the well-known story, found in many sources, about Antiochus I, who fell in love with his stepmother Stratonice, wife of his father Seleucus I. By a similar stratagem to that reported in our letter the doctor Erasistratos persuaded Seleucus to give her up to his son. This was in about 292 BC, and the story can be found in Appian, *Syr.* 59 ff.; Plut. *Demetr.* 38; Lucian, *De Syria Dea* 17–18; Val. Max. 5.7 ext. 1. Aristaenetus' debts to Lucian at least might well include this tale, and he seems also to know a variant of it in Heliodorus 4. 7.

The theme of the letter is also reflected in the elaborately named writer and addressee: 'Lucky-counselling' and 'Cure-gifted'.

Structurally, we should note the sententious beginning and proverbial ending, which may be deliberate devices to adapt the narrative to the epistolary form.

1 τέχναι... τύχης...: the tragic poet Agathon expressed a similar thought more pungently: τέχνη τύχην ἔστερξε καὶ τύχη τέχνην (fr. 6 N²). But a contrasting claim was made for the father of doctors himself, Hippocrates, in an epitaph in the Greek Anthology, that his fame depended entirely on his skill and not on fortune (*Anth. Pal.* 7. 135: the last line runs δόξαν ἑλὼν πολλῶν οὐ τύχᾳ ἀλλὰ τέχνᾳ).

2 διακοσμεῖται: lit. 'is ordered, regulated' for the benefit of professional skills. (Alternatively it might mean 'acquire adornment or lustre', roughly anticipating εὐδοκιμεῖ below.)

5 μακρόν... προοίμιον: very similar is Plato, *Rep.* 432e μακρὸν τὸ προοίμιον τῷ ἐπιθυμοῦντι ἀκοῦσαι.

10 Πανάκειον: lit. 'Cure-all', from πανάκεια, English 'panacea'.

12 μετάρσιον: used of elevated and speculative thoughts already in Euripides (*Alc.* 963), and increasingly in Patristic Greek. There is a similar phrase to ours in Gregory of Nazianzus, *Or.* 8. 13, νοῦν ἀπλανῆ καὶ μετάρσιον: see also Lampe s.v. A. 2. a.

20 ἐταμιεύετο: Panaceus 'husbanded, stored up' his insight until he could make the best use of it (εἰς καιρὸν).

29–30 τὸ βλέμμα... ἀλλοιότερος ἦν: lit. 'he was a different man with respect to his look and his pulse'.

32 τὸ τρίτον τῷ σωτῆρι: lit. 'the third (cup) to (Zeus) the Saviour': a proverbial expression derived from the practice of dedicating the third cup of wine to Ζεὺς Σωτήρ, which made it a lucky drink. For other examples of the saying see Plato, *Phlb.* 66d, *Charm.* 167a; and LSJ s.v. σωτήρ I. 2. Panaceus means that on his third visit he will sort out the problem.

42 τά τε στήθη... ἁπτόμενος: both actions express humble and heartfelt entreaty.

44 ἐκτόπως ἐρᾷ: Lucian similarly uses the phrase ἔρως ἔκτοπος (*DMeretr.* 15. 2) of an 'out of the way', extraordinary passion.

47 τῆς φύσεως γεγονὼς: lit. 'belonging to, under the control of, his own nature': for γίγνομαι with this sort of genitive see LSJ s.v. II 3. a.

50 διωλύγιον κατεβόα: 'gave a tremendous shout': cf. Chariton 3. 3. 15 διωλύγιον ἀνεβόησεν.

53 συλλαβεῖν: Lesky's supplement, or something like it, seems required to complete the sense.

55 ὡς ἐν ὑποθέσει … ἀντεπάγων: lit. 'bringing up in return as a supposition': ὑπόθεσις is the technical word for a logical assumption or supposition, matching the doctor's description as συλλογιστικός.

57 ἐκαρτέρεις … ἐκδοῦναι: the infinitive with καρτερεῖν is very rare (see LSJ), but natural on the analogy of τολμᾶν.

66 μὲν: as in classical Greek, μὲν here on its own (without a following correlative δέ) is simply emphatic and affirmative (Denniston, *GP* 359 ff.).

Aristaenetus 2. 3

Newly married Glycera complains to Philinna that her sophist husband spends his nights practising his speeches instead of making love to her. Can Philinna please help her out with a replacement?

We have here a variation on the familiar theme of a disparate marriage, often an older man married to a young girl, with the attendant strains and difficulties. Theognis expressed it pungently: οὔ τοι σύμφορόν ἐστι γυνὴ νέα ἀνδρὶ γέροντι (457), and Aristaenetus has another letter exploiting a disparate marriage (1. 5).

1 σοφῷ ῥήτορι: Strepsiades is a sophist, a professional declaimer or rhetor, who teaches oratory to students and gives public performances to illustrate his own skill, and also practises in court. Here Strepsiades has been instructed in a case (ἐδιδάχθη), and he works late into the night, getting every detail of his delivery right. On the whole subject of declamation and its performers in the Graeco-Roman world see G. W. Bowersock, *Greek Sophists in the Roman Empire* (Oxford, 1969), D. A. Russell, *Greek Declamation* (Cambridge, 1983), esp. chap. 4. The name Strepsiades ('Twister') is appropriately uncomplimentary (cf. δικορράφος at the end), and must also be intended to recall Strepsiades in Aristophanes' *Clouds*.

3 πραγμάτων: for πράγματα meaning 'law-business' see LSJ s.v. III 4.

4 ὑπόκρισιν: the technical term for an orator's delivery: he is essentially acting a part. For the importance of delivery see Russell, op. cit. 82, and Quintilian's long section (11. 3) on delivery, including the need to practise gestures.

8 γυμναστήριον: used metaphorically, but Glycera of course means he should be 'stripping off' for a different activity.

11 ὑποθέσεως... ῥήτωρ... δίκης: Glycera punningly adapts legal and rhetorical terms to her own situation, but the word-play is hard to retain in translation. *Hypothesis* was the formal subject of a declamation.

16 θεραπεύειν: the 'cure' Glycera is requesting is of course that Philinna find her a lover. Philinna had acted formally as her go-between when her marriage was being arranged, and must now do so rather more informally. The προμνήστρια (matchmaker, go-between) was a girl's older woman friend, who assisted the courtship by recommending her charms to the prospective husband in order to win him over. See Aristoph. *Nu.* 41 (with Dover's note), Plato *Tht.* 149d, Xen. *Mem.* 2. 6. 36.

19 τὸν λύκον... ἔχω: a proverbial expression with the sense of the English 'to catch a Tartar'. The Latin version appears in Terence, *Phormio* 506 'auribus teneo lupum'. (See Leutsch–Schneidewin, ii. 220.) Glycera finds her husband unbearable, but cannot risk leaving him for fear of legal consequences.

21 ἀναίτιον αἰτιάσηται: Glycera continues her sententious strain. The phrase ἀναίτιον αἰτιάασθαι (from Homer *Il.* 13. 775) is quoted twice by Lucian as a poetical 'tag': *Prometheus* 4, *Hermotimus* 63.

ARISTAENETUS 2. 15

Chrysis and her widowed friend Myrrhina have a mutual problem: Chrysis has a passion for Myrrhina's slave and Myrrhina is in love with Chrysis' husband. Chrysis offers a solution.

This letter takes us straight into the world of mime and the novel, especially with the theme of sexual relations between mistress and slave. We find a lively treatment of this, for example, in Herodas, *Mime* 5 (see Headlam's discussion of the motif in his edn., pp. xlv f.). The scheming, domineering mistress and the exploited slave are by now well established types, and play their parts in this little picture of unscrupulous sexual intrigue.

4 τῆς Ἀφροδίτης: Hercher's supplement, accepted by Lesky and Mazal, supplying an object for ἐδεήθην to be picked up by ἡ δαίμων.

7 δόκει οὖν: οὖν is very irregular this late in the sentence (Hercher deleted it), but it might be defended by regarding the words τὸν... ἐρωτικὸν as essentially a unit describing one individual.

12 ἐξαποστέλλω: the present tense used vividly for the future, expressing certainty of intention (Weir Smyth, §1879).

17 ἔρρωσο: see above on Alciphron 4. 7.

19 εὐτυχοῦσα: transitive εὐτυχεῖν is late and mainly non-literary: see LSJ Rev. Suppl. s. v.; Russell–Wilson on Menander Rhetor 439. 10.

ANACHARSIS 1

I know my Greek is not perfect, but it is unfair to make fun of people's difficulties with a foreign language. What matters is the meaning and intention behind what is said.

According to Diogenes Laertius (1. 101) Anacharsis had a Greek mother and was bilingual, but we may imagine that he spoke Greek with a foreign accent: his imperfections in Greek are reported elsewhere: Fronto, *Ep. Graec.* 1. 5 τὸν ᾿Ανάχαρσιν οὐ πάνυ τι ἀττικίσαι φασίν; *Gnomol. Vat.* 16 (Sternbach) (᾿Ανάχαρσις) λοιδορούμενος ὑπ᾿ ᾿Αθηναίων ἐπὶ τῷ σολοικίζειν εἶπεν, ᾿Ανάχαρσις ᾿Αθηναίοις σολοικίζει, ᾿Αθηναῖοι δὲ ᾿Αναχάρσιδι.

As elsewhere in the letters Anacharsis is here a spokesman for a Cynic theme—the importance of judging people by inner worth and not by external trappings. This letter also resembles many passages in the others in its idealizing of the Scythians.

1 γελᾶτε…: a common reaction then as now to verbal infelicities: see too Dion. Hal. *Comp.* 18 γελᾶν δὲ ὁ σολοικισμὸς ἐποίει.

2 ᾿Ανάχαρσις…᾿Αθηναῖοι…: cf. the quotation from *Gnomol. Vat.* above.

2 σολοικίζει: here in the sense of faults in pronunciation rather than in grammar (cf. below, φωνῇ ἄρθρα οὐκ ἐχούσῃ). This seems to be an earlier meaning of the verb, which helps to date the letters to the 3rd cent. BC (Reuters, 4–5). The traditional derivation of the word was from the Athenian colony of Soli in Cilicia, whose inhabitants spoke a corrupt form of Attic (LSJ s.v. σόλοικος).

4 Σπαρτιᾶται: Herodotus reports (4. 77) that Anacharsis had a particular admiration for the Spartans.

6–7 λόγον…τοῦ δέοντος: according to Maximus of Tyre (25. 1) Anacharsis' own brand of wisdom was characterized by βίος ἀκριβὴς καὶ γνώμη ὑγιὴς καὶ λόγος βραχύς, εὔστοχος.

8 ἄρθρα: the correct articulation of syllables which is difficult for those speaking a foreign language: for this sense of the word cf. Arist. *HA* 536ᵃ3 ἄρθρον τῆς φωνῆς.

9–10 ὠνεῖσθε ... λαμβάνετε ...: the point is: you are not tempted to pay more to vendors just because they speak fluent Greek, in contrast with foreigners.

20 φωνὰς ζητεῖτε ἐμμελεῖς ...: another variation on the theme: by all means judge technical perfection in performances to be all-important; but when it comes to speakers (in politics) think of the sense (rather than the words).

24 γυναιξὶ καὶ τέκνοις: (don't judge others) and don't let yourselves be judged on the domestic scene for slips in language.

ANACHARSIS 2

The Greeks have no monopoly of wisdom: other peoples are wise and good by the same standards; so why do you, Solon, decline my friendship?

Solon was the great early statesman, lawgiver, and poet of Athens, and chief archon in 594/3. This letter, in which one of the Seven Sages addresses another, reflects the tradition that Anacharsis visited Athens and Solon in about 592; and this visit (legendary or not) generated other anecdotes about the meeting. Plutarch (*Solon* 5) and Diogenes Laertius (1. 101 ff.) have a very similar story to ours of Anacharsis knocking on Solon's door, though it ends with Solon complying with his request; and Lucian in his *Anacharsis* brings them together for a long discussion about athletics.

5 στῆλαι ...: again the Cynic stress on essential qualities opposed to outward show (see above, introductory note to Letter 1). Adorning buildings with elegant columns symbolized luxury, and not just for the Cynics: see the Stoic Musonius, τί δ᾽ αἱ περίστυλοι αὐλαί; (p. 108. 5 Hense); Sen. *Ep.* 115. 8 'nos (delectant) ingenium maculae columnarum'; Tib. 3. 3. 13.

11–12 ἐκείνῳ ἀνδρὶ κύνα τοῦτον: our author decorates the letter with an obvious chiasmus. Spartan dogs had long been highly regarded and should therefore be welcome presents. (See Pindar, fr. 95 Bowra, Soph. *Ajax* 8, Xen. *Cyn.* 3 ff., Virg. *G.* 3. 405.)

DIOGENES 30

Diogenes tells his father how he made a choice between two roads leading to happiness, and how he was equipped for the journey.

The letter follows a long tradition of discussions of moral choices, often using the imagery of a road or roads which the chooser has to decide upon: e.g. Hesiod, *Op.* 256 ff. (κακότης or ἀρετή: see West's note on this for other parallels and the proverbial background to the imagery); Xen. *Mem.* 2. 1. 21 ff. (the 'Choice of Hercules' between κακία and ἀρετή); 'Diogenes' again in *Ep.* 37 (the road to εὐδαιμονία). For further discussion of this kind of imagery see Capelle, 31 ff.

The 'companion of Socrates' referred to here is usually assumed to be Antisthenes, associate of Socrates and the original inspiration for the Cynic movement. Some of our sources report that Diogenes was a personal pupil of Antisthenes (Plut. *Quaest. Conv.* 2. 632e; Dio Chrys. 8. 1; Diog. Laert. 6. 21), and though this is chronologically difficult it is certain that he was strongly influenced by Antisthenes at whatever remove, and himself became the most famous Cynic among the sect.

6–7 ἐπειδὴ ... καὶ ὃς ...: the construction has a slight anacoluthon, with καὶ ὃς introducing the main clause.

10 δύο τινὲ ὁδώ: Pausanias (1. 22. 4) tells us firmly that there was only one road up to the Acropolis, and he must refer to the gently sloping path from the west side (the smooth and easy one here). But there was another point of ascent located through a deep cleft to the east of the Erechtheum, which might be the second one here. A modern authority supports Antisthenes: 'There are two ways up to the summit: one on the west side, where the slope is comparatively gentle, and another about half way along the north side, where a deep fold in the rock forms a very steep and difficult natural approach. Elsewhere the sheer sides of the hill are unscalable' Spyros E. Iakovides, *Late Helladic Citadels on Mainland Greece* (Monumenta Graeca et Romana; Leiden, 1983), 73.

12 καθιστὰς ἅμα γάρ ...: the text may be corrupt: καθιστὰς is not very clear (presumably 'brought back' from the Acropolis), and γάρ is displaced. (For καθιστάς we might consider καθίσας 'making us sit down'.)

18 διὰ πυρὸς ἢ ξιφῶν: proverbial as in English: LSJ s.v. II. But the combination seems to be commoner in Latin with the similar *ferrum et ignis*: see Otto, *Sprichwörter*, s.v. *ignis* 1.

20–3 τρίβωνα... πήραν... βακτηρίαν: cloak, pouch, and staff are the standard equipment of the itinerant Cynic, and as Diogenes' mentor Antisthenes gives him his kit: Plut. *Quaest. Conv.* 2. 632E (Antisthenes gave Diogenes rags and made him a beggar); and cf. 'Diogenes', *Ep.* 37. 4.

22 λήκυθον καὶ στλεγγίδα: oil and scraper were the ancient equivalents of soap and flannel for washing, as explained allusively below.

27–8 χειμῶνος... ταλαιπωρίαν: the single cloak was insufficiently thick for the discomfort of winter cold. Presumably the double cloak was not too hot for summer.

29 οἰκίαν: 'house' here in the natural extended sense 'household necessities'.

31 ὄψῳ ἑτέρῳ...: ἔφη is otiose after εἶπε, and the text may be corrupt. (Capelle suggested, perhaps rightly, that a question from Diogenes, say, about the relish, has dropped out before ὄψῳ ἑτέρῳ.)

31 κάρδαμον: sometimes translated 'mustard', seems to be some type of cress used as a garnish. It occurs in the similar context in 'Diogenes', *Ep.* 37. 4.

33 ἀρωγόν... πόνων: from Plato, *Menex.* 238a7 (the earth gave us) ἐλαίου γένεσιν, πόνων ἀρωγήν. After hard work or exercise the oil cleans you, and the scraper wipes you dry of the accumulated oil and dirt, γλοιός.

35 πρὸς τοὺς ποιητάς: presumably in punishment for their sometimes uncomplimentary references to the gods. Plato had famously accused the poets of this, *Rep.* 3. 388b8 ff., and Euripides, for one, was notorious for his alleged irreverence. Antisthenes warns Diogenes to expect ribaldry from the poets—and to retaliate.

CRATES 34

Crates, himself a disciple of Diogenes, writes to his brother-in-law Metrocles with an account of Diogenes' courageous and clear-headed behaviour when captured and offered for sale by pirates.

The addressee Metrocles was a fellow Cynic and the brother of Crates' wife Hipparchia.

The story of the 'sale of Diogenes' was a favourite anecdote among the Cynics, and we have many versions which reproduce details in this letter or offer variants on the tale. Menippus of Gadara wrote a Διογένους πρᾶσις, and see also Philo, *Quod omnis probus* 121–4, Epictetus 2. 13. 24, 3. 24. 66, 4. 1. 114 ff.; Diog. Laert. 6. 29–30, 36, 74; Lucian, *Vit. Auct.* 7 ff.

4 ἤνεγκε …: this begins the verbatim report of the ex-prisoner, which continues to ἀφήσειν (5).

5 οὗτοι: the vocative has as commonly a tone of peremptory impatience or scorn: LSJ s.v. C I 5.

20 καὶ γάρ … σίτου: from *Iliad* 24. 602, where Achilles similarly exhorts Priam to eat in spite of his grief: even the archetypal mourner Niobe remembered to eat.

22 εἰρωνευόμενοι: Diogenes suggests that their lamentations are contrived and unrealistic, since in fact they have always been slaves of a sort.

28 ἀπαθείας: here used generally of insensibility to disaster, but the word must have resonances of its technical Stoic use as freedom from strong emotions.

32–3 ἡδονήν … μέγιστα τῶν κακῶν δελέατα: perhaps a reminiscence of Plato, *Ti.* 69d1: ἡδονήν, μέγιστον κακοῦ δέλεαρ.

35 τοῦ λίθου: the stone block from which slaves were sold by the auctioneer, like the πρατὴρ λίθος in the Athenian agora.

SOCRATES 5

Xenophon is on his way to assist Cyrus to take over the Persian throne from his brother Artaxerxes II, and Socrates writes to his old pupil to warn him that this venture has its strong critics in Athens. But now he has begun he must carry on with vigour and courage.

Although Socrates had actually advised Xenophon against this expedition in 401 BC (*Anab.* 3. 1. 5 ff.; and cf. Chion 3.4 *n.*), on the same grounds as expressed here of Cyrus' support of Sparta against Athens, this letter shows him now generously associating himself with the venture, and offering moral support and encouragement in the face of Xenophon's critics. There seems to be no other clear evidence of this particular opposition to Xenophon's activities, but there may have been some residual resentment against him in the restored democracy relating to his apparent acceptance of the Thirty Tyrants (404–403), and his opposition to the democratic insurgents during their rule.

1 **Θήβαις ... Πρόξενον**: the letter is sent to Thebes, where Xenophon is supposed to be meeting Proxenus, a Boeotian friend who had persuaded him to join the expedition (*Anab.* 1. 1. 11; Diog. Laert. 2. 49–50).

4 **οὐ γὰρ ἄξιόν ...**: the same point is made in Xen. *Anab.* 3. 1. 5. The strength of feeling is stressed by the repetition ὑπὲρ ἐκείνου, δι᾿ ἐκεῖνον.

7 **μεταπεσούσης τῆς πολιτείας**: this might refer to either future change or change that has already happened, i.e. the restored democracy: the translation assumes the latter.

12 **περὶ ἀρετῆς**: Socrates reminds him of a stock subject of philosophical discussion. He underlines his point with a famous quotation from Homer—part of his father's injunction to Glaucus: αἰὲν ἀριστεύειν καὶ ὑπείροχον ἔμμεναι ἄλλων, | μηδὲ γένος πατέρων αἰσχυνέμεν (*Il.* 6. 208–9).

17 **οἰκεῖα ... παραδείγματα**: i.e. I don't have to spell this out to you: you know the types of men I mean.

SOCRATICS 21

Aeschines writes a friendly letter to Socrates' widow, offering support to her and her children, and encouraging her to remember the ideals and the noble qualities of Socrates' life.

The writer is supposed to be Aeschines 'the Socratic', famous as a loyal and devoted disciple of Socrates (see also above, note on Philostratus 73). Allatius in his edition (1637), followed by Hercher, assigned the letter to Xenophon, but there seem no good grounds for doing this: see Köhler's note on this letter.

Several other members of the Socratic circle appear in the letter. Eucleides and Terpsion are mentioned as Megarians in *Phaedo* 59c2. (Aeschines is supposed to be visiting them in Megara when he writes this letter.) Eucleides was the founder of the so-called Megarian school of philosophy. Apollodorus of Phalerum was another great admirer and constant companion of Socrates. Dion is mentioned briefly at *Menex.* 234b10. Aeschines, Eucleides, Terpsion, and Apollodorus were all present at Socrates' death (*Phaedo* 59b6 ff.).

This letter of course ignores the traditional account of Xanthippe as a nagging scold who made Socrates' life a misery: e.g. Sen. *Const.* 18, *Ep.* 104. 27 (where we are also told that his children were undisciplined, and more like their mother than their father).

1 **Εὔφρονι:** presumably a local friend entrusted with the errand to take the presents to Xanthippe.

14 **ὁμολογουμένως:** i.e. sympathetically consistently with what you and I do at present: cf. Xen. *Oec.* 1. 11.

17 **ὁ μαλακὸς:** this nickname of Apollodorus is found also in Plato, *Symp.* 173d8. (The variant μανικὸς in the Plato passage is read here by Köhler (following Allatius), but μαλακὸς must be the right reading there: see Dover's note ad loc.)

18 **παρ' οὐδενὸς οὐδὲν λαμβάνεις:** as 'Socrates' said of himself in *Ep.* 1. 2 παρ' οὐδενὸς οὐδὲν εἰληφὼς εὑρεθήσομαι.

22–3 **ὁποῖα... καὶ ὁποῖα:** Westermann's correction καὶ for the MSS μὴ is necessary to make sense of the next sentence: both Socrates' life and his death were exemplary.

EURIPIDES 5

Euripides writes to Cephisophon in Athens to tell him about his arrival and reception in Macedonia. He goes on to discuss his enemies in Athens who are spreading malicious gossip about him, and urges Cephisophon simply to ignore them.

We hear about Cephisophon from Aristophanes as a friend of Euripides and collaborator in his plays (*Ra.* 944, 1408, 1452–3). There was also a story, found both in the ancient *Vita Eur.* 6, and in Satyrus' biography, col. XII, that Cephisophon seduced Euripides' wife; but this is usually discounted on the grounds that Aristophanes would surely have made capital out of it, and the writer of our letter obviously regarded the two men as enjoying a friendly relationship. See Dover's edition of Aristoph. *Ra.*, pp. 53–4 and note on 1046–8; and Gösswein's judicious note.

1 **Μακεδονίαν:** Eur. went to Macedonia in about 408, at the invitation of Archelaus (reigned *c.*413–399), who was interested in improving not only the military but also the cultural strength of his kingdom. Whether his departure from Athens was due to unpopularity and adverse criticism there is debatable and quite uncertain. We do not know whether he was as impervious to backbiting as this letter portrays him; and though there is an allusion to a cogent reason for his departure (ἀπηνάγκασε, 2), we are not told here or elsewhere what it was.

2 **οὐ μοχθηρῶς διατεθέντες:** a touch of complacency, as it must have been a gruelling journey for a man in his seventies.

4 δωρεαῖς: Plutarch has a relevant anecdote (*Mor.* 531D–E) about Archelaus' discriminating generosity: he gave a golden cup to Euripides who had not asked for it, instead of to another guest who had requested it.

6 Κλείτωνα: apparently an official or courtier attached to Archelaus and on friendly terms with Eur.; but this letter contains the only allusions to him, apart from Letter 1 to Archelaus, which mentions him in a similar context.

10 φροντίζειν ... καὶ ποιεῖν: Eur. does indeed seem to have continued to write in Macedonia (*Bacchae* and *IA* probably date from these last years); and Gösswein suggests that there must be a reference here to the lost play *Archelaus*, which the *Vita* tells us Eur. composed as a thank-offering to his host.

17 Ἀγάθων, Μέσατος: if Agathon is the famous tragic poet it is not clear why he was criticizing Eur. They were said to be on friendly terms, and Agathon was in fact at Archelaus' court at the same time as Eur. (Aelian, *VH* 13. 4; Aristoph. *Ra.* 83–5). Perhaps another rival poet of the same name, unknown to us, is referred to. Mesatus is a more shadowy 5th-cent. tragedian (Schol. Aristoph. *Vesp.* 1502; *POxy* 20. 2256), and nothing is known of relations between him and Eur.

17 Ἀριστοφάνους: for most of his creative life Aristophanes never tired of poking fun at Eur., the most extended parodies occurring in *Acharnians*, *Thesmophoriazusae*, and *Frogs*.

22–3 μὴ δεῖν ... ἀποδημεῖν: presumably Eur. is portrayed as having previously stated that he did not need the protection of a royal patron, but something subsequently made him (ἀπηνάγκασε) change his mind.

24 τοῦτον δὲ: an example of the 'apodotic' δέ: it is strictly superfluous, but used for emphasis in the apodosis of a conditional sentence, especially after a personal or demonstrative pronoun, as here. See Weir Smyth §2837; Denniston, *GP* 177 ff.

24 τοῦτον ... αὐτῷ: a slightly loose repetition designed to give emphasis: '*that* is the person you can tell ...'.

28 οὐ γάρ που δὴ: = οὐ γὰρ δήπου.

29 Τριβαλλοῖς: a people living on the borders of Thrace who became the proverbial type of far-off, uncivilized barbarians: see e.g. Aristoph. *Av.* 1529 (with Dunbar's note). The allusion is geographically apt here, as the Triballi were not very distant from where Euripides is supposed to be writing his letter.

31 δηλονότι: used here with obvious irony: I must of course want to enrich myself. In fact Eur. must have been well-to-do, as Aristotle reports (*Rhet.* 3. 1416ᵃ29–30) that he was once challenged to an *antidosis* (an exchange of properties when an expensive public service was in question); and Aristophanes' jibe about his mother Cleito being a greengrocer (*Thesm.* 387) is probably not to be taken seriously. (The *Suda* entry quotes Philochorus' statement that she was of high birth.)

43–4 οὐ λαμβάνοιμεν...: this correspondence consistently portrays Eur. as refusing Archelaus' generosity: in *Ep.* 1 he writes to Archelaus, returning a gift of silver Archelaus had sent him. The forty silver talents mentioned here seems a very large sum. Possibly numerical symbols have become confused (as frequently in manuscripts); or the author, writing in Roman imperial times when the talent was worth less, has unhistorically projected back a figure which is too large for Euripides' time.

49 ἀποδημῆσαι... ἀποδημίαν: the *figura etymologica* is a self-consciously stylistic touch.

50 ἀλαζονείαν... τοῦ δύνασθαί: Eur. then replies to these charges in reverse order: ἡ μὲν δύναμις ... ἀλαζονείας τε ἕνεκα.

51 'Αλλ' ἡ μὲν δύναμις: the sentence is elaborate and the text in places uncertain (see Gösswein's note), but Eur. seems to be saying that if his motive for going to Pella was supposed to be to acquire influence with Archelaus, he already had it at Athens, particularly through his powerful friend-at-court Clito: so that was no reason for a major disruption in his life. With the printed text ἡ δύναμις governs the three substantival infinitives τοῦ ... βιοῦν ... ἀποθανεῖν ... παρέχειν.

57 εἰς τὰ τῆς πόλεως: this might mean that Eur. helped to persuade Archelaus to offer Athens the support he gave her towards the end of the Peloponnesian War; but if so, a clearer reference to this would have strengthened his point.

63 Σοφοκλέους: our author takes the reasonable view that, at least in their later years, Eur. and Sophocles were on friendly terms. (In *Ep.* 2 Eur. commiserates feelingly with Sophocles on the loss of some of his plays on a sea voyage.) This is supported by the well-attested story (in the *Vita* and other sources), that at the first *proagon* after the death of Eur. Sophocles appeared dressed in mourning and his chorus did not put on the traditional crowns.

66 φιλοτιμότερον: this must allude to Sophocles' obvious willingness to take on public duties: he was *Hellenotamias* or treasurer of the Delian League in 443/2; he was twice elected *strategos*; and he served as one of the *probouloi* appointed to cope with the crisis following the Sicilian disaster. But φιλοτιμότερος is a derogatory term, so Eur. is supposed to be admitting to a touch of jealousy or suspicion at these activities.

69–70 ἵνα... αὐτοὶ: the text follows Gösswein's conjectures for the MSS reading εἶναι ἄν τοι, which gives no construction.

71 διαβεβλήμεθα: for this rare sense of the verb, 'dupe', 'deceive' ('outwit' seems right here), see Herod. 9. 116, Plato, *Phaedr.* 255a5, Aristoph. *Av.* 1648; LSJ s.v. VI.

76 εὖ ποιεῖς περὶ τούτων... ἀδικεῖν... ἀντιλέγοντα: the letter closes with an emphatic restatement of the opening theme of sect. 2.

THEMISTOCLES 9

Themistocles writes a bitter letter to his political enemy Callias, who, while Themistocles is exiled from Athens, is attacking him and seeking to be elected general himself. The city does not need men like Callias, who is acting just like a cowardly intriguer.

The context of the letter is the acrimonious political bickering that was taking place at Athens in the late 470s against the background of the struggle between Greece and Persia. Themistocles was ostracized in around 472 because his policy towards Sparta was not acceptable to the Athenian people, and he went to live in Argos. While there he was implicated in Pausanias' Medizing manoeuvres and condemned to death, but the Athenians agreed to try him before the court of the Greek League. Before he could be escorted back for trial he escaped from Argos and went initially to Corcyra. After further wanderings he arrived at Ephesus, from where Letters 6, 7, 8, and therefore presumably 9 were written, though our letter has no indication of its source.

1–2 Καλλία... πλούτου: Callias was very rich, being the leader of the wealthy Ceryces clan; he was also a cousin of Aristides, one of Themistocles' strongest political opponents. Subsequently he led the negotiators for the peace treaty between Athens and Persia, *c*.448, which has been called the 'Peace of Callias'. The reference to Aristides' malice must be to something he had said about Themistocles which Callias would like to have said himself. Aristides' comment about Callias' wealth seems to refer to a story found in Plutarch (*Arist.* 25), that Aristides had declined an offer of financial help from Callias because he prided himself more on his poverty than Callias did on his wealth.

6 ἐκ τῶν ἀναξίων ... εἰς ἐμὲ αἰνιττόμενος: the implied slur might be because Themistocles' mother was not an Athenian: Plut. *Them.* 1; Nepos, *Them.* 1. 2.

10 ἄλλους Θεμιστοκλέας: i.e. other generals who were as distinguished as I was. As *strategos* in 480 Themistocles had been responsible for the decisive defeat of the Persians at Salamis.

12 τῶν τυμβωρυχησάντων: Callias was nicknamed λακκόπλουτος ('pit-wealth'), which might have derived from the mines he owned (Nepos, *Cim.* 1. 3). But the reference here is clearly to the story we have in Plutarch (*Arist.* 5), that Callias tricked a Persian prisoner at Marathon into revealing some gold hidden in a pit. The version in our letter seems to link the pit with the graves of the Persians who fell at Marathon, which Callias dug up to find the gold.

13 ἐν Εὐβοίᾳ: in 490, when Euboea was attacked by the Persians under Datis.

21 οὓς ... ἐκληρονομήσω: a sardonic reference to Callias stealing the Persian gold at Marathon, pressing home the following words ἀφελόμενος ... τὰ λάφυρα.

30–1 σὺ ... ἐμπίπλασο: in similar vein Themistocles tells Leagros (*Ep.* 8. 4) that the Athenians feasted on him as on a beast that had fallen.

33 δημηγορίας: there is no other reference to Callias attacking Themistocles in a speech, but the writer might have known of one, or assumed it.

34 δώσει ... δώσει: the letter-writer affects this kind of repetition: see too εἰμί γε, εἰμι (10. 3); ἤραμεν εἰς Πέρσας ... ἤραμεν (12. 1).

34 οὐκ ἀρετᾷ κακὰ ἔργα: one poet anyway: Homer, *Od.* 8. 329 (the gods comment on Ares and Aphrodite caught in adultery).

HIPPOCRATES 14

Hippocrates writes to a friend in Rhodes, requesting the use of a good boat to take him to Abdera. He has been summoned there to cure Democritus of his incessant laughter, which is thought to be a sign of madness.

This particular Damagetus cannot be pinpointed, but the name is found repeatedly in the famous Rhodian family, the Diagoridae, with whom the author of the letter assumes Hippocrates to be acquainted.

2 Ἅλιος: an appropriate name for a Rhodian boat, as Rhodes was an important centre for the worship of the sun god.

6 πτεροῖσιν ἐρετμώσας: the idea may come from Aesch. *Ag.* 52 πτερύγων ἐρετμοῖσιν ἐρεσσόμενοι. The image was popular in the Latin poets: Virg. *Aen.* 6. 19 'remigium alarum'; Lucr. 6. 743; Ovid, *Met.* 8. 228.

15–16 χαριέστατος ... φροντιστής: i.e. both socially charming and a serious philosopher, the usual sense of φροντιστής.

27 μελαγχολᾷς: 'mad', 'crazy', not 'melancholy'. Hippocrates himself in some of his earlier treatises pointed to 'black bile' as a symptom of physical and mental disturbance. See H. Flashar, *Melancholie und Melancholiker in den medizinischen Theorien der Antike* (Berlin, 1966).

28–9 Ἀβδηρίτης ... πόλις: the Abderites were proverbial for being simple and stupid (Otto, *Sprichwörter*, s.v.), yet his city shows more sense than Democritus in his present mood. Cicero makes a similar comparison: 'omnia sunt patria Democriti quam Democrito digniora' (*ND* 1. 120).

HIPPOCRATES 17

This long letter is the last in the series (10–17) within the Hippocratic corpus of letters dealing with Democritus and Hippocrates' visit to Abdera. In it he gives Damagetus an account of his meeting with Democritus and the long discussion he had with him. The upshot of the meeting is that he is convinced that Democritus is not mad: rather he is truly wise in his analysis of human nature and men's wayward activities, and so far from trying to cure him Hippocrates will proclaim Democritus' wisdom to the world.

5 Ὑγιείην: Hygieia was the personification of good health; she was the daughter of Asclepius and shared his cult. We know from Letter 14 above that the boat was named 'Helios'.

10 οὗτοι μέντοι...: understand something like κατηφεῖς ἦσαν from the previous clause.

11 ὁ δέ... ὑπερεφιλοσόφει: as Hippocrates subsequently discovered. This is a very rare compound ('up to his ears in philosophy'): apart from this passage only Philostr. *VA* 7. 37 is cited (LSJ Rev. Suppl.).

19 ἐτησίῃσιν ὥρῃσιν: i.e. the summer when these winds blew (cf. below, Chion 13.17), so Democritus might be suffering at worst from a mild hot weather ailment. Hippocrates' *Epidemics* have many references to fevers which occur in the summer (e.g. *Epid.* 2. 1. 2; 7. 82).

25 ἀμφιλαφεῖ... πλατανίστῳ: this description of a *locus amoenus* as the scene for a philosophical discussion obviously recalls the setting of Plato's *Phaedrus* (230b2 ff.), where there is also a πλάτανος ἀμφιλαφὴς and a shrine to the nymphs. (For this kind of influence of the *Phaedrus* on later Greek literature see M. B. Trapp, in D. A. Russell (ed.), *Antonine Literature* (Oxford, 1990), 141 ff.)

72 ἐκ πατέρων... ξεῖνος: from Homeric times the bonds of ξενία, reciprocal hospitality, were very strong in Greek society and passed down from generation to generation in the families concerned.

77 προὔπεσεν: προπίπτειν has the sense here of 'make a slip of the tongue': LSJ s.v. II 2.

78 τί... ἄλλο ἢ τίς πέλει: 'its precise nature': for the form of the expression see LSJ s. v. ἄλλος III 2.

81 χολῆς: see above, 14.27 *n.* on μελαγχολᾷς for Hippocrates' own professional interest in bile and its link with physical and mental dis-orders. For Hippocrates to be receiving a lecture on the nature of bile is part of the turning of the tables upon him by Democritus which this letter is largely about.

84 ὕλης: used of 'matter' in the human body by medical writers: LSJ s.v. IV 2.

87 ἡμῖν δὲ μετέχειν ταύτης...: there is obvious humour here in the complaint of the great physician that he has no time to pursue his researches because of domestic and social distractions. But it may also be a device to keep Democritus talking.

99 τίνος ἄξιος... γέλωτος: the construction is slightly loose, with ἄξιος joined to both genitives: 'for what reason I seemed to deserve laughter'.

[For the omitted section of the letter see summary in the translation. In effect Democritus delivers what might later be described as a Cynic diatribe on the follies and vices of men, and explains that they are the real cause of his laughter.]

105 παιήονα: = παιώνια (which is read by one manuscript): for the phrase cf. Aesch. *Ag*. 848.

105 σὸς πρόγονος Ἀσκληπιὸς: πρόγονος has its derived sense of founder of a school or sect. Asclepius was destroyed by a thunderbolt from Zeus, who was enraged because he had restored Hippolytus to life: Virg. *Aen*. 7. 765 ff.; Ovid, *F*. 6. 746 ff.

107 κακίης μοῖρά εἰμι: Democritus admits that he shares the lunacy of men that he has been castigating in misdirecting his researches onto animals rather than humans.

108 κατακτείνω: the translation assumes this reading: the variant κατατείνω ('torment', 'torture') would suggest more brutal vivisection.

110–11 ἄνθρωπος ἐκ γενετῆς...: Democritus' version of the Ages of Man—deeply pessimistic in accordance with his general creed.

114 λύθρων: talking to a doctor Democritus uses a medical term: the word is applied to the blood in the womb or appearing at childbirth.

117 ὄφελον: in this construction found in later Greek ὄφελον is used semi-adverbially with a finite verb (ὑπῆρχεν) attached to it paratactically (here = ὤφελον δύναμιν ἔχειν): LSJ s.v. ὀφείλω II c.

124–5 βαθύτεραι πρήξιες ... κευθομένων: this rather arcane statement resembles a similar remark attributed to Democritus in Plut. *Animine an corporis* 500 D, about the store of evil hidden inside men. He seems to suggest that we all have within us the potential for even more nefarious activities than we visibly indulge in.

150 ἀναισθήτοισι ... ψῆφοι: the adage summarizes this rather wordy homily on the thesis that fools only applaud other fools and have no respect for talent.

151 οἱ πάσχοντες: the unexpressed object is τὸ κρέσσον: 'those who experience superior talent (in others)'. Then a fresh point is added, that fellow professionals (ὁμοτεχνεῦντες—in this case other doctors) are jealous—as you well know.

155 φιλοτωθάσσοντα: the text is uncertain, but the sense is clear and this reading will serve.

155 ἀτρεκείης ...μαρτυρίη: Democritus' coda that we cannot know the real truth about people both consoles Hippocrates for having been misjudged by others and applauds him for not himself maliciously misjudging others.

160 κῆρυξ: W. D. Smith in his edition (p. 22) suggests that we have here a sly literary reference to a joke about the Abderites reported by Athenaeus (8. 349). He quotes some lines by the New Comedy poet Machon about the musician Stratonicus visiting Abdera. There he found that each Abderite employed his own herald, so that there were more heralds than citizens. If the allusion is intended, Hippocrates is volunteering his services to Democritus as his personal crier.

161–2 τῆς τοῦ σώματος τημελείης: hunger or the natural functions.

166 τοὺς ἐόντως Ἀβδηρίτας: the point of ἐόντως is presumably 'the genuine Abderites', i.e. the real fools, in contrast with Democritus, similar in sense to αὐτὸς Ἀβδηρίτης in *Ep.* 14 (see note there).

CHION 3

Chion writes to tell his father that a meeting with Xenophon has convinced him that philosophers are capable of vigorous and decisive action. Previously he had thought that the weakness in philosophical teaching was that it did not encourage men to be brave or heroic. If we ignore the wide gap between this episode (400/399 BC) and the murder of Clearchus (353/2 BC), we might regard this letter as revealing an impetus given to a student of Platonism towards the heroic act of killing a tyrant.

Behind the letter lie the traditional philosophical alternatives of the active and contemplative lives (βίος πρακτικός and βίος θεωρητικός). The Stoic Panaetius had divided virtues into the practical and the contemplative (Diog Laert. 7. 92), and the division is reflected in many later writers (e.g. Seneca, *Ep.* 94. 45). Another traditional aspect of our letter is its picture of Xenophon as a role-model: he was widely admired, particularly by Stoics, both for his literary style and for his heroic personal qualities. (See K. Münscher, *Philol.* Suppl. xiii 2 (1920); Russell on 'Longinus' 8. 1.) So too he serves here as a model of active virtue.

Chion's account of his meeting Xenophon at Byzantium is based very loosely on *Anabasis* 7, which deals with events at Byzantium when Xenophon arrived there after his return from the famous expedition. More precisely it is a very fanciful version of *Anab.* 7. 1. 18 ff., as a comparison with Xenophon's account will show, Chion's aim being to stress the dominance and charismatic power of Xenophon in a crisis. Also, the reason given here for Seuthes' need of Xenophon's mercenaries does not tally with Xenophon's account, where Seuthes says he is trying to regain power in his own kingdom (*Anab.* 7. 2. 34). See Düring's note for a discussion of these divergences, and for references to other views of the letter.

4 γνώριμος: for the sense 'pupil' see LSJ s.v. I 2 b. In fact it was against Socrates' advice that in 401 Xenophon joined the expedition to assist Cyrus to wrest the Persian throne from his brother Artaxerxes II (*Anab.* 3. 1. 5 ff.).

9 ἀπετμήθησαν τὰς κεφαλάς: as reported by Xenophon (*Anab.* 2. 6. 1).

31 ἀνάγετε ἐπὶ πόδα: i.e. retire still facing the enemy, in a leisurely manner.

37–8 μηδὲν … πνέοντας: a touch of the high style: the phrase echoes the Homeric μένεα πνείοντες and more particularly Aesch. *Ag.* 375 τῶν Ἄρη πνεόντων. With the very rare ἁρπακτοῦ Chion also seems to have his eye on Callimachus' famous Heraclitus epigram and its reference to ἁρπακτὴς Ἀΐδης (*Epig.* 2. 6).

44 παρίστατο: the sense 'dispose', 'induce' someone goes back to Herodotus, but the acc. and inf. construction is unusual: see LSJ s. v. C II 2.

45–6 εἰς Θρᾴκην …: see introductory note for Xenophon's own version of this.

53 καθ' ὁτιοῦν … μέρος: the conventional divisions of philosophy were physics, ethics, and dialectic (Diog. Laert. 1. 18 and many other authorities).

55 ἐδόκει: the understood subject is φιλοσοφία.

59 ἀπραγμοσύνη … καὶ ἠρεμία: more or less the same states of mind as those described by the technical Stoic term ἀπάθεια and the Epicurean ἀταραξία. Chion is saying that he had formerly only been aware of philosophers' arguments in favour of the βίος θεωρητικός. Seeing Xenophon in action persuaded him that philosophy equips you for the βίος πρακτικός too.

76 τοῦ ἱκανοῦ: with πέρα. The text here is uncertain and follows Düring's suggestion: see his note.

78 τὰ τῶν ἀνέμων: simply = οἱ ἄνεμοι. Such expressions (neuter article and genitive) are occasionally used as a plain periphrasis: see Weir Smyth, §1299. Chion has another example in *Ep.* 17.1: τὰ τῶν δορυφόρων.

CHION 13

Chion writes to describe to his father how he was assaulted in Athens by a henchman of Clearchus, but managed to overcome his attacker. He urges his father to allay Clearchus' suspicions by persuading him that Chion has no intention of getting involved in public life. (This is the burden of Letters 14 and 16 too.)

Two of the men referred to here have the names of historical characters from Heraclea, but not at the time of the dramatic date of the letter. Silenus (here an opponent of Clearchus) was a general in the early 1st cent. BC, and Nymphis a historian of around the first half of the 3rd cent. BC. As Düring says (p. 16), our writer is adding verisimilitude to the letter by bringing in local characters even though they come from different periods.

5 ὕστερον ἢ γραφῆναι: a very rare construction, found also in Thuc. 6. 4. It follows the analogy of πρότερον ἢ with infinitive: see Weir Smyth §2459. There is no letter in the collection about Chion's illness, so this remark looks like a deliberate attempt by the writer at the sort of chatty allusiveness characteristic of real letters.

7 περὶ ἕκτην ὥραν: this is an important clue to the date of the letters. According to Herodotus (2. 109) the 12-hour division of the day and the night was adopted by the Greeks from the Babylonians; but there is no trace of this time-reckoning in our literary sources until late Hellenistic times. From the 1st cent. AD we find it in Plutarch and the Gospels, so we have a cautious pointer to this period onwards as our author's date. See above, p. xviii; and for the 12-hour reckoning LSJ s.v. ὥρα II 2 b; E. J. Bickerman, *Chronology of the Ancient World* (London, 1968), 14–16.

8 ἐν τῷ 'Ὠιδείῳ: the Odeum of Pericles, dating originally from the mid-5th cent. BC. It was a large hall next to the Theatre of Dionysus, used for musical contests and for rehearsals of the tragedies presented in the Theatre at the Great Dionysia.

8 σκέμματος: σκέμμα is a subject for speculation, a philosophical question.

10–11 μεταλαμβάνοντα…μετειληφότος: this seems to refer to the action of 'transferring' the dagger from its sheath to his right hand, which now (ἤδη) gripped it.

16 τοὺς στρατηγούς: at Athens it would strictly be the polemarch who dealt with a case involving a resident foreigner; but the chief magistrates of cities in Asia Minor and elsewhere were called στρατηγοί (like the ten ministers of war at Athens), which may have led our author to use the term in this context.

17 τῶν ἐτησίων: the ἐτησίαι (ἔτος, 'year') are annual summer winds blowing from the north-west, and so of no use for Chion's sailing purposes.

22 πεῖθε τὸν Κλέαρχον...: the same appeal to his father is made at 14.50 ff. below, and his own arguments to persuade Clearchus of this appear in 16.

24 Νύμφιδος: for Nymphis see above, introductory note.

CHION 14

Chion reports to his father that he has got as far as Byzantium on his way home. He reflects on the evils afflicting Heraclea under Clearchus' tyranny and the long-term demoralization which will affect the people. Chion himself through his philosophical studies can never be enslaved, as his soul will be free. He plans to do what he can to save his city from Clearchus, and with this in view urges his father (as in Letter 13 above) to divert Clearchus' suspicions from him.

4–5 οὐκ ἐπὶ Κλεάρχῳ: 'not (only) Clearchus' seems to be the sense: as Chion goes on to explain, there is also a wider danger to confront in the damage done by tyranny to the moral fibre of the state, and the example Clearchus sets to others like him to become tyrants.

7 τε γάρ: may simply = γάρ. (This combination of particles is regarded where it occurs with varying degrees of suspicion by editors: see Denniston, *GP* 536.) Yet νῦν τε might be picked up by καὶ εἰσαῦθις, though the construction is broken.

12 περιστῇ: the verb is often used of things 'turning out' for the worse: LSJ s.v. B II 3.

Much of this section draws on traditional Greek political theory. The comparison of a sick state with a sick body goes back to Plato's *Republic* (556e: and note μικρᾶς ῥοπῆς there and μικραὶ ῥοπαί here), with echoes in Aristotle, *Pol.* 1320^{b}33 ff., and Demosthenes, *Olynth.* 2. 21. In particular, tyranny was regarded as a disease of the state: Plato, *Rep.* 544c6–7 τυραννὶς ... ἔσχατον πόλεως νόσημα; Isocrates, *Helen* 34. Chion exploits these *topoi*, and then moves on in sect. 3 to contrast the situation in Heraclea with his own moral freedom.

13 σχεδὸν εἰπεῖν: an absolute infinitive, giving a mild parenthetic qualification: cf. σκοπεῖν below.

17–19 μέχρι...πλήθους: confusion and corruption reign in the MSS in this sentence, but the general sense seems clear, and the text follows Düring's suggested emendations. For παράταξις in the sense of 'resistance' see Marcus Aurelius 11. 3. πρὸς βουλομένου τοῦ πλήθους: literally 'on the part of the people who still have the will (for resistance)'.

It was common philosophical currency, especially among the Stoics and Cynics, that the soul could be free even if the body was enslaved. Our souls can be slaves to vices like greed and lust, but not to external forces; and one of the advantages enjoyed by the Stoic ideal *sapiens* is that fortune has lost control over him. (So below, 4 'it is the body which is always subject to fortune'.) Chion's argument here is that no one is truly a slave who is unafraid of a present or future evil.

31 καὶ πῶς: sc. δουλεύσει.

35 σῶμά... συντυχίας ἧττον: see note above.

37 ἦν γὰρ οὐδὲ...: the antecendent is ψυχή. For οἰκονομία in the sense 'control', 'power of management', 'function', see Lampe, s.v. A.

39–40 Κλέαρχος...δοῦλος γενήσεται: another Platonic touch: ὁ τῷ ὄντι τύραννος τῷ ὄντι δοῦλος, *Rep.* 9. 579d9–10.

42 τὰ μὲν οὖν ἐμὰ... ἀσφαλέστερα: both phrasing and thought pick up εἰ μὲν αὐτὸ...ἀσφαλής εἰμι above (23–4). σκοπεῖν is a rather loosely attached absolute infinitive used parenthetically: 'My own situation (if you look at it) is more secure...'. For the absolute infinitive, with and without ὡς, see Weir Smyth §2012.

45 τὰ... συνημμένα μοι: literally 'the elements...bound to me' (συνάπτειν).

50 πολιτεύου: in later Greek the verb can, as here, mean dealing with private affairs: LSJ s.v. B VI.

51–52 πείθων...ἐρασταί ἐσμεν: cf. above, 13. 22.

CHION 16

This letter is a miniature ἀπολογία in which Chion defends himself to Clearchus against the charge of active hostility to him. There is no motive for hostility as he has no cause to feel injured by Clearchus, and his own inclinations are for philosophical study and a quiet life.

The letter is closely linked with Letter 15 to Chion's father, who has been calming the tyrant's fears about him. There Chion suggests that Clearchus' cruelty will actually make it easier to overthrow him, and he tells his father that he himself will write to Clearchus to allay his suspicions. This letter will be exalted in tone (⟨ἐπιστολὴν⟩ διθυραμβικωτέραν ποιήσας, 15.3), which will induce Clearchus to disregard him as a harmless pedant. Letter 16 is the resulting letter, and we have the writer's cue to note its 'dithyrambic' elements, especially the address by Tranquillity which adds a tone of grandeur at the end.

A parallel to this intentionally misleading letter can be found in Richardson's novel-in-letters *Clarissa* (vol. 4 no. 60, Everyman edn.): Clarissa similarly writes to deceive Lovelace about her own prospective death. (I owe this reference to Professor D. A. Russell.)

The letter falls into two parts. In sects. 1–3 Chion pleads that he has no motive for hating Clearchus: he has been living abroad and he was not even present in Heraclea at the crucial time when Clearchus seized power. In sects. 4–9 he argues that his retiring disposition and philosophical interests preclude any desire to meddle in public affairs.

10–12 ἠπόρουν ... ἠπόρουν: ἀπορέω has two different constructions, first the genitive ἀπολογίας, then the dative τῷ ... ἐννοεῖσθαι, followed rather loosely by the participle ἔχων ('I am in no difficulty. ... being also able to convince you ...').

13 εὐέμβατος: a very rare word which Chion uses metaphorically here and literally at 15. 3.

16 παιδικῶν ἐπιτηδευμάτων: we might consider deleting ἐπιτηδευμάτων as a gloss and translating 'the objects of their love'.

22 λόγου: for the legal sense of λόγος see LSJ s.v. III 1 b. It would also make sense with the meaning 'rumour'.

22 καθαρεύω ...: lit. 'I am clean in my mind of these things' (Clearchus' suspicious charges).

25 τριήρεις ... ἱππεῖς: forces supplied by the Athenians to assist Chion, according to Clearchus' implied suspicions.

25 ἵνα: not final, but used for consecutive ὥστε. The usage belongs chiefly to later Greek, e.g. Plut. *Mor.* 333A, and many examples in the NT: see Arndt–Gingrich, s.v. II 2.

38–9 θεατὴς ... λόγων: θεατής is used in philosophical contexts of one who contemplates or studies knowledge and truth: Arist. *EN* 1098ᵃ31 (truth), Plut. *Mor.* 80F (virtue). Chion was an earnest student of the principles, λόγοι, underlying the natural order, φύσις.

44 εἰς Ἑλλήσποντον...: this refers to the hostility between Athens and Sparta in the early 4th cent. BC, when naval engagements took place in the Hellespont, as elsewhere: see N. G. L. Hammond, *A History of Greece* (2nd edn., Oxford, 1967), 462–5.

46 ἡσυχίας: the quiet life of tranquillity, though associated most notably with the Epicureans as their *summum bonum*, was widely recognized as desirable by other philosophical creeds, here Platonism. It is the βίος θεωρητικός, opposed to the hurly-burly of public engagement (cf. πολιτείαν καὶ πολυπραγμοσύνην below). See above, Chion 3, introd. *n.*

52 τηνικαῦτα ἤδη: 'only then', suggesting that it took him some time.

52 ἐπόπτην: a common epithet both of pagan gods and of God in the Septuagint. (The phrase τὸν πάντων ἐπόπτην θεόν occurs in Esther 5: 1a.) See LSJ and Arndt–Gingrich, s.v.

56 ἄνθρωπον... θεοῦ κεκραμένον μοίρᾳ: the idea that mortal man has yet a share in God would be characteristic Platonic teaching absorbed by Chion: see e.g. Plato *Prot.* 322a ὁ ἄνθρωπος θείας μετέσχε μοίρας, *Critias* 121a, *Rep.* 611e. Of course Platonism had no monopoly of the doctrine: the Stoics had their own explanation of man's share in the divine, believing that the individual human soul derived from the fiery air, πνεῦμα, that informed the whole cosmos as its basic principle.

62 ἄριστον: adverbial (as more often in the plural): 'in the best way', 'ideally', picked up rather loosely by εἰ δὲ μή γε, 'but failing that'.

66 οἰκείων ἔργων τρέψειε: the genitive with the simple verb τρέπειν ('turn from') is rare and poetic (e.g. Homer *Il.* 18. 138): the Aldine reading, ἀποτρέψειε may be right.

71 ἀπολιτεύτους ὧν σὺ βούλει: a typically condensed Greek relative construction: 'stay out of (the sort of) public activities you wish them (to stay out of)'.

75 Ἡσυχία... λέγοι: this is an instance of the rhetorical figure called προσωποποιία, a speech attributed to a dead character or, as here, some personified virtue or force conjured up for the occasion. It was thought to be characteristic of the 'grand' style of oratory: see introductory note. Tranquillity here represents the teaching of the Academy, and the obvious model for Chion is Plato, *Crito* 50a ff., where Socrates imagines the Nomoi, the personified Laws, to be addressing him. See Demetrius, *On Style* 265, and for Cicero's use of the technique, Austin on *Cael.* 33–4.

77–8 δικαιοσύνην ... σωφροσύνην: these virtues are routinely associated in Plato, e.g. *Gorg.* 507d, 508b.

82 νόμῳ ... ψυχῇ: the philosophical law and spirit which Chion learnt at the Academy and should not now abandon.

88 πρὸς ἐμαυτὸν ἀεὶ λέγω: speaking one's thoughts to oneself brings in another touch of Plato: see *Tht.* 189e, 190c, *Soph.* 263e. Chion ends by assuring Clearchus that this letter is not a sudden reaction to events: his attitude is deep-rooted and secure. οὐδὲ γὰρ οὐδέ is very emphatic, and ἡσυχία delayed till the end of the sentence stresses his complete detachment.

INDEX